POPULAR CULTURE IN MODERN FRANCE

'Culture' in France has long been understood as the 'high' culture of great names and great works. But it is popular culture, as much as high culture, which has preoccupied the French themselves in the last 50 years, to an extent where 'culture' is now one of the most frequently used terms in the French vocabulary. It sells not only books, newspapers and magazines, but also consumer products and political parties. But what are the meanings of 'culture populaire'? What do the French understand by it, and what is its history?

Brian Rigby's lively and cogent study traces changing notions of French Popular Culture from 1936 – the year of the Popular Front – to the present day. He shows how the post-war democratic project of taking high culture to the people was redefined in the wake of profound social, ideological and cultural change, and how intellectuals and the state came to embrace a pluralist notion of popular culture which recognised the centrality of the mass media. Asking why 'culture' remains a fiercely contested term in French society, Rigby considers the work of major French theorists, including Barthes, Bourdieu and Baudrillard.

Brian Rigby is a lecturer in French Studies at the University of Warwick. He is editor of the journal *French Cultural Studies*, and the co-editor (with N. Hewitt) of *France and the Mass Media*.

POPULAR CULTURE IN MODERN FRANCE

A study of cultural discourse

Brian Rigby

London and New York

First published 1991
by Routledge
11 New Fetter Lane, London EC4P 4EE

Simultaneously published in the USA and Canada
by Routledge
a division of Routledge, Chapman and Hall, Inc.
29 West 35th Street, New York, NY 10001

© 1991 Brian Rigby

Typeset in 10/12 Bembo by
Falcon Typographic Art Ltd., Edinburgh & London
Printed in Great Britain by
T. J. Press (Padstow) Ltd., Padstow, Cornwall

British Library Cataloguing in Publication Data
Rigby, Brian
Popular culture in modern France: a study of cultural discourse.
1. culture, history   I. Title
944.08

Library of Congress Cataloging in Publication Data
Rigby, Brian.
Popular culture in modern France: a study of cultural discourse/
Brian Rigby.
p. cm. Includes bibliographical references and index.
1. Arts and society – France – History – 20th century.
2. France – Popular culture.   I. Title.
NX180.S6R54   1992
700'.1'0309440904–dc20   90–27020

ISBN 0–415–01246–5
0–415–01247–3 (pbk)

CONTENTS

ACKNOWLEDGEMENTS

I would like to acknowledge the financial help given by the University of Warwick in the preparation of this book. I would also like to thank Pauline Wilson for her help with the typescript.

1

FROM HIGH CULTURE TO ORDINARY CULTURE

In this study my aim is to set out significant elements of the discourse on culture which has been such an important feature of modern French intellectual life. My primary focus is postwar France, but I also look to the time of the Popular Front in 1936 as an important point of reference for later debates on culture. In fact, since the terms of the modern debate on culture were, to an important extent, established at the time of the Popular Front, I hope to point out the links not only between 1936 and the periods of Resistance and Reconstruction, but also to indicate the significant continuities up to the early 1960s and even beyond. However, although I take my examination of cultural discourse up to the present day, my principal aim is to sketch out the general field of cultural discourse, and for this purpose I take the key period for my investigation to be from 1945 to the late 1960s. I consider this period to be without doubt the high point of intellectual and political debate about such issues as popular culture, mass culture and State intervention in culture. This is not to say that the questions have ceased to be discussed. Cultural discourse in France is apparently infinite in quantity. Every French intellectual seems to want to have his or her say on cultural matters and the books and articles continue to be produced at an alarming rate. There seems no prospect of this flood diminishing and for some optimists this is clearly a sign of cultural health: 'If there were no cultural discourse, that would basically mean there would be no future and, therefore, no hope and no dynamism.'[1]

I do not pretend, however, to give an exhaustive treatment of all areas of cultural discourse. Rather, I am simply trying to circumscribe and give access to the abundant discourse on culture, by setting out some of the main issues and pointing to

1

the typical themes and characteristic arguments that are to be found in this discourse. I am looking almost exclusively at the writings of intellectuals and academics, although these writings do take a great variety of forms: doctoral theses, scholarly monographs, book-length 'essais', journalistic articles and so forth. Within the vast area of writing upon modern culture, I am focusing particularly on questions relating to popular culture, mass culture, and the State and culture. I see myself as carrying out an introductory and preliminary survey of the ways in which French intellectuals and academics have dealt with these related issues since the time of the Popular Front and the Second World War. I am only too aware that this is a very selective approach to the study of popular culture, but it does, none the less, seem to me a worthwhile one. At the very least, I hope it can clear some ground and help to lay some foundations for the developing study of modern and contemporary French popular culture. I have chosen to approach the study of French intellectual treatment of popular culture by looking at a range of French writers who seem to me to have played a significant role in constituting the specifically French discourse on culture. I imagine that only a few of the names will be known to Anglo-Saxon readers. However, I am not so much interested in expounding the separate theories, arguments and attitudes of individual writers, as I am in building up a general picture of how the issues of popular culture have been handled in France. Few of the texts I refer to have been translated, and I hope that I can familiarise readers with important aspects of French intellectual and cultural debates which are little known outside of France.

Since my primary interest here is in what has been written about popular culture, I have felt the need to pay close attention to the specific terms used by French writers in their treatment of cultural matters. Some of the French terms might be self-evident, even to readers without much French (or without any French at all), but I have, none the less, given translations where appropriate. It seems to me that one cannot deal with specifically French debates about culture, if one does not also point out how the terms used in the debate play a role in constituting these debates. Without in any way claiming to provide a comprehensive vocabulary of modern French cultural discourse, I hope I can contribute to the understanding of this discourse by picking out and glossing many of the key words.[2] My aim is to focus on those terms which have actually played a significant role in the writings on culture in the relatively

2

limited period of the last fifty years, and to try and assess what meanings they have had, and often still have, within the framework of these writings.

If one were to believe Philippe Bénéton in his *Histoire de mots: culture et civilisation* (1975) ['History of the words "culture" and "civilisation"'], one would be perhaps discouraged from such a venture from the beginning, for he thought that some of the key words used in the cultural debates in the period with which I am concerned had no real 'operative' function:

> Allowing for a time-lag of a few years, scientific terms and intellectual fashions in France . . . follow a development parallel to that which takes place across the Atlantic. Thus, the French debate about 'mass culture', 'elite culture', and 'high culture' evolved at the time when it was already losing some of its vitality in the United States, and French intellectuals in the 1960s engaged in the same controversies that had occupied their American colleagues ten years earlier. Several monographs and numerous special numbers of journals were published on this theme, and they helped to put into circulation a new terminology, at the centre of which is to be found the notion of mass culture, defined sometimes by the number of people reached in the process of communication (the masses), sometimes by the means of communication (the 'mass media'), and finally sometimes by the two at once. The concept is imprecise and appears to have very little use, as is also the case with such other notions as 'higher culture', 'average culture', 'high culture' . . . which mix scientific observations and normative considerations.[3]

Bénéton was, therefore, aware that, from a 'scientific' point of view, the various terms used in the debates on culture were too imprecise. This is no doubt true, but is not my concern here, which is rather to show which terms are actually used in the cultural discourse and to attempt to explain how they have been used and what significance they have had in these debates.

I am, however, in agreement with Bénéton, when, in considering the contemporary use of the terms 'culture' and 'culturel', he concluded that there had been a shift from a universalist, all-embracing notion of culture. Bénéton observed that the field of application of the term 'culture' had become very extensive, and it is this extension of the term which is part of my interest in this study.

It is not simply a case of everything having become 'cultural' in French life, whereas not so long ago everything seemed to be 'political', although this is part of the story. (It is the substantive 'le culturel', which is now sometimes used to render this sense of everything being 'cultural').[4] Already in the 1960s, Henri Lefebvre was remarking that in 1946 people had used the term 'intellectual' in contexts where 'cultural' would later come to be used.[5] Certainly the word 'culture' has been particularly pervasive in French life in recent years, and one does need to have some way of interpreting the range of meanings it has taken on, as well as some idea of the innumerable contexts in which the word is now to be found. Anyone who is at all acquainted with French publishing, media or politics (just to mention a few key areas) will recognise the fact that 'culture' is one of the most overused words in the modern French vocabulary. It sells not only books, newspapers, magazines, but also consumer products and political parties. In fact, so important is the word and concept of 'culture' in French society that, if one were to attempt to locate and interpret its every manifestation, one would be trying to encompass virtually the whole range of activities in every area of French life. Fortunately, my task is more modest, but, even within the limited compass of my concerns, I would hope to give an idea of how important and extensive is the use of the word 'culture' and consequently how important is the reflection upon cultural questions in modern and contemporary French intellectual life.

To begin with, it is important to stress that a universalist, human-ist notion of 'Culture' with a capital C still survives strongly in French society, despite many vigorous attacks upon it.[6] Attacks on humanist Culture have, of course, been a central feature of French intellectual life throughout the twentieth century, and have been particularly associated with Marxists and Marxist sympathisers from the 1930s onwards. (One thinks especially of Paul Nizan's *Les Chiens de garde* (1932) and of Sartre's *Qu'est-ce-que la littérature?* (1948).) The universalist, humanist values of Culture have been seen by Marxists and Marxist sympathisers as simply a bourgeois strategy designed to mask the underlying economic exploitation of the working class. The task of demystifying Culture has been taken up throughout the postwar years by the intellectual avant-garde, whether by the protesters of 1968 or by the various representatives of anti-humanist, anti-rationalist thought who have played a promi-nent role in Parisian intellectual life both in the 1970s and the 1980s.

But it is not only the deliberate attacks of intellectuals on Culture that have called it into question and supposedly undermined its existence. The economic progress of postwar French society is also said to have undermined the premises of a humanist Culture through the growth of materialism, acquisitiveness, consumerism and so forth. Added to this is the crucial development of the mass media (radio, cinema, television) which have often been thought to offer short-term, low-grade satisfaction and mere entertainment in place of the more worthwhile and lasting experiences of Art and Culture.

The defence of Culture has, of course, been taken up throughout the period by various traditional, conservative figures. For instance, Pierre-Henri Simon was a notable example of someone who took up the cause of humanist Culture during the student demonstrations of 1968.[7] Other Right-wing authors and journalists such as Jean Cau, Paul Guth and Jean Dutourd have since then kept up an untiring struggle in the name of 'true' culture in their books and in the Right-wing press (*Le Figaro-Magazine, Paris-Match etc.*).[8] Left-wing commentators have seen this 'tenacious reactionary resistance' as being much stronger in France than in other advanced capitalist countries.[9] There are also, of course, famous institutions such as the Académie Française which seem specifically designed to enshrine and celebrate traditional ideas of Culture. But one can hardly claim that the Académie still plays a visible and important role in French society, and one can doubt whether this institution still represents a cultural elitism significant enough to criticise. Patrick Combes, for instance, has pointed out in his study of literature and 1968, that during the May events hardly anyone even bothered to single out the Academy for criticism.[10]

There are, however, many more people who believe that the educational system is still geared to perpetuating traditional, elitist notions of Culture, and to serving that small minority who have access to Culture and the competence to talk about it: 'Culture, that is to say, true Culture, High Culture, Culture with a capital C, is almost by its very essence verbal . . . what counts more than paintings or statues is what has been said about them.'[11] In fact, the best testimony of the continuing existence of the notion of a dominant or high Culture in French society is, perhaps, to be found in the importance attributed to it by its opponents, whose vociferous attacks upon it demonstrate that it still exists as a very powerful idea and force in French life,[12] whether or not it corresponds to what actually goes on inside cultural and educational institutions, and whether or not in reality Culture plays the legitimating role which, for instance, the sociologist Pierre Bourdieu has attributed to it in his works. Bourdieu himself is, of course, in no doubt that Culture does still have real power in French society, and that it remains one of the most important ways in which classes demarcate themselves from one another and in which certain classes exert power over other classes.[13] Few people in French society, according to Bourdieu, are prepared to call into question the importance and legitimacy of Culture. Few are willing to be cast as 'barbarians', by asking what value Culture has, and by analysing what purposes it serves.[14] In Bourdieu's terms, few people seek to understand how an interest in Culture actually works in the 'interest' of certain sections of society.[15] In fact, it is not only the already cultured who believe in the worth of Culture.[16] According to Bourdieu, the petit bourgeois is reverence itself in the face of Culture.[17] What is more, even the working classes can be found to have high-flown notions about the value of Culture, although, for Bourdieu, this just goes to indicate the extent of the power wielded by dominant culture, which enables it to impose its values even on those who, strictly speaking, are outside its sphere.[18] All Bourdieu's analyses of the relationship to Culture of different social groups (especially 'dominated' social groups) depend on a belief in the actual existence of 'high culture', 'dominant culture', 'legitimate culture', all of which are deemed to be possessed by dominant social groups. This legitimate culture sets a standard which, by definition, cannot be attained or matched by other dominated forms of culture possessed by inferior social groups.

There are a considerable number of French terms used to express the notion of Culture with a capital C, and this abundance seems one of the clearest indications of the importance attributed to it in French life. The word 'la Culture' itself by no means rules exclusively over the field. One finds 'la Grande Culture', 'la Culture classique', 'la haute culture', 'la culture supérieure', 'la culture unique', 'la culture universelle', 'la culture générale', 'la culture désintéressée', 'la culture désincarnée'.[19] All these terms come together to confirm the notion of Culture as one of the mind and spirit, made up from the great works of writers and artists. It is a unified culture, whose values are permanent and universal. Many other terms stress the notion that Culture is the emanation of the State and its institutions (here one sees how the educational system is regarded as inseparable from ideas about Culture): 'la culture officielle', 'la culture légitime', 'la culture consacrée', 'la culture cultivée', 'la culture savante', 'la culture universitaire'. Almost identical with these terms are those which express the idea that Culture is the preserve of dominant social groups: 'la culture dominante', 'le pouvoir culturel'. Those who possess Culture are 'les cultivés', 'les intellectuels', 'les esthètes'. Culture is seen as an inherited possession, and is often described as 'a private hunting-ground' ['une chasse gardée']. Culture is something that is kept within a small, privileged group, a favourite image here being that of the closed circuit ['le circuit fermé'], which is sometimes taken to be the fashionable social and cultural world of Paris ['le tout-Paris de la culture', 'la culture mondaine'], but also sometimes the overlapping worlds of the fashionable Parisian intelligentsia and the University and other higher education establishments. Hence the assault on the watchdogs and guardians of culture ['les chiens de garde', 'les gardiens de la culture'], which links up explicitly with Nizan's earlier attack on university professors and their bourgeois, humanist, universalist Culture. In a more humorous vein, Pascal Ory's volume *Mots de passe* (1985) ['Passwords'], reinforces the view that French culture is a secret and private domain into which one can only be admitted by knowing the secret formulas,[20] a view already held by Emmanuel Berl earlier in the century, when he wrote: 'The primary function of bourgeois culture is to supply passwords.'[21]

Inseparable from notions of high culture in France is the view that it is French culture itself which best embodies the values and forms of high culture. However, just as elements of the avant-garde intellectual Left have throughout this century consistently attacked the notion of Culture, so they have attacked the idea of the Nation. And just as there has been a traditional, conservative Right-wing defence of Culture, so there has been a traditional, conservative, Right-wing defence of the Nation. In fact, of course, the two are seen as inseparable. Notions of 'la culture française' are inseparable from notions of 'la patrie'. One still comes across writers who have a virtually mystical view of the special and transcendent qualities embodied in the French language, French literature, the French countryside and French ways of life. The not uncommon belief in 'la francité' [essential Frenchness] does of course imply not only a belief in the essential qualities, but also in the essential superiority of French culture. In fact, as France's political, economic and military power has declined in relative terms, so has the tendency grown among some French people to see France's special contribution to the world as being a cultural one, this special contribution being namely its language, its writers and its artists.[22] No doubt many French people would scoff at the idea that France had a special civilising mission, but the fact remains that the State and its agencies still take extremely seriously the question of the protection of French language and culture from foreign corruption, and take equally seriously the question of the promotion of French language and culture abroad, a policy and attitude expressed in the phrase 'le rayonnement de la culture française' ['the influence of French culture'].[23] The term 'la culture française' traditionally denotes a culture characterised not only by its unity and homogeneity, but also by its aesthetic superiority. In general, 'French culture' means the works produced by France's great writers, philosophers, painters and so forth, works which are taken to be quintessential expressions of 'le Génie français', and which serve to demonstrate 'la Grandeur française' and 'le Prestige français'.[24]

As to the traditional notion of France itself, the country is, of course, supposedly the land of liberty, equality and fraternity, united in its Republican traditions and in its language and culture. However, France's national identity and cultural unity were themselves not a natural given but needed to be constructed. Historians have suggested that it was particularly in the late nineteenth century that national identity and cultural unity were forged on the basis of myths and symbols drawn from history and disseminated through the curriculum of the national educational system.[25]

French culture became truly national only in the last years of the [nineteenth] century . . . . We are talking about the process of acculturation: the civilisation of the French by urban France, the disintegration of local cultures by modernity, and their absorption into the dominant civilisation of Paris and the schools. Left largely to their own devices until their promotion to citizenship, the unassimilated rural masses had to be integrated into the dominant culture as they had been integrated into an administrative entity. What happened was akin to colonisation.[26]

Much of what I want to say in this study is related to different notions of popular culture, and this is a first instance to be noted.

This new national culture, which the State sought to impose on a France notable for its diversity of local and regional languages and cultures, has been referred to as 'la culture populaire nationale'.[27] It was a *national* popular culture because it was intended to replace the different forms of popular culture to be found in all the various localities of France. According to one historian, there were 40,000 villages in France at the close of the eighteenth century and no two villages were alike, so the task of providing a uniform national culture out of such diversity was no small task.[28] It was also a national *popular* culture, because the State intended to replace what was perceived as an archaic culture of the people – a folk culture of superstition, ignorance, irrationality, violence and local factionalism – by a modern culture of the people, a secular, rational and national culture, which was seen as the only possible culture that could lead France into the twentieth century. One of the fundamental meanings of 'la culture populaire' is, of course, popular culture in the sense of folk culture and traditional culture, a meaning it carries much more dominantly than does its English equivalent of 'popular culture'. So, for instance, when Jean Cuisenier's book *L'Art populaire* was translated into English in 1977, it became not *French Popular Art* but *French Folk Art*.[29] A very important aspect of what I am attempting to investigate is precisely the way in which the French term 'culture populaire' carries a different range of meanings from those conveyed in English by 'popular culture'. What also makes the term 'culture populaire' interesting and rather complex is the fact that its meanings in French are unstable and overlapping. Throughout this study I hope to set out and disentangle different usages and meanings of the term 'culture populaire', and thereby hope to illuminate the discourse on modern and contemporary culture by clarifying one of the principal terms in this discourse.

Needless to say, the major reason why 'culture populaire' readily means popular culture in the sense of folk culture is that France remained a rural country with a living peasant and village culture for much longer than, for example, did England. All historians wishing to chart and understand the process of the modernisation of France over the last two centuries find themselves time and again trying to pin down and locate how and when the ever disappearing (yet never quite totally disappearing) traditional life of the countryside was gradually and inexorably transformed and replaced by modern urban models. In fact, so strong is the memory of France as a rural country, and so visible are the signs of its having been so (and even still remaining so to a significant degree, despite the thoroughgoing processes of modernisation) that the term 'culture populaire' even now tenaciously carries as one of its dominant meanings that of folk culture.

It is, however, fairly safe to say that the controlling ideology of postwar France has been a modernising, technocratic one. Bourdieu has picked out those vogue words which express and embody this ideology and which denote the desire of France to become a modern industrial nation, turned towards the future, and open to rapid change and growth.[30] In the context of this prevailing ethos, it is, of course, traditional, rural France which has been seen as the old world that had to be left behind, characterised as it was by its agricultural, artisanal world of work, its small-scale parochial networks, and its attachment to the ways and values of the past. In the immediate postwar years, not only was there a need and a will to proceed to the modernisation of France, but the folk image of old France also now carried the stigma of the Vichy period, since the traditional folk values and folk ways had been harnessed by Vichy propaganda in the service of collaboration. It was probably not until the 1970s with the folk revival and the growth of a culture of nostalgia that rural France became once more the focus of attention and was again for a time thought to be the carrier of important values.

It is true that in recent years there has been a massive historical interest in the traditional rural past of France, some of it without doubt fuelled by the 1970s fashion for folk culture. Apart from the vast amount of academic, literary and journalistic work devoted to the 'popular culture' of the ancien régime and modern France (there has, for instance, been a considerable body of work on nineteenth-century society), one of the most striking testimonies to the persistence of the interest in folk culture is the considerable network of museums that has grown up throughout the country. These museums, dedicated to local and regional culture (and of which the most celebrated example is the Musée National des Arts et Traditions Populaires in Paris), present their material in a lively and innovative manner, and constantly search for new ways of interesting the public in France's traditional past. Despite the appeal of such museums, there is, however, a general recognition that France's folk culture is only of historical interest, and the more serious professional ethnologists seem to want to have little truck with the folklore industry which attempts to keep old ways artificially alive or, indeed, pretends that the old ways remain alive and kicking. What is more, the word 'le folklore' itself is now used most frequently in a pejorative manner.[31] There does also seem to be a growing tendency among ethnologists to turn their attention away from the folk culture of the past to the popular culture of modern urban societies. One can, perhaps, find an objective indication of this by looking at the principal French ethnological journal, *Ethnologie Française*. This was the title taken by the periodical in 1971, and it is the title which it still bears. Previously – from 1953 to 1970 – the periodical was entitled *Arts et Traditions Populaires*. Between 1971 and 1976 there were very few articles devoted to modern popular culture. From 1977 to the present, however, there has been a steadily growing number of articles on such diverse features of modern life as gardening, post-cards, hunting, advertising, 'fêtes', hairdressing, sport (wrestling, cycling), political demonstrations, music (accordion) and popular images. This list is not exhaustive, but it serves to show that the ethnologists themselves seem also to be registering the view (which many others have often expressed in postwar France) that the traditional past is well and truly dead, and that popular culture should not be exclusively identified with the folk culture of the past, nor be enclosed within the walls of a museum.[32]

Paul Yonnet, who has written a recent work on modern mass culture,[33] to which I will return in more detail at a later stage, is, however, not so confident of the French academic establishment's ability and readiness to accept this broadening of the definition of 'culture populaire' to incorporate modern popular culture. Yonnet rails at academic sociologists for their totally negative attitudes to such modern popular cultural practices as betting on the horses ['le tiercé'], which is such a widespread activity among French people, and especially of lower social groups:

the 'tiercé' is one of the few cultural practices to be devoid of all social or intellectual prestige, and even in these respects to carry highly negative connotations. The Amerindian potlatch is noble, as all University people will tell you, but the 'tiercé' is vulgar. It is not cultural, it does not even constitute a subculture (like strip cartoons); it does not produce enough original sublinguistic phenomena, and structuralist analysis has not deigned to apply its method to it. In brief, it is only seen as despicable stupidity, shameful mindlessness, sordid greed; in other words, the 'tiercé' in the eyes of sociologists is nothing but a ritual performed by slaves and morons, a sacrifice offered up once or twice a week to this new 'opium of the people'.[34]

Allowing for possible overstatement, and also for the aggressiveness of one who is outside the academic establishment, there are, none the less, several important interrelated issues here. Firstly, there is the question of what is regarded as fit for the scrutiny of French academics and intellectuals, who are characterised by Yonnet as having a very limited and circumscribed notion of what constitutes the cultural domain. According to Yonnet, culture needs to have intellectual or social prestige before a French academic will accept it as worthy of attention. Secondly, French intellectual and cultural life is presented as being governed by fashion, according to which only certain cultural forms and practices (e.g. strip cartoons) come to be regarded as worthy of examination by modish intellectual approaches (e.g. structuralism). Betting on the horses, for example, has clearly failed to satisfy these fashionable criteria. Thirdly, 'le tiercé' falls foul of another crucial element in much of French intellectual and academic life, namely its deep aversion to many aspects of mass culture. In this quotation Yonnet has touched on several important issues to which I shall return in the course of this study, but at this point one can simply observe how the field of French cultural discourse is marked by a preoccupation with the question of who determines, or arbitrates upon, what should enter into the domain of culture.

Michel de Certeau's *La Culture au pluriel* ['Culture in the plural'], first published in 1974,[35] is an interesting collection of essays to look at within the context of what has already been said. In this volume one sees how a contemporary apologist of the liberties gained in May 1968[36] turned his attention not only to folk culture but also to mass culture and forms of modern popular culture. Initially, I want to look at the essay De Certeau wrote with Dominique Julia and Jacques Revel, called 'La Beauté du mort' ['The beauty of the dead']. One of the most characteristic indications of the complexity, slipperiness and shifting nature of the term 'culture populaire' is the frequency with which French writers feel the need to surround it with inverted commas. In doing so, they are obviously acknowledging that the term does not have an agreed significance, or rather that its connotations or possible meanings are so varied that the writer wants the reader to realise that there is a question mark over the term, as well as inverted commas around it. Just as 'culture populaire' takes inverted commas, so the adjective 'populaire' and the substantive 'le peuple' ['the people'] require similar warning marks in 'The beauty of the dead', as they also do so often elsewhere.[37] The reason for the inverted commas in this essay is that the authors wish to disabuse the readers of any innocent, pre-political or non-political understanding of the terms, which according to them have been subject to a good deal of folkloric and sentimental idealisation.

We are told in 'The beauty of the dead' that in the latter part of the eighteenth century there was a fashion for idealising the people and rural life, and that this aesthetic vogue depended upon an actual distance from the people. In fact, the people were never allowed to speak for themselves, and a sentimental halo was simply cast over them and their supposedly natural way of life. Passing from the theme of the sentimentalisation of the people to that of the repression of the people, the authors then go on to consider the policy of the Constituent Assembly at the time of the French Revolution which was designed to suppress local and regional dialects in favour of a universal use of the French language (a subject to which they have elsewhere devoted a whole volume).[38] But it is on the mid-nineteenth century that they principally choose to focus, in order to demonstrate how the State repressed popular culture, not only because it prevented national unity, but also because it was seen as a danger to the social and moral order. They also point out how the folklore movement in the later years of the century went on to 'castrate' popular culture. It is the case of Charles Nisard that particularly interests them. Nisard was the author of *Histoire des livres populaires et de la littérature du colportage* ['History of popular books and chapbooks'] (1854). He was the most famous collector and recorder of popular literature at this period. The authors of 'The beauty of the dead', however, see it as highly significant and symbolic that Nisard was, in fact, also appointed by the Minister of Police in 1852 as secretary to the commission set up to scrutinise, control and censor the material being carried to the rural population in pedlars' packs. Charles Nisard's view of his dual activities was given by himself in the preface to his book. As the authors of 'The beauty of the dead' point out, he described his attitude with 'a disarming naïveté':

I estimated that if, in the interest of those people who were easily seduced, as are the workers and the inhabitants of the countryside, the Commission had to forbid the pedlars from selling three quarters of these books, this prohibition did not concern those people who were not in any danger from evil reading matter, that is to say, scholars, bibliophiles, collectors and even those who were simply curious about all kinds of strange literature.[39]

The authors see an inextricable link between the exorcising of the political danger inherent in an unregulated popular culture, and the arrival on the scene of specialists of popular culture in the middle of the century, and particularly following on from the Revolution of 1848. The intellectual interest in popular culture is seen as a complicity with a State system concerned only with controlling and repressing this culture. Once this culture has been deprived of its true life and its capacity to trouble the powers that be, then one enters the next stage, that of the later nineteenth-century folklore boom. Situating and cataloguing popular culture is a form of 'reasonable integration' of popular culture into the dominant culture.[40] No longer is popular culture a living, sometimes subversive culture. It is now a 'heritage' ['un patrimoine'] and can be safely assimilated into the comforting setting of a museum. Within the context of the folklore movement, the connotations of 'popular' are those which relate it to a state of childhood: 'the natural, the true, the naïve, the spontaneous'.[41]

'Popular' is also exclusively identified with all that is related to peasants and peasant life, and explicitly opposed to all that is urban and connected to the life of the urban working classes. According to the authors, this idealisation of the 'folk', and this rejection of modern industrial life, helped to prepare the ground for the later neo-Fascist Vichy 'National Revolution'. But the authors are in fact concerned with a more general point, relating to how academics and intellectuals treat popular culture. When intellectuals choose to look at popular culture ['le regard des clercs'], they think they are being neutral or even sympathetic. In reality, the attention of the early folklorists masked 'a social violence'.[42] According to the authors, the contemporary situation is no different. When intellectuals and academics deal with the subject of popular culture, they are incapable of understanding its true nature, and they are incapable of keeping it alive and intact while subjecting it to their intellectual scrutiny. By definition, the particular frame of reference of those who are within the dominant culture deprives them of the capacity to understand what does not enter into that frame of reference. The dominant culture interprets what is different and external to it in terms of its own values and norms, and it sees in the alien what it wants and needs to see for its own purposes. Is this not what 'we' all still do when we talk of 'the people', the authors ask? By 'we' they no doubt mean the academic, intellectual classes.

The authors scrutinise the work on popular culture done by various acknowledged academic experts – R. Mandrou, M. Soriano, G. Bollème. They conclude (and with particular reference to Soriano), that on reading their work, we, in fact, learn less about popular culture than we do about 'what is involved when a progressive academic today talks about popular culture'.[43] This could, of course, stand as an epigraph to my own present study of French intellectual and academic discourse on popular culture. Somewhat ruefully, I add yet another dimension of self-consciousness and reflexivity to a discourse that is itself often characterised by self-consciousness and reflexivity. In the case of the authors of 'The beauty of the dead', this consciousness of the intellectual's need to become aware of how he or she is actually positioned in relation to what he or she is discussing is raised to a very acute level. This heightened awareness was, of course, typical of Parisian intellectuals who had been deeply involved in May 1968 and who were still deeply influenced by that experience, as is the case with these authors. After criticising Soriano for his liberalism, his non-commitment and his stance of free-floating objectivity, the authors then turn their critical scrutiny upon themselves, and ask: 'Where are *we* speaking from?'[44] This, they say, is a political issue since it calls into question the social function of 'learned culture' ['la culture savante']. The authors are themselves in no doubt that this social function is essentially one of repression. They acknowledge that they, as much as the 'progressive' writers they criticise, exist within the confines of 'learned culture', and that they may well be as guilty as those writers of 'suppressing' popular culture by talking about it. But they at least lay claim to having a utopian dream of a time when the relationship between popular culture and learned culture would not be a hierarchical relationship. They dream of 'a kind of cultural democracy' which would be the reverse of the violence now done to popular culture. They reject the distinction between 'the elite' and 'the people', but are, however, obliged to conclude, in a realistic or rather resigned vein, that their writing cannot seriously pretend to form the basis of new cultural relationships in French society.

This final touch of intellectual defeatism, or even masochism, by which the authors express their feeling of marginality within the 'real' social and political processes, rounds off an article which contains so many of the characteristic cultural and intellectual positions of the French left-wing intellectual in the late 1960s and early 1970s. Not least, we see popular culture being characterised as a separate and potentially (or even essentially) subversive culture. However, rather than rebelliousness it is perhaps the essential 'otherness' of the people and its culture that the authors choose to stress, an otherness which, they say, male bourgeois intellectuals and academics within the dominant culture are unable to understand but which, in seeking to understand, they only succeed in destroying since they inevitably end up by assimilating it into their own culture. As for the authors' notions of the people and popular culture, and the intellectuals' relationship to these, one has here elements which recur time and again in the discourse of French intellectuals on culture. French intellectuals seem to be acutely aware of their actual distance from the people in social, cultural and intellectual terms. Yet their political sympathies lead them time and again to try and ally themselves with the people. But in the end the gaps between intellectuals and the people prove to be so wide that French intellectuals constantly feel that the alliance is never successfully forged and, indeed, can never be forged. Hence the constant fear of populism and the constant accusations of populism which are to be found throughout all French intellectual discourse on the people and popular culture.

When Michel de Certeau, in the other essays in *La Culture au pluriel*, moves on to a treatment of popular culture and mass culture in contemporary life, a slightly different picture emerges. Firstly, he does not seem to be sure if he believes that there is still a dominant, monolithic culture in France, or if this 'unitary', State-supported notion of culture has been effectively undermined and exploded by other developments such as the mass media. However, at one point he states quite categorically:

A monolithic culture prevents creative activities from becoming significant. It still dominates. Real forms of behaviour, carried out by the majority of people, are culturally silent and are not acknowledged.[45]

But if he does think that this monolithic culture still dominates French cultural life, he certainly also thinks (and it is his usual emphasis throughout the essays) that it is now being so forcefully challenged and outflanked that what we are observing are, in fact, its death throes. For instance, when De Certeau treats the question of culture and the universities, he focuses on the clash between the teachers with their traditional notions of culture (its transcendent value, what constitutes the canon etc.) and the students, who form a massive hetereogeneous group with completely differing notions and perceptions of culture. For the students, the culture promoted by the university is only one of many cultures on offer to them, and they do not see it as the dominant, encompassing culture. According to De Certeau in this essay, 'Les Universités devant la culture de masse' ['Universities and mass culture'], culture is no longer the sole preserve of one milieu, and it no longer belongs to professionals and specialists of culture.

In the related essay, 'La Culture et l'école' ['Culture and school'], De Certeau conveys a similar picture of a system that is engaged in fighting a losing battle by trying to impose a 'unitary' notion of culture. This is evident in the prevailing approach to the teaching of French language, where pupils are taught 'a unitary, backward-looking and chauvinistic form of language, that of the established canon of writers, that of one specific social category, that of one privileged region'.[46] In contrast to this, De Certeau argues in favour of teaching language as it is spoken by the whole range of French speakers, and not as it is written (or, rather, as it has been written) by one privileged group. This example serves to point to what De Certeau wants modern culture to be in general. He wants it to be a 'culture éclatée',[47] that is, one that has shattered the constraints of a monolithic culture, represents the true diversity and vitality of all people and is allowed to express the way they live in all its reality and difference. Therefore, not only do we see De Certeau observing and welcoming the shift from a fixed, 'unitary' notion of culture to 'plural' notions of culture, but one also notes that he is moving from a definition of culture based largely on the works of high culture to an ethnological definition based on the whole range of human practices.

This point allows me to link up with what was said earlier in connection with De Certeau and his co-authors' treatment of nineteenth-century popular culture and the people. De Certeau believes that for intellectuals ['les clercs'] the culture of the people is 'the silent culture', 'the oceanic night'.[48] Using self-consciously Hugolian metaphors and symbols in order to render this sense of the unknown and infinite quality of the life of the people, De Certeau speaks of walking along the shore-line, looking at the silent immensity, and having an overwhelming feeling of one's own smallness and one's own limitations. De Certeau describes himself as 'obsessed with the noise coming from the other country':

> I have to admit that there is no text, nor any institution that can ever take the place of, or compete with, the distant murmur that can be heard coming from machines, tools, kitchens – the thousands of noises of creative activity. Innumerable lexicons, strange vocabularies. They grow silent as soon as the museum or writing seizes fragments from them in order to make them speak their own interests. That is when they cease to speak for themselves or when they cease to allow others to speak for them.[49]

De Certeau is here reiterating his belief that the dominant culture in which intellectuals are immured prevents them from making contact with the living multifarious culture of the people, which in turn cannot be contained in, or encompassed by, the existing forms of the dominant culture (words and museums). De Certeau believes that the dominant culture has a model of culture which is 'aristocratic and museographic',[50] that is, which only attaches value to *durable* forms. If one were to try and understand the culture of the people, and the creativity of the people, one would, on the other hand, have to give full weight and importance to what is by definition ephemeral and instantaneous: the element of play, celebration, transgression and subversion in the life of the people, none of which tends to leave permanent traces. It is not surprising, therefore, that De Certeau considers 'la fête' as a quintessential element within popular culture, and as a crucial notion for understanding it.

I will touch on some other uses of the notion of 'la fête' in the modern discourse on culture at a later stage, but for the moment I simply want to stress that for De Certeau 'la fête' is an exemplary instance of how people escape from the definitions and systems of control that the dominant culture endeavours to apply to them. However, De Certeau by no means restricts popular culture to such exceptional moments as those which have the qualities of 'la fête'. The otherness of popular culture is, in fact, to be found in more mundane activities, which are far from being legitimated by the dominant culture but which form the 'everyday' tissue of the life of the people. De Certeau insists that culture is not just literary and artistic culture, produced with typewriter, paper and leisure. It is also

> houses, clothes, do-it-yourself, cooking, the thousand things that people do in the town and in the country, that families and friends do together, the multifarious forms of professional work – all these are spheres in which creativity can be seen on all sides. Daily life is scattered with wonders and casts up a foam that rides as dazzlingly on the crest of the rolling waves of language and history as the creations of writers and artists.[51]

Like 'la fête', 'le quotidien' ['the everyday' or 'daily life'] is a key word in the modern French discourse on culture. As indicated here, it tends to convey a sense of the interest, worth and vitality of the ordinary, everyday life of all people. It does, however, only take on its true significance within French discourse on culture, when one recognises to what degree French writers believe that this ordinary, everyday life has traditionally been subject to neglect, indifference and even contempt within the dominant system of French intellectual and cultural life.

Pierre Gaudibert, an important writer on modern cultural questions in France, and a man much involved with, and much marked by, the events of May 68, believed that it was specifically after 1968 that the anthropological/ethnological definition of culture gained general currency, a definition which he saw as rooted in notions of the 'quotidien'. However, Gaudibert admitted that the notion of culture he used in his own work, *Action culturelle: intégration et/ou subversion* (1972), ['Cultural action: integration and/ or subversion'],[52] was too restricted to fine art and literature:

> There exists another more all-embracing notion of culture, which derives from anthropology and ethnology. Since 1968 it has ceased to be restricted to this specialised area, and has come to be applied to the spheres of cultural action as well as to political thinking: according to this definition, culture is the totality of those representations, values, actions, models and rules which control the mentality and the life-style of a social group, and hence of all the individuals who make up the group. Creative works, where they exist, are only one

component part of the totality of objects, signs, gestures, and rituals, a totality which is at one and the same time much greater than individual creative works, but which also exists on a more everyday level.[53]

It is certainly true that notions of 'le quotidien', like notions of 'la fête', run through all modern French cultural discourse.[54] They are talismanic words, used by everyone at every available opportunity, and in a great variety of ways. But, despite all the differences in usage, and despite all the superficialities in usage, these words do clearly express, or appeal to, some fundamental needs and aspirations in modern French society. The 'everyday' seems to be a concept developed by intellectuals who feel that the dominant culture is repressive of the lives and practices of ordinary people. However, one is perhaps justified in supposing that, whether ordinary people do or do not, in reality, feel oppressed by the dominant culture, they would in all probability find the suggestion preposterous that they need their everyday practices legitimated by intellectual discourse. It is, perhaps, only certain intellectuals who, finding themselves for a whole variety of reasons caught between high culture and popular culture, experience the need to have everyday culture legitimated by having it enter into intellectual discourse and by seeing it given as much weight and significance as high culture within this discourse. 'La fête', on the other hand, seems to be a notion that expresses the more general need of all people to branch out, not only from the straitjacket of dominant culture, but also from the monotony, oppression and alienation of modern existence in all of its many dimensions. These two notions do, of course, coincide in the prevalent conception of culture as public festivity, an idea which has dominated much of French thinking about culture in recent years.[55] In this notion of culture the street is the privileged site which unites the quotidian and the festive. The importance attributed to the street in French cultural discourse conveys a sense of a general desire for a culture that is more open, fun-loving, and free-wheeling, as opposed to the allegedly stifling, pompous and enclosed world of high culture.

Since notions of 'la fête' occur in most areas of modern French cultural discourse, I shall keep returning to the question of the festive when it is appropriate. For the moment I wish to take a little further my consideration of the notion of the everyday, by looking at two texts published together and prefaced by Michel de

Certeau in a volume entitled *L'Invention du quotidien* (1980), ['The invention of the everyday'].[56] The first text is by Pierre Mayol and is entitled 'Habiter' ['Living' or 'Inhabiting']; the second is by Luce Giard entitled 'Faire-la-cuisine' ['Doing-the-cooking']. This is the second volume of a work with the title, *L'Invention du quotidien*, the first volume being by Michel de Certeau himself.[57] The text by Pierre Mayol is a sympathetic, not to say empathetic, study of contemporary working-class family life in the old silk-workers' area of Lyon, la Croix-Rousse. Mayol does, in fact, come from this district and is also a member of the family being studied. He regards what he is doing as a socio-ethnographic study of daily life, mixed with a certain amount of urban sociology. It is also a rather literary evocation of the 'banal' details of everyday existence. Mayol sees himself as scrutinising the 'pratiques culturelles' ['cultural practices'] of the inhabitants, which on the whole involves him in finding underlying patterns, rhythms and meanings in such 'cultural practices' as how the inhabitants use the facilities of the neighbourhood, how they relate to other people, how they negotiate the relationship between private space and public space, and how they relate, from the vantage-point of the 'quartier', to the city centre. There is also a considerable amount about eating and drinking, particularly the latter. In addition, there is some consideration of the different mentalities of men and women, and particularly of their different cultural practices (particularly going to the café).

Given the fact that the author has himself such a personal stake in the text (it is his local district and his family), the study is not surprisingly also an exercise, however academic, in retracing his steps, in locating and understanding his roots. However, the study has a more general significance and exemplifies the interest in the everyday and the local which followed on from 1968 and gathered pace in the early and mid-1970s. On the one hand, this concentration on the everyday and the local represents a positive legacy of 1968, in that it shows a genuine interest in, and sympathy for, the life of the people. On the other hand, it marks a rejection of 1968, in that it signals a retreat from the national, political spheres, and is therefore part of a more general process of depoliticisation. At the end of his study, Mayol says that the 'quartier' is a 'powerful site of social apprenticeship . . . an apprenticeship to daily life'.[58] He does, however, add that the complex and profound life of the 'quartier' cannot be captured by political rhetoric or

by statistics. Mayol has, therefore, tried to write a text in which
he consciously avoids foisting political categories and political
interpretations on his material. In fact, his 'socio-ethnographic'
approach leads him away from politics and into a consideration
of the 'culture populaire' of his district, conceived of not as a
politicised working-class culture, but as a popular culture which
is the modern equivalent of the old folk culture:

> To be a member of the working class is . . . not so much
> to be yoked to a specific job, as to participate (and this is
> fundamental) in a form of urban popular culture, in which
> what are most important are those essential values of identi-
> fication which revolve principally around *practices of solidarity*.
> Lacking the rituals and peasant tales collected by folklorists,
> urban culture is based on a practice of relationships (with
> friends or family).[59]

Here is another interesting example of how the French term 'culture
populaire' has rather complex ramifications. The 'popular culture'
referred to in this quotation is popular culture in the sense of the
old folk culture. 'Urban popular culture' is, therefore, presented
as a culture which has replaced the old rural folk culture with
different modern forms, but these are forms which perform the
same function as did the rituals of the old folk culture. According to
Mayol, this new urban popular culture binds communities together
by 'the practice of human relationships'. Mayol acknowledges that
the family he is studying is 'steeped in a working-class cultural
tradition with which it is intimately identified'.[60] But even in a place
like la Croix-Rousse, with its venerable history of working-class
political action, Mayol does not see the working-class cultural tradition as political in the usual sense of the term. For Mayol, the chief
component of this tradition is a sense of local community, a sense
of one's family having lived from generation to generation within
this specific urban context. As we will see in chapter 3, the term
'culture populaire' in modern French usage is often the equivalent of
'culture ouvrière' ['working-class culture'] and often signifies a very
politically conscious culture. It is indicative of Mayol's approach
that he chooses not to use 'culture populaire' in this way, but gives
it a meaning close to 'modern folk culture'. This is no doubt,
once again, a striking testimony to the importance of France's
peasant past, in that most writers on modern French life at some
point feel the need to propose their version of how the popular

culture of the past has been converted into the popular culture of today.[61] It is also a striking testimony to the extent to which writers on modern France have expressed an overwhelming sense of the repressions and distortions that modern city life engenders. Mayol clearly falls into the category of someone who believes that small is beautiful, but he is at pains to stress that it is the inhabitants of cities themselves who break down the experience of city living into manageable, human-size proportions. In fact, for Mayol, 'cultural practice' of the city seems primarily to mean the way in which inhabitants create in the 'quartier' a local environment which is deeply satisfying on an everyday level:

> Faced with the whole complex network of the city, entangled as it is with codes over which the user does not have control, but which he needs to assimilate in order to be able to live there; faced with the way in which town-planning has organised urban space; faced with the general lowering of the quality of social life within the urban setting, the user of the city, nevertheless, always succeeds in creating for himself places to which he can withdraw; he always manages to devise itineraries for his use or pleasure, which are the marks he himself has contrived to make on the urban landscape. The 'quartier' is a dynamic notion which requires a gradual apprenticeship: by repeated physical contact with the public space, the user reaches the point at which he is in a position to appropriate it. The daily banality of this process, shared by all the city-dwellers, conceals the complexity of this cultural practice, and masks how important a role it plays in satisfying the 'urban' desire of the users of the city.[62]

According to Mayol, people have an intense desire to feel part of a community, a feeling which is constituted by the actual experience of growing up within a 'quartier', and which is reinforced daily when one 'practises' [or uses] one's 'quartier'. What the local inhabitant gains from knowing his 'quartier' well is not something that can be quantified, nor can it be cashed in. What the local inhabitant gains is nothing less than the improvement of the quality of his life ['l'amélioration de la "manière de faire"'].[63] On the streets of the 'quartier', or in the living-rooms and kitchens of their homes, the inhabitants are described as following quite strictly the established rituals of shopping, exchanging courtesies and gossip, taking a drink in the café, preparing food, eating at the dinner-table. The dominant impression that Mayol wants to convey is of a stable, self-sufficient and enclosed working-class community, happily going through the rituals of daily life and sticking to traditional gender-based roles. Not only does Mayol give a picture of an unchanged 'working-class culture', but he is also keen to show that the new consumer society has been appropriated and assimilated by the working class in a relatively uncomplicated and painless way. Not for Mayol any tirades against 'la société de consommation' ['consumer society'], and certainly not for him any nostalgic lament over a working-class life threatened or destroyed by the new glossy world of consumerism. For Mayol the coming of the five-day working week has meant a liberation for the working class. The workers are now able to become not only consumers but also spectators at the feast of consumption. This may seem a rather strange distinction, but, according to Mayol, workers who previously worked on Saturdays were obliged to do their shopping through mail order catalogues. Now, however, they are able to take a more active role in consumer society and can exercise this freedom by choosing to wander round the shops on Saturdays and look at all the shop window displays. Workers are now free to have an aesthetic relationship to the city. Mayol talks of 'the extraordinary build-up of the desire to "practise the city", a desire that had to remain repressed, as long as Saturdays were still not free and the worker did not have the space and the time to spread his wings'. For Mayol, this liberation of Saturday is tantamount to 'a revolution in daily life':

> Now that the free Saturday has become a part of everyone's life, it is hard to imagine the revolution which it introduced into daily existence: the city has truly become an open city, a profusion of symbols, a poem. Over and above the mystifying strategies of consumer society, the freeing of Saturdays has made possible the appropriation of urban space by the desire of an itinerant subject who, discovering the city when he is in full control of his natural vitality, begins truly to love it, because at last he can now see himself as a consumer and no longer only as a producer.[64]

Mayol describes in affectionate detail the trips to the big city-centre stores, and describes these outings as an opportunity for the workers to savour the multi-sensory experience offered by the centre with its conspicuous luxury. He stresses the way in which these trips have become part of the tissue of existence of the inhabitants of la Croix-Rousse, by highlighting the significance the inhabitants attach to the various routes they take into the centre. These various routes appear to be, in fact, so many umbilical cords radiating from the maternal 'quartier' but binding the inhabitants to it. For, although the inhabitants of la Croix-Rousse are only too happy to go into the centre, they are, none the less, described as being very happy to come back. They are said to be even happier still to return to base after their functional shopping expeditions to the out-of-town hypermarket Carrefour, and on their way home make a point of stopping off at the local café:

> The excursion into modernity demands this kind of expia-
> tory ceremony; the café is a place of reconciliation with the
> 'quartier' and the place where one celebrates its qualities.[65]

What I have said so far suggests that Mayol concentrates exclu-sively on how the people of la Croix-Rousse live within a limited framework dominated by the values of cohesion, a cohesion largely obtained by the performance of repeated and consoling rituals, which work to ensure and reinforce the sociability of the 'quartier'. But Mayol is, in fact, also interested in those forces that threaten the stability and well-being of the community. He principally focuses on wine as representing an element that is central to la Croix-Rousse's 'urban popular culture', but which, because of the possibilities it offers for excess, is an ever-present threat to the community. Bread, on the other hand, represents thrift and restraint within the culture. Mayol has clearly been receptive to current notions of carnival and 'fête', and he constantly evokes those aspects of this culture (sex and drink) which threaten to subvert the everyday order.[66] It does, however, seem to contradict his dominant approach when he is tempted into defining cultural practice itself either as a 'playing' with the system, or even as a deliberate flouting of the system.[67]

Mayol gives a prominent place to the mythical figure of Gnaffron, who is said to play an important role in local Lyons folklore. He is a kind of folk hero, a carnivalesque figure who represents the poten-tiality for rebelliousness and subversion through drunkenness. But, although Mayol is clearly aware of 'la fête' as being the potential occasion for subversion, he points out that the local community recoils from such excesses and refuses to give in to its destructive

energies. None the less, Mayol's text is peppered with the term 'la
fête' and with notions of the festive. For example, going to the city-
centre stores is a 'festive' experience, as is the family Sunday lunch,
because both are based on excess and gratuitous expenditure ['la
dépense'], but perhaps, above all, because they are both occasions
on which the people participate in a celebration of collectivity and
solidarity.[68] This is, indeed, what Mayol also sees as the primary
festive function of drink and its accompanying rituals in the Croix-
Rousse district. Wine-drinking is even seen by the inhabitants as an
activity specific to their class, other groups (and in particular the
bourgeois) being perceived as stuffy and inhibited 'water-drinkers'.
Ordering a 'pot' of wine (a half-litre measure) in the local café is
described by Mayol as an affirmative act of class solidarity, since
the bourgeois of Lyons, it is claimed, would never venture to order
this particular measure. Mayol's socio-ethnographic approach is,
perhaps, best seen in the passage in which he describes the ritual
of Sunday-morning drinking, when the men gather together in
one particular café in the 'quartier', to drink white wine before the
Sunday meal. The passage is reminiscent of that famous section in
Mass-Observation's *Pub and the People* (1943), in which the arcane
rituals of drinking in a Bolton town-centre pub were recorded by
middle-class intellectuals, like the anthropologists they were, come
to study the natives of Lancashire.[69]

The second part of 'The invention of the everyday' is given over
to Luce Giard's study of women and cooking. In her section
Giard gives particular prominence to the term 'culture ordinaire'
['ordinary culture'].[70] This term is also much favoured by Michel
de Certeau and it underlies much of his thinking on modern culture.
It is a very interesting formulation, and it is clearly being proposed
by these writers as an alternative to 'culture populaire', precisely
because it does not carry the many ideological and historical connotations evoked by this term. In an earlier text, De Certeau had made
his reasons for adopting the term 'ordinary culture' quite clear:

> I would simply like to present to you some work in progress
> on 'ways of doing' and 'everyday practices' to which I would
> like to give the name of 'ordinary culture', in order to avoid
> the accepted expression 'popular culture', in which the word
> 'popular' carries too many ideological connotations.[71]

Much of the thinking of De Certeau, Mayol and Giard on popular culture is concerned with the ways in which modern society has

developed a new folk culture appropriate to an industrial, urban society, and therefore the term 'culture populaire' is plainly too closely associated with the old peasant folk culture. What is more, the meaning of 'culture populaire' as 'working-class culture' is likewise not a meaning with which they wish to be burdened. As we have seen, even Mayol, who is mainly concerned with the culture of the urban working class, tries to avoid using the term 'culture populaire' in this sense of a politically conscious working-class culture, and develops a notion of 'culture populaire' as modern urban folk culture. Giard's attitude to the term 'culture populaire' is even clearer on this point. She wishes to expunge any suggestion of class from her notion of 'ordinary culture'. What is more, in her desire to give a classless portrait of ordinary culture, Giard seems particularly to want to avoid what she sees as the mechanistic and imprisoning schema of Pierre Bourdieu's analysis of popular culture in *La Distinction*, a text which I discuss later (see chapter 4). In her view, Bourdieu rigidly assigns people to a class position which is shown as determining all their cultural attitudes and practices. Within such a dogmatic framework, 'popular culture' is always an inferior, illegitimate, degraded form of culture in the face of higher, dominant forms of culture. By using the term 'ordinary culture' in preference to 'popular culture', Giard was therefore hoping to escape from Bourdieu's class-controlled analysis of cultural practices.

In addition to objecting to the importance Bourdieu accords to class, Giard also objects to the fact that to date he had given almost no consideration to the specific experience of women. In her own study of women and ordinary culture, Giard says she was inspired by the film *Jeanne Dielman* by the feminist director Chantal Akerman. In this film Akerman tried to show 'the true value of the daily experience of women'[72] by slowly and patiently evoking the daily rituals and gestures of women in the home. Giard admits that she found in Akerman's film a confirmation of her own project of making visible, and giving value to, those women's activities which had previously been neglected or despised:

> In that voice, in its gentleness and its violence, I recognised the same need to return to insignificance in order to break out of the feeling of being hemmed in by an ideology and by the intelligentsia. The same wish to learn how to look away from 'educated culture' . . . . The same feeling of distance from

27

those who sing the praises of the naïve marvels of so-called 'popular culture', while, in reality, they destroy it all the more effectively. The same refusal to despise 'mass culture', as do those who deplore its commercialised mediocrity, while they willingly share the profits that this industry brings in. These are some of the reasons which make me want to turn my attention to people and things of the present, to ordinary life in its infinite variety . . . . To accept those ordinary cultural practices, which are so often taken to be insignificant, as worth taking an interest in, recording and analysing. To learn how to look at those 'ways of doing' which are fleeting and modest, which concern everyday series of events, and which are often the subject's only site of possible creativity: precarious inventions with nothing to consolidate them, no language to articulate them, no recognition to give them value.[73]

Giard's project is, therefore, to reject the criteria laid down by the dominant culture and bring to light what is invisible in daily life ['l'invisible quotidien'], a 'zone of silence and shadows'. In a series of interviews she attempts to give a voice to women, 'the voice of the people in the kitchens' ['la voix du peuple des cuisines']. She wants to hear their 'ordinary words' ['paroles ordinaires'] describing 'ordinary practices' ['pratiques ordinaires']. She has chosen ordinary middle-class and lower middle-class women, articulate enough to express themselves, but not so highly educated that they are totally in control of, and aware of, the discourses they use. She does not see this middle-class sample as itself having any significance, since, as already stated, she does not believe that cooking is to be thought of in a class-specific way. In fact, she regards cooking as an important part of all 'ordinary culture', because she sees it as playing a central role in all women's lives, 'independent of their social situation and their relationship to high culture ['la culture cultivée'] or to mass culture ['l'industrie culturelle de masse']'. She likes to see cooking as 'a site of happiness, pleasure and creativity ['invention']', which requires as much intelligence, imagination and memory as those activities traditionally regarded as superior, such as music or weaving.

As well as giving a voice to other women, Giard is also, of course, giving herself the opportunity to speak. In fact, much of the study is taken up with a consideration of her own attitude to cooking. She describes herself as someone who, as an adolescent and a young woman, violently rejected the traditional female role of cook played by her mother, grandmothers and indeed all her female forebears. To the whole business of buying, preparing and serving food she had always shown indifference and even contempt. She had wanted to follow a purely intellectual destiny, that of a writer or a mathematician. As a student, her indifference to and contempt for food had been reinforced by noisy, impersonal cafeteria-type student restaurants, and she had at this time maintained her scornful attitude to the 'knowledge' and 'skills' required to be a good cook. It was only later, when she was in a place of her own, and when she had to do her own cooking, that she slowly came round to abandoning her former attitudes. Not only did she begin to take a positive delight in the whole activity of preparing and serving food, but she began to think carefully about the role of cooking in the lives of the preceding generations of women in her family. She says that it had been her 'intellect' which had kept her away from cooking and traditional women's activities. Now she had begun to feel an enduring worth in the endlessly repeated gestures of generations of women, their daily activities, their unrecognised fund of knowledge expended on ephemeral tasks. She experiences a profound desire to make contact with these women of past genera-tions, to render homage to them, to demonstrate a loyalty towards them, to acknowledge an indebtedness and also a connection. She obviously feels, therefore, a deep need to affirm her solidarity with women of the past and the present in their ordinary tasks, to be herself part of 'ordinary culture', and indeed to be fused into this ordinary, everyday life. She even defines her ambitions as a writer in this way:

> Women eternally destined to do housework and to pro-vide the necessities of life; women removed from public life and the world of knowledge; illiterate women, who, in my grandmothers' generation, barely received any schooling, and whose memory I would like to keep active, alive and true. Following their example, I have always dreamed of practising a 'poor' form of writing, in the manner of the public letter-writer to whom words do not belong, a kind of writing from which one's own name disappears, which aims at its own self-effacement, which produces its own dispersal, a kind of writing which, in its own way, renders the humble service to others which those unknown women

(no one any longer knows their names, their strength, or their courage) performed throughout the generations, in the ceaseless, elementary gestures demanded by the endless repetition of domestic tasks through the remorseless succession of meals and days.[74]

In the cases of both Mayol and Giard we find, therefore, notable examples of French intellectuals who feel a profound desire and need to understand, give value to, and connect with the life and culture of 'ordinary' people, the life and culture of the 'everyday'. There is even a desire to fuse themselves into this ordinary, everyday culture, and to feel an anonymous, consenting, even unconscious part of this culture. There is also, and not least, the desire to escape from what is seen as the tyrannical habit of viewing culture in terms of the 'cultivated' and the 'popular', the latter supposedly being granted no value or importance in French society.

A crucial element in the desire to give value to ordinary, everyday culture, and to be part of it, is the wish to connect with the past and to feel that one belongs to continuing, enduring traditions and practices. This is clearly what leads both Mayol and Giard to seek out the 'folk' element in their different areas of study. In the modern discourse on culture, and particularly throughout the 1970s, one constantly meets this attempt to counter the alienations of modern existence by returning to, or re-creating, some version of peasant or folk culture. There is no need to stress here that it is not a case of *actually* re-creating or returning to the authentic folk culture of the past. Almost all writers agree that the old folk culture is, and has been for some considerable time, well and truly dead. In such studies as Eugen Weber's *Peasants into Frenchmen* (1977) and the collected volume of essays *The Wolf and the Lamb. Popular culture in France from the old regime to the twentieth century* (1977),[75] we find, charted in fascinating detail, the story of the passing of the old peasant culture and the coming of the new urban mass culture. These scholars in general select the period 1870-1914 as being the moment when the old folk culture finally died. Other scholars have even suggested that the old culture survived into the 1950s and was only finally killed off by the consumer society and the mass media.[76] But, whatever the truth of this might be, one can safely say that what is not dead is the desire of people to relate to the old folk culture, and to make it in some way part of their modern lives.

In *La Politique du patrimoine* (1980) ['The politics of the heritage'][77]

Marc Guillaume, however, casts a very jaundiced and critical eye on this interest in folk culture, particularly as shown by the State and various public agencies, which, he claims, use the past for their own political and economic purposes. Firstly, Guillaume acknowledges that there is, indeed, an overwhelming passion for conserving the heritage in industrial societies, whether it be buildings, communities, the countryside or whatever. But he sees this passion for conservation as profoundly at odds with capitalism and its devotion to 'uprooting, obsolescence and destruction'. Guillaume believes that there has occurred a loss of collective memory and social identity in the modern world and that people do feel a need to find their roots. The politics of the heritage are, however, based on the reassuring fantasy that change can be reconciled with continuity and that creating the new can be reconciled with conserving the old:

> 'Preserving a living culture', 'a memory of daily life', 'putting the past into the shopwindow of the present', are the formulas that one most frequently finds coming from the pen of conservationists today, formulas which struggle against the very logic of conservation.[78]

According to Guillaume, the State works hard to make its version of the past dominate the public space through such varied means as museums, monuments, street signs and national celebrations. But none of these has, in reality, the capacity to touch people. None of these has any true symbolic significance for them. The more the State works at accumulating and preserving the material remains of the past, the more it becomes apparent that people are cut off from it. People do, indeed, feel a great sense of loss, and do desire to surround themselves with what Guillaume calls 'objets de suture' – things that will help them to stitch together symbolically the wound inflicted by what has been lost. The State obviously wants its monuments to be the objects that bind people to their past. But such monuments clearly do not perform this role, for people do not identify with the past that they symbolise. Equally, Guillaume believes that the massive trade in 'bygones' functions in a similar way. The nostalgia industry has produced a veritable mania for emptying attics and selling and displaying folk objects, which in reality no longer mean anything important to us. Guillaume sees the nostalgia for old rural ways and old rural objects as an 'ideology' to be found particularly among the 'new lower middle-class intelligentsia', a group which, in his view, has been especially affected by the changes brought about by economic growth, and which has sought stability and identity by retreating into the past. Guillaume sees such people as caught in an impossible dilemma. They find the present state of society so unbearable that they turn to the past as the only habitable space. But by definition this past is irretrievable and can now only be found either in fake reproductions or in 'mute' objects. Guillaume particularly likes the story of Lamartine's house in Mâcon in Burgundy, which the local council is said to have demolished to make way for a car park. Having done this, however, the council was not deterred from simply putting Lamartine's commemorative plaque on another house nearby.[79]

In the end, Guillaume's main concern is with what he believes to be the State's project to monopolise the past and to appropriate it for its own use. This approach is similar to that of De Certeau examined earlier, in which he described how he believed that in the nineteenth century the State succeeded in destroying local cultures in order to create its own dominant culture. In the same way, Guillaume claims that the modern State endeavours to manufacture a 'collective memory', a popular memory, which is not in reality the memory of the people themselves. A truly collective memory would not have one single meaning but a multiplicity of meanings, because it would be true to all the experiences of 'everyday life' and would not just be made up of those experiences which the State found useful to its own ends. Guillaume believes that the official collective memory dominates the public space of French towns:

> Surveys that have been done on the place-names used in towns show that the great majority of town-centre streets bear the names of important people connected to the town: lawyers, mayors, doctors, benefactors, war victims. On the other hand, the streets in outlying districts, and particularly in housing estates, generally bear names *that have no memory*: names of plants, countries, towns etc. These cultural and spatial hierarchies, which are carefully promoted by all the authorities, denote a strict topography whose values are clear to see. No less clear is all that is left out and cast into oblivion: women, the manual professions, the popular arts such as song, and the new arts such as cinema.[80]

Whatever one thinks of the validity of some of Guillaume's claims, one is none the less struck by the way in which French culture is yet again described as a system in which the experience of the people, and the culture of the people are not given any value nor even acknowledged at all. But there is an optimism in Guillaume which is also certainly to be found in the other writers considered so far. Although the powers that be try as hard as they can to impose their law, it remains a fact that they never actually succeed in containing and directing the life that goes on beyond their reach. Here again we find the word 'ordinary' being made to assume a very important task, for Guillaume sets 'ordinary memory' against collective memory to name what he feels to be the real process by which people actually invest the place they inhabit, and the daily lives they lead, with authentic symbolic significance, as opposed to the false process by which the State and public authorities attempt to foist an alien national popular culture upon them.

One of the most celebrated French works on 'everyday life' is Henri Lefebvre's *La Vie quotidienne dans le monde moderne*, ['Everyday Life in the Modern World']. It was published in 1968, and is often considered to have had a decisive influence on the ideology of May 1968 and on the Situationists in particular. In this text Lefebvre gave central importance to the notion of cultural revolution and the revolutionary transformation of everyday life. It is, of course, a striking testimony to the changes in French intellectual life since 1968 that the various writers I have already looked at in connection with notions of popular culture, everyday culture and ordinary culture, do not embark on a full-scale assault upon capitalist society. It is now commonplace to observe that, during the 1970s and indeed up to the present day, there has been a steady erosion of Marxist and neo-Marxist beliefs among French intellectuals.[81] In fact, it may be fairer to say that this process of erosion had been going on throughout the postwar period, despite intermittently spectacular increases in the popularity of Marxist and neo-Marxist ideas, for example at the time of the Liberation and in 1968. The abandonment of revolutionary ideology can be seen quite clearly in the discourse on popular culture and mass culture. In the work of a writer like De Certeau one notes how he began by seeing popular culture as having a revolutionary potential. He stressed the extent to which the State (particularly in the nineteenth century) regarded popular culture as dangerous and hence worked to control or repress it. But, as De Certeau proceeds to consider modern popular culture, one observes a distinct tendency for him to believe that people can actually attain a plenitude of experience within existing capitalist

33

society. Capitalist society may repress, but it does not, in fact, destroy the creativity of the people. In the case of Mayol and Giard, one also observed a willingness to see the virtues of accommodating oneself to society as it existed and of being a part of a traditional and enduring community.

Henri Lefebvre, however, was not interested in making a reasonable accommodation with modern society and with the everyday life that has to be suffered in it. For Lefebvre, the everyday was inseparable from mass society, mass culture, mass consumerism and the mass media. It was therefore subject, as they were, to the relentless process of planning and organisation by capitalists and bureaucrats ('la société bureaucratique de consommation'). According to Lefebvre, the majority of people had now become little else but passive consumers and passive observers, locked into the logic of a system which constantly created and promoted new desires and needs, which, by definition, it always failed to satisfy. The passive consumer/observer was always left with a sense of emptiness and meaninglessness. True happiness was not, in fact, attainable in this system, but could only be achieved by the revolutionary project of disengaging true creativity from the everyday. Lefebvre in this text was no classical Marxist, but was more of a utopian socialist, who ended by proposing a rousing but rather vague cultural programme of the kind which became very familiar in 1968. There seems little doubt that Lefebvre himself did much to popularise the optimistic, alternative, not to say 'gauchiste' discourse on culture. He called for a sexual revolution. He also called for an urban revolution, in which the city would no longer be the property of rationalising capitalists, but would be appropriated by the people themselves in a spirit of play and creativity. He called for a rediscovery of 'la fête' and for the elimination of the distinction between the festive and the everyday. Indeed, he saw it as an essential part of the revolutionary moment that it would do precisely this: it would break with the everyday and restore 'la fête'.

> The future Revolution will put an end to the everyday by shattering all constraints, and by investing the everyday, immediately or gradually, with the values of prodigality and waste. The Revolution is not, therefore, to be defined only on an economic, political or ideological level, but in a more concrete way as the end of the everyday. As for the much-talked about period of transition, this also takes on a

new meaning. For it is a period which challenges the everyday, reorganises it, and, in so doing, dissolves and transforms it. In destroying the importance and the illusory rationality of the everyday, it also puts an end to the opposition between the everyday and 'la fête' (between work and leisure) as the foundation of society.[82]

This revolutionary discourse is not only reminiscent of 1968; it also recalls 1936 and 1944–5. In fact, in this passage Lefebvre was thinking above all of those two moments of recent history. He admitted that he was deeply influenced by the experience of both the Popular Front and the Liberation 'which both took on the appearance of gigantic "fêtes"'.[83] But with the benefit of twenty to thirty years' hindsight, Lefebvre came to believe that these historical examples of how the everyday could be transformed by the festive were no longer relevant. 'Revolutionary romanticism' had been betrayed and the notion of revolution had itself become a degraded notion, trapped in the everyday structures and concerns of a bureaucratic and institutional party. Lefebvre believed that capitalism had succeeded in 'integrating' Marxism and working-class ideology. The working classes themselves had been effectively incorporated into the system by capitalism's powerful dual strategies of repression and persuasiveness. In particular, the workers had been seduced into accepting and believing in the ideology of consumerism. In so doing, the workers were, of course, deluding themselves, and failed to see that they were still exploited and could never appropriate the things and the life-style that were held tantalisingly in front of them. According to Lefebvre, the social groups that had refused to be seduced and integrated into consumer society were now not the working classes but the young, the ethnic minorities, women and intellectuals. Although such groups had a real stake in consumer society, and were profoundly compromised by it, they none the less retained a capacity to react against it and even to reject it. But, while Lefebvre allocated to such groups a central role in the cultural revolution, he did not in fact give any consideration to what forms their creativity might take in practice. Instead, he devoted virtually the whole study to a critique of how mass culture, as it at present exists, represses and alienates all its members.

According to Lefebvre, mass culture prevents its members from achieving genuine creativity, because it relegates them to the passive condition of spectators. Here one can see the close links between Lefebvre's critique of mass society and the Situationists' denunciation of 'the society of the spectacle'.[84] I do not intend here to consider fully Lefebvre's critique of mass culture, but I do, however, wish to stress the general point that, for Lefebvre, mass culture was so oppressive and alienating that it prevented people from achieving any genuine plenitude in their lives. He believed that citizens of mass society lived in a world of manufactured fantasies, based on the lives of film stars and other personalities (throughout the 1960s, French intellectual observers of mass culture liked to call such figures 'Olympians'). On the practical level, people could only express their creativity in drastically diminished forms. Lefebvre was, for instance, scathing about hobbies such as gardening and do-it-yourself. He talked of these activities as 'ghettos of creativity, scaled-down, hygienic and functional'.[85] In his view mass society was scrutinised, organised and planned down to the last detail, with the result that there was no room for individual creativity and spontaneity. Even joy and freedom were catered for and contained within the ghettos of 'holiday villages'.[86] Everyday life for Lefebvre was, therefore, nothing but a manufactured illusion, a domain in which people were controlled and manipulated, while being made to feel that they were making free choices and living the good life. In calling for the revolutionary transformation of daily life through grandiose and daring acts of destruction and creativity, Lefebvre was heralding the utopian dreams of 1968.

Writers such as De Certeau, who in the wake of 1968 experienced the failures and disillusionments of these utopian dreams of cultural revolution, could not write of cultural matters in the same way as Lefebvre, even though after 1968 De Certeau still shared some of Lefebvre's attitudes to mass culture. For instance, one of De Certeau's favourite words to describe a key aspect of mass society is 'quadrillage', a word also to be found in Lefebvre. This word has the meaning of a tight military or police surveillance of an area. It also means the squared, criss-cross pattern on a piece of checked material or paper, and it can also mean the grid pattern of a group of streets. The word 'quadrillage' conveys, therefore, the notion that modern society is completely controlled and organised, and that there is no room in such a society for individual creativity and action. De Certeau's repeated use of the word 'quadrillage' clearly shows that he was drawn to this view of mass society. However, De Certeau was willing, in a way totally contrary to

Lefebvre, to see value in the everyday cultural practices of people within this society. In fact, he saw the proliferation and variety of such everyday practices as do-it-yourself, gardening and cooking as evidence of the irreducible vitality and creativity of people. It is true that Lefebvre also saw that mass society was not a monolithic block. He believed that it did have 'fissures, holes, lacunae',[87] and that there were irreducible elements within it. But for Lefebvre these 'fissures' were not the creative spaces that ordinary people opened up for themselves. They were the defects in the apparently perfect structure of 'bureaucratic consumer society', and these fissures could serve as the points at which pressure could be applied in order to destroy this society. In other words, Lefebvre did not accord any worth to existing everyday culture, but only saw value in the practices of marginal and discontented groups who could transform everyday culture into revolutionary activity.

It is not surprising that Lefebvre thought that the 'festive' and 'revolutionary' experiences of the Popular Front and the Liberation were no longer relevant to the situation of the late 1960s. He clearly believed that some of the principal aspirations of these periods had come to nothing. Two of the key words of both the Popular Front and the Liberation periods were without doubt 'leisure' and 'culture'. As for leisure, Lefebvre was far from impressed by the claim made by many sociologists and journalists, particularly in the late 1950s and early 1960s, that the 'leisure society' had already arrived. Lefebvre was more cautious and sceptical. For him, leisure was, in fact, just another facet of mass culture:

> At the present time, leisure is for almost everyone principally a break, and that only momentary, with the everyday. We are living through a difficult period of change, during which the old 'values' have been prematurely and thoughtlessly lost from sight. Leisure is no longer 'la fête', or the reward for hard work, nor is it yet free activity done for its own sake. It is a universal spectacle: television, cinema, tourism.[88]

As for culture itself, in the sense of high culture, this had also become in Lefebvre's eyes simply another consumer product. To consume culture was for him an activity which was only 'a little less passive a way of accepting things as they are'.[89] Above all, culture had simply become a 'State ideology', another way of exercising control by imposing a false image of unity and coherence:

The ideology of culture, or 'culturalism', props up the crumbling thesis of the coherence and oneness of Culture. That is the official thesis, whereas everything points to the fact that Culture has been smashed into smithereens. For a long time now, there have been only subcultures of diverse origin: countryside and rural life, urban life, aristocracy, proletariat, bourgeoisie, countries and sectors dubbed 'under-developed', mass culture and so forth. Several 'subcultures', even if subsumed under one blanket definition of classical culture, do not in reality make up one single culture. In any case, is culture not after all a myth? No. It is more than that: it is a State ideology. The unity of culture is, in fact, situated at the highest level – that of cultural institutions.[90]

We see here how Lefebvre believed that the State, through its institutions, tried to impose high culture on the nation. In doing so, it was attempting to present high culture as the unifying culture of the nation, whereas the unified notion of 'Culture' had, in his view, been shattered into a multiplicity of 'sub-cultures', of which 'classical' culture was now only one. In 1936 and in the postwar years, 'leisure' and 'culture' had been the key words and the guiding myths of those who sought to improve the quality of life for the majority of people by extending leisure time, offering leisure facilities and giving access to high culture. Having looked at Lefebvre, one can already see that 'leisure' and 'culture' were later to be subjected to considerable critical scrutiny and found, in particular by the far left, to be merely the mystifying constructs of capitalist ideology. But, before returning to developments in the later 1960s, and afterwards, I want to go on to discuss in some detail the more optimistic notions of leisure and culture that were current between 1936 and the early 1960s.

2

POPULAR CULTURE AND POPULAR EDUCATION: LEISURE, WORK AND CULTURE

In 1962, Jacques Charpentreau and René Kaës published a volume entitled *La Culture populaire en France* ['Popular culture in France'],[1] which provides a useful starting-point for the analysis of one of the dominant meanings of 'culture populaire' in France from the 1930s until at least the late 1960s. Essentially, Charpentreau and Kaës used the term 'culture populaire' to characterise the educational and cultural movement that emerged at the time of the Popular Front, was nurtured during the Resistance and took form at the time of the Liberation. This movement was seen as a socialist movement of 'cultural emancipation', which sought to obtain 'cultural rights' for the people ['le droit à la culture'] in the same way that political, economic and social rights had been fought for. As these writers were always keen to stress, this 'right to culture' was in fact acknowledged for the first time in the French Constitution of 1948 and, at the same time, in UNESCO's 'Declaration of the Rights of Man'. This educational and cultural movement did, of course, have important historical antecedents, particularly in the many projects concerning working-class education which were initiated throughout the nineteenth and the early twentieth centuries.[2] Charpentreau and Kaës were, however, happy to take the story even further back to the French Revolution, and to see there the first instances of the attempt, not only to take education and culture to the people, but also to create a new 'authentic culture of the people'. In the modern period, the educational and cultural movement for the 'cultural emancipation' of the people had, according to Charpentreau and Kaës, expanded beyond recognition, and they pointed to the thousands of national and local 'associations' which were committed to enhancing the cultural life of the people. Indeed, it was in the work of these associations that they saw the true meaning of 'popular culture'.[3]

The way in which Charpentreau and Kaës used the term 'culture populaire' was, to say the least, ambiguous.[4] But they used it in exactly the same way as all those others writers who from the 1930s to the 1960s identified it with this movement of cultural emancipation. On the one hand, 'culture populaire' seemed to mean simply 'popular education', 'culture' here having the force of 'educating and cultivating' the people. On the other hand, 'culture populaire' also meant, in the way that Charpentreau and Kaës used it, the actual 'culture of the people', that is, their own cultural practices, very broadly defined. Charpentreau and Kaës, in fact, accepted this ambiguity as the necessary and even healthy 'tension' of popular culture, a tension which embodied 'the desire to have access to cultural life, and the desire not to disown one's origins':

> On the one hand, popular culture wants to favour this enormous movement for the diffusion of culture. This diffusion of 'works of art and works of the spirit', and the participation of the mass of French people in a real cultural life were the tasks that André Malraux assigned to his new Ministry of Culture. On the other hand, popular culture claims to take on board the real daily lives of people, and refuses to accept a split between 'cultural activity' and everyday existence. Working-class traditions teach us that workers must take their cultural destiny into their own hands, as well as their political, economic and social destiny. In this respect, popular culture is to some degree inseparable from a rejection of a monolithic notion of 'national culture', as this is worked out behind closed doors by professionals of culture.[5]

In fact, modern movements of popular culture and popular education in France never did resolve this particular ambiguity. Although they continued to stick to the ambition of being true to the actual culture of the people and of encouraging the people to take control of their own cultural lives ['autogestion culturelle'], it became very clear that these ambitions could not really be reconciled with the constant appeals to the State to assume the task of improving the life of its citizens. It was taken for granted that, in order for the 'average French person' to lead 'a normal cultural life', he had also to lead 'a decent daily life', which involved the State in improving everyone's standard of living, in terms of higher salaries, better housing, better education, more leisure facilities. Charpentreau and Kaës were writing at the tail-end of the 'heroic' period of the popular culture movement's fight for the right to culture. They were, therefore, still largely bound by the definitions and perspectives laid down by the movement from 1936 to just after the war. They seemed to be happiest when they could define popular culture in terms of small-scale, human initiatives. They identified it with those privileged moments when the 'militant', the 'animateur', or the 'educator' with few means at his disposal, took culture to a small number of eager but culturally deprived people, and succeeded in conveying to them the morally and spiritually uplifting potential of art:

> Popular culture is the effort put in by many people so that all those, who are not among the two million privileged individuals, can actually enjoy the right to culture. It is the age-old affirmation of human values in the context of modern civilisation, and the living proof of a will to confront the mass era and to meet the claims of 'the person'. That is why it is interested both in the great works of modern art, as well as in the life of the village. That is why it does not hesitate to operate on the most modest of scales, to pass through the humblest channels, to tread the most obscure bypaths, and to penetrate into the most hidden corners: to gather a few friendly 'persons' around a record-player in a deprived suburb. It is an attempt to respond to the cultural aspirations of people ('les gens').[6]

It is worth noting a detail in that last sentence. Charpentreau and Kaës did not, in fact, use the term 'le peuple' (the people) in their books. They preferred the more noncommittal and certainly more pluralist term 'les gens', that is to say, not 'the people' but simply 'people'. The willingness or unwillingness of writers to use the term 'le peuple' is a central issue in all the texts with which I am dealing. In general, it is, of course, a question of whether the writer feels happy with the notion of a unified nation, or with the idea of a unified working class, since 'le peuple' can mean both. In the case of Charpentreau and Kaës, there was no doubt an underlying recognition that social structures were changing and that it was no longer possible to talk in such a confident way of the working class as a homogeneous entity. When they used the term 'les gens', they put the word in inverted commas, and thereby signalled the fact that they were using the word in a new way. They also were pointing out that they were consciously choosing not to use the term 'le peuple'.

There are other reasons why these writers might not have been happy to use the term, and one can see evidence of these reasons in the extract above. In the development of the popular culture movement from the 1930s onwards, an important part was played by the personalist philosophy of Emmanuel Mounier.[7] Many members of the popular culture movement explicitly acknowledged their debt to Mounier (Charpentreau, for instance, also wrote a study of Mounier's aesthetics). It would, in fact, seem fair to claim that the ideology of the popular culture movement between the 1930s and the 1960s was made up of a vague blend of socialism and personalism. Charpentreau and Kaës's resistance to the collective term 'le peuple' must, therefore, have derived to a certain degree from their personalist attachment to the notion of individual 'persons'. In the extracted passage above, the influence of personalism is evident in the vocabulary itself ('the claims of the "person"', 'a few persons around a record-player'). This influence is also evident in the central belief that what mattered in popular culture was making contact with individuals on a personal level and contributing to their moral, spiritual and cultural development within a broader social context that was defined by cultural dispossession, massification and alienation. Charpentreau and Kaës, like other writers in the popular culture movement, used a vocabulary of moral heroism to define their ambitions: they saw themselves as confronting and contesting the prevailing culture and as refusing to adapt to it. They were fighting for higher moral values within a degraded society and struggling to protect human values in an inhuman society.

Given such views, it is hardly surprising that the popular culture movement was highly critical of mass culture and the mass media (called 'les moyens de masse' or 'les arts de masse' at this period).[8] At the same time, it tried hard to be resolutely modern and claimed to take full account of the technological realities of the modern cultural world. It solved this apparent dilemma by adopting a thoroughly educational approach to the mass media. A very characteristic initiative of the popular culture movement was the creation of 'ciné-clubs' and later 'télé-clubs'. These were seen as ways of introducing people to the best examples of cinema and television as well as of helping people to understand and analyse these new media. They were also, of course, seen as ways of criticising, controlling and even eliminating the undesirable aspects of the new media. One of the principal ambitions of the popular culture movement was to create a vast corps of 'animateurs' or 'militants', who would perform the crucial task of leading people into an appreciation and understanding of culture. These 'animateurs' would also play the role of civic educators, for their main object was not only to introduce people to high culture, but also to provide them with the necessary awareness to enable them to judge the aesthetic, social and moral worth of the culture that surrounded them (that is to say, mass culture and everyday culture). These 'animateurs' would also encourage people to develop their practical creativity in their everyday life. In fact, popular culture was defined by Charpentreau and Kaës as the attempt 'to reunite daily life and culture'. 'Animateurs' would have the job of bringing 'the cultural level of the mass' up to their own, but they had also to be sensitive to the daily life of people and to their own culture, as it was actually lived and practised. Ideally, 'animateurs' should be of the mass and live with the mass, not only in order to know them well, but also 'to make the mass more militant':[9]

> In reality, one has to be sensitive to what might seem to be the most insignificant happenings of life at its most familiar. Only 'animateurs' who have themselves come from the masses can be made sufficiently sensitive to these. And when this occurs, all is possible. As it happens, we have participated in cultural events which deliberately took their starting-point in everyday life: poetry evenings, which began with the reading of evening newspapers; sessions in which one got people to respond to art on the basis of the most ordinary objects (such as wax tablecloths with abstract designs), or by looking at problems of interior decoration (polychroming of kitchen cupboards) or by looking at shop windows of big stores to see the wonderful surrealist effects to be found there. In their daily lives, 'people' ('les gens') already have the possibility of personal choice and personal expression. What is more, one can systematically draw on all the riches offered by the 'mass arts' (cinema, radio and television).[10]

If everyday life is mass culture, then, as this passage indicates, people must not experience it passively but must learn how to respond actively to the given environment and select the best aspects on offer, in order to enhance their moral, social and aesthetic awareness. On occasions, Charpentreau and Kaës did not so much seem to be attacking mass culture as advocating a pluralist position. That is to say, they seemed to be simply recommending that people should have the chance of enjoying both mass culture and high culture. Thus, we find the following passage:

> People refuse to believe that, in order to participate in culture, they need a daily diet of Romanesque art, abstract painting and the works of Mauriac – and of course they are right. But equally, they refuse to limit themselves to television and wrestling on a Saturday evening. A double refusal and a double difficulty. This is the painful and unsatisfactory dilemma of popular culture, for, after all, one can like wrestling *and* the works of Mauriac.[11]

Charpentreau and Kaës themselves seemed to be willing to accept that one could like elements of both high culture and mass culture, but they also made it clear that this was not a solution readily available to the popular culture movement. In any case, this passage represents an untypically open and relaxed attitude to mass culture on the part of Charpentreau and Kaës. It seems fair to say that, like other writers in the popular culture movement, whatever they might say about staying true to the 'everyday life' of people, they were above all interested in taking high culture to them, and in using high culture as a way of counteracting the alienations of modern city life and the vicious and degrading influence of mass culture. For instance, Charpentreau and Kaës constantly used the image of 'inserting culture' into the everyday life of people.[12] By choosing the image of 'insertion', they wanted to convey their belief that introducing culture into the lives of people had to be done in such a way that it did not alter the structure of their lives. Hence the view that popular culture 'unites everyday life and culture'. However, this image also implied a realisation on the part of the 'animateur' that he might be forcing his values on other people. To 'insert' culture into daily life sounds very much like slipping it in unbeknown to people. In retrospect, one may well think that this is an important part of the truth about the popular culture movement, but it seems clear that the popular culture movement itself did not consider that people were in any way resistant to culture. On the contrary, the starting point of the movement was the belief that not only did people have a 'right' to culture, but that they also had a 'need'. The notion of 'besoin culturel' ['cultural need'] underlies most of the discourse of the popular culture movement. According to Charpentreau and Kaës, 'the average French person' suffered from a real sense of 'cultural

frustration' at not having 'free access to culture'.[13] It was precisely
to respond to this frustration and to break through into the closed
'cultural circuit' that the popular culture movement developed. The
thousands of cultural organisations to be found in modern France
were designed to be cultural relay stations ['relais culturels'], which
passed culture down the line to people.[14] It is also because this need
for culture was perceived as a vast and ever-growing one that the
popular culture movement appealed to the State to invest massive
resources in the cultural sector, while at the same time looking
nostalgically back to that heroic period when lack of equipment
and facilities had gone together with a profound commitment to
'cultural action' ['action culturelle'] 'on a human scale'.[15]

Charpentreau and Kaës's *La Culture populaire en France* was published in 1962. In 1967, Charpentreau published his own work *Pour
une politique culturelle* ['For a cultural policy'],[16] in which one can
still see all the important elements of his previous analysis of popular culture and mass culture. In fact, his assault on mass culture was
even more virulent in this text, and his call for a truly democratic
cultural policy even more passionate than before. Yet one also notes
Charpentreau's sense that, even though there was more than ever a
crying need to combat mass culture and to bring people into contact
with culture of real worth, there had been a distinct falling-away of
purpose and belief in the ranks of intellectuals and militants. Even
popular culture organisations were said to be beginning to treat
culture as just another consumer product. Charpentreau attacked,
in particular, those who had abandoned their idealistic, moral and
cultural positions in the face of a general, fashionable capitulation
to mass culture:

> At the present time, there is a tendency to minimise the
> particularly harmful effect that the usual content of the mass
> media has upon children and adolescents. Some educators
> have a bad conscience, fearing to appear 'square'. They do
> not know how to stand up to the sarcasm of those who are
> 'with it'. In the last few years, a kind of 'intellectual terrorism'
> seems to have paralysed those who used to call into question
> the content of the mass media. In certain aesthetic coteries,
> which feel they are above the influence of the mass media, it
> is regarded as the in-thing not to reveal the true nature of the
> products which are packaged in this way, but to make fun of
> those who question their value.[17]

Many of the key figures of the popular culture movement had, however, resolutely refused to give in to what they saw as the prevailing fashionable views of mass culture. The most dominant intellectual force in the movement was without doubt the sociologist Joffre Dumazedier, and to this day his approach to cultural issues is still substantially the same as it was in the early days of the popular culture movement.[18] Having been active in this movement since 1936, he stands as a crucial example of the continuity of this movement in French society.[19] What is more, as an influential figure in French academic sociology, he has also played an important part in defining the way in which cultural questions have been addressed. Probably his most famous text, though not his most recent or most scholarly, is still his *Vers une civilisation du loisir?* [*Toward a Society of Leisure?*][20] published in 1962, at the height of French intellectual debates on mass culture. In this text, Dumazedier was keen to make a case for the sociology of leisure as a valid and respectable area for academic study. Here I am not so much interested in analysing Dumazedier's sociological methods as I am in placing his work in the context of the French discourse on culture, popular culture and mass culture. According to Dumazedier, leisure has three functions: 'délassement, divertissement, développement' ['relaxation, diversion, development'].[21] Although he claimed not to disparage or underestimate the functions of relaxation and diversion, it is more than clear that Dumazedier, as a leading figure in the popular culture movement, attributed dominant significance to the function of personal development. In fact, elsewhere in the text Dumazedier used the personalist word 'épanouissement' ['blossoming, opening-out'], to convey his view that leisure should ideally be the occasion on which individuals strove to become complete persons.

In Dumazedier's writings, as in all the discourse of the popular culture movement from 1936 onwards, the word 'loisir' ['leisure'] is made to seem almost precisely synonymous with the word 'culture', so that the term 'culture populaire' becomes interchangeable with 'loisir populaire' ['popular leisure']. But his identification of leisure with culture is totally misleading, if it encourages one to think that Dumazedier respected and admired the culture of the working class as it then existed. There is, it is true, in Dumazedier's works an acute awareness of what the 'daily life' of the working class involves, and his pedagogic concerns lead him to insist on the need to take full account of this 'daily life', when attempting to bring 'a broader culture' to the working class. That is to say, Dumazedier stresses that pedagogical initiatives must start from a point which can be understood by working-class people, and must also only move to a point which can be assimilated by them. But this sensitivity to the daily life of the working class and to its 'limited' perspectives is hardly the same as respecting and admiring the existing culture of the working class. In fact, far from admiring working-class culture, Dumazedier did not actually believe that it existed at all. His main thesis in *Vers une civilisation du loisir?* was that mass culture, as provided by the mass media, was now to all intents and purposes the culture of the vast majority of people in modern society. The empirical basis of his study was designed to show the extent to which mass culture had taken hold of French society since the war, through cinema, radio, television, the motor car, tourism and so forth. Dumazedier came up with yet another alternative to 'everyday culture', in the formulation 'culture vécue', and he made it clear that this 'lived culture' of the working class was largely characterised by the consumption of what was on offer through the mass media. Not surprisingly, Dumazedier attacked the mass media for its violent, sensational and vicious material, but, in fact, his attack on the mass media for being a vehicle for 'pure entertainment' was more fundamental to his case.

Dumazedier has a rather primitive way of analysing cultural forms and he is, for instance, quite happy to make a crude distinction between 'escapist' and 'realist' values. He constantly accuses mass culture of promoting unrealistic fantasies. In fact, he sees it as an enduring characteristic of 'popular taste' that the imaginary is preferred to the real. He clearly regards this as undesirable, since, in his view, an excessive indulgence in the imaginary turns people away from their real social responsibilities:

> The mechanisms of projection and identification provoked by fiction can deaden the critical and discriminating spirit. The imagination can go astray, and there can arise a confusion between the real world and the fictional world. If this happens, then the personality loses itself in the lives of the film stars. Life by proxy comes to replace real life. Instead of offering an agreeable dream, the pleasure of fiction turns people away from all individual activity, or promotes anti-social behaviour. Fictional games, like real games, run the risk of leading the individual beyond the real world into

a fantasy world, where he is nothing but a refugee or an exile, indifferent to all active participation in the life of his time.[22]

This passage indicates Dumazedier's view that leisure should not mark a turning away from social and personal responsibility, nor a slackening of the desire for social and personal development, but, on the contrary, should be the occasion when high social and personal ideals are pursued and reinforced. It is for this reason that Dumazedier, despite his desire to give an accurate account of modern leisure practices, and despite his desire not to look down upon the leisure practices of ordinary people, could not summon up any enthusiasm for such activities as do-it-yourself and gardening:

> For most of the time, these new Sunday craftsmen retreat into a life of gardening and do-it-yourself. Some Parisian workers studied by Chombart de Lauwe claim to devote up to five hours a day to these activities! They are indifferent to those questions which transcend their private lives . . . . They are diminished citizens, for whom political, social, and cultural questions do not exist. The vehicles of mass information are all around them, but they do not use them. They are isolated; they adopt the attitudes of craftsmen turned in on themselves, almost like in the days when there was no press, no cinema, no division of labour, no class struggle.[23]

Political and civic indifference was obviously not something to be condoned by Dumazedier. In fact, the popular culture movement as a whole saw itself as a massive movement of civic education, dedicated to the promotion of a new humanist culture that would train people to be active and useful citizens in the modern technological society. At the same time, it sought to teach them (following the example of personalism) to work towards the fullest development of their own 'person', and to have the greatest possible respect for the dignity of others. This 'new culture' would, of course, also be a 'popular culture': 'a popular culture appropriate to the needs of a modern, democratic society'.[24] It would be 'less abstract than classical culture, more disinterested than a "polytechnic" culture, more complex than a militant culture, and would be a culture closely linked to the active attitudes of the Man of Leisure'.[25]

Notions of active and passive leisure were central to all Dumazedier's concerns. To participate actively in culture meant, for instance, not just passively watching TV or going to the nearest cinema to watch any film that happened to be playing there. The ideal active participant in culture was, according to Dumazedier, someone who was a member of a 'ciné-club' and selected those films he judged to be worth seeing. He sought to learn about cinematic conventions; he became aware of the difference between form and content; he analysed the film after the event, deepened his understanding and tried to fit the film into broader historical and cultural contexts. Not least, the 'active spectator' tried to assess the relationship between the film and reality. Finally, the active spectator became a kind of cultural 'animateur', and took his knowledge and awareness into his family, among his friends, and into the workplace, so that he could share his knowledge, and also so that he could develop the critical sense in others.[26]

Dumazedier was constantly concerned with the 'content' of leisure and culture, as he was with the 'level' ['niveau'] of leisure and cultural activities. For him one of the chief aims of 'popular culture' was to raise the level of leisure and cultural practices of mass society and also to improve the content of what was provided in the mass media. Together with the aim of giving the masses access to culture, these all added up to what Dumazedier understood by 'cultural development' ['développement culturel']. Dumazedier believed that the State education system alone was not adequate to the task of ensuring cultural development and that is why he insisted that a 'modern democratic society founded on the right to culture' needed a vast system of cultural education and cultural 'animation', which would be rooted above all in local associations of leisure and popular culture:

> These associations are the effective intermediaries between the distant sources of information and the local public. They contribute to the raising of cultural levels ['niveaux culturels'] by an egalitarian system of information and a form of mutual education.[27]

Dumazedier's approach to culture was dominated by his educational aims, as is demonstrated by his view that the mass media performed their function best when they operated as an information and cultural service. In fact, he liked to show that he was not against mass culture by demonstrating his readiness to detect the positive potential that could be found in all aspects of mass culture. For instance, he refused to join in the universal assault on advertising, even though he said he was fully aware of what simplistic and vicious mythologies it promoted, because he also saw that it could render a useful service. So, for instance, Dumazedier pointed out in this optimistic vein that the advertising of toothpaste and shampoo had improved hygiene, and claimed that one had even to recognise that advertising had been responsible for 'the diffusion of art', since many advertising companies had displayed great works of art on the walls of towns. In his treatment of all mass culture Dumazedier adopted the same approach: a criticism of the lamentable state of mass culture (the inferior cultural content, the antagonism to true moral and social values, the indulgence in fantasy and stereotype to the exclusion of the real world, the purveying of vacuous and infantile entertainment) was followed by a recognition that there was always a potential for education and information which should be exploited by cultural 'animateurs'. In fact, Dumazedier often made no distinction at all between 'culture' and 'information' or 'knowledge'. The French notion of 'culture générale' seems to have contributed to the blurring of these distinctions. 'Culture générale' means general knowledge or general education, but it carries more weight than these English terms might indicate, since having a 'culture générale' has been widely regarded in France as an essential qualification for being a cultivated and well-educated person.[28] Dumazedier clearly thought it of the highest importance that a citizen of a modern democratic society should have a 'culture générale' and that the mass media, with the help of leisure and popular culture associations, should play an important part in supplying this. Looking at the results of a survey he conducted in the resort town of Annecy in eastern France on attitudes to learning, Dumazedier noted that certain groups displayed 'a veritable cultural atony', by which he meant they were not interested in acquiring knowledge about a whole range of subjects. In other words, the autodidactic impulse was not present in large numbers of people. This was an important point for Dumazedier, because he, like the rest of the popular education movement, always saw the autodidact as a kind of ideal, symbolic figure. In fact, he thought that a primary function of popular culture associations was precisely to stimulate the autodidactic impulse in people:

Autodidacts, that is to say, those who spend a large part of their leisure developing their knowledge, number about 10% of the urban working-class population (manual or clerical). . . . Studious forms of leisure are the pre-condition for the 'continuing culture' which is more and more necessary if one is to keep up with the rapid and complex evolution of our society. What is more, this quest for serious information presented in an agreeable way might one day bring about profound changes in the way knowledge is communicated to adults by radio, television, newspapers, or through voluntary associations.[29]

The entertainment values of the mass media are here reduced to simply presenting information in a pleasing way. In recommending that the 'cultural content' of the mass media should be improved as a way of raising the 'cultural level' of the masses, Dumazedier was calling for a more educational and pedagogic approach, despite the fact that the statistics showed that the public did not have any great desire to learn. On this topic Dumazedier was somewhat ambiguous. One can understand that, as a 'popular educator', he himself believed in the desirability of providing an improved 'cultural content'. Yet for much of the time he also claimed that people themselves had these cultural needs. It is true that he mainly talked of 'leisure needs' ['besoin de loisir'], but since we know that for him leisure, ideally defined, was indistinguishable from culture, then it is evident that he also believed that people had 'cultural needs'. However, the logic of Dumazedier's arguments would seem to suggest that it was more a case of the need felt by certain 'educators' to stimulate and create a cultural need in people, in order that they could save themselves from the perils of mass culture.

As mentioned earlier (p. 46), Dumazedier had been a part of the popular culture movement since 1936. At the time of the Liberation, he played a leading role in setting up the most famous popular culture organisation in France, *Peuple et Culture* ['People and Culture'], of which he remained the head for many years. The continuity of Dumazedier's preoccupations from the time of the Popular Front to the 1960s can be seen, for example, in his treatment of sport in *Vers une civilisation du loisir?* On looking at the situation of sport in modern mass society he could not help but lament the betrayal of earlier sporting ideals:

Coubertin had wanted to use sport as a way of bringing to the nation 'tranquillity, philosophy, health and beauty'. The sporting press, with its specialised columns becoming more

51

and more dominant, whips up the excitement of those who go to stadiums and velodromes, turns all the attention on the professionals and transforms them into demigods, the fans becoming just so many customers who keep up business. After fifty years, almost all Coubertin's ideas have been betrayed; mass sport is not the essential thing, but is of secondary importance. Champions are not 'animateurs' but stars – no one is trying to encourage them to play a social role. Outside educational circles one never sees anyone seriously trying to encourage people to use sport as a way of developing a style of life, whether in the form of an aesthetic, theatrical culture, or in the form of a social or human culture. How can the majority of those who play sport find in it a form of cultural expression? Even the Olympic Games, which were supposed to be 'an educational event which is intended, as in former years, to bring together the idea of a collectivity of people, around the cult of youth', have now become in the eyes of the specialised press and the majority of those in charge of sporting federations simply the championships of the world, with no significant educational meaning.[30]

One sees here important aspects of what Dumazedier understood by a democratic popular culture: it was one in which all citizens actively participated, and in which the highest civic and moral goals were set as the ultimate purpose of cultural activity. Dumazedier was hostile to the very notion of spectators of sport. His preference was for everyone to play sport, rather than simply watch a few gifted professionals do it for them. What is more, if there were to be leaders or performers, they should fulfil the role of 'animateurs', and draw out of the sport they were playing all the social, aesthetic and moral lessons that it could offer. In Dumazedier's terms, sport should not, therefore, be a passive entertainment, it should be a 'means of cultural expression', a means of moral and social self-development.

One of the principal heroes of the popular culture movement was Léo Lagrange, appointed by Léon Blum in 1936 as the Under-Secretary for Sport and Leisure in the new Popular Front government, and whose name has since been frequently honoured by being given to sporting, leisure and cultural facilities. It is Léo Lagrange who is credited with carrying out a policy of democratising culture, leisure and sport – of promoting, in brief, a truly 'popular' cultural policy. The adjective 'populaire' has been much used in French history, but never can it have been used to the extent it was in 1936, and never can it have carried quite the euphoric force it did then. Everything suddenly became 'popular': of the people, by the people and for the people, people here meaning chiefly the underprivileged working class, who, it was claimed, were for the first time being given access to leisure and culture, and were, thereby, being allowed to achieve human dignity. The word 'populaire' expressed the idealism and the enthusiasm of a political movement which celebrated the access of the workers to a life that had been previously denied to them, and which welcomed the breaking down of barriers and compartments and the breaking out into freedom and the open air. Reduced rail fares, designed to help people to take holidays and profit from the new paid free time, were called 'billets populaires de congé annuel' ['popular annual holiday tickets']; the certificate which was awarded for general sporting attainment was called the 'Brevet sportif populaire' ['popular sporting certificate']. Speaking on the radio in 1936, Léo Lagrange set out his aims in the following way:

> Our simple, human aim is to offer the mass of French youth the chance to play sport, and to find joy and health in this activity; to build an organisation of leisure, such as will allow the workers to relax and be rewarded for their hard labour.[31]

Lagrange, like Dumazedier, rejected the notion of what he called 'sport-spectacle', that is to say, sport as played by a few privileged people and simply watched by the rest. He preferred that sport be played by the great mass of French youth, which at the time was not possible due to lack of facilities and to the lack of money and time available to young workers. Because of the German fascist model, Lagrange was, however, sensitive to the word 'mass' and to any suggestion of the regimentation and militarisation of youth. He made it clear that no such intention lay behind his sporting policy. He saw the 'organisation of leisure' as having become a necessity, simply because of the new situation in which a reduced working week and paid holidays had created the phenomenon of 'free time'. In order that the workers could profit from this free time, facilities and opportunities had to be provided. Hence the need for 'loisirs sportifs, loisirs touristiques, loisirs culturels' ['sporting leisure, tourist leisure, cultural leisure']. The vision emerged, therefore, of a popular culture which was a fusion of healthy outdoor activities and cultural self-improvement.

Lagrange put more stress than did later representatives of the popular culture movement, including Dumazedier, on the simple 'joy' of physical activity. Leisure for the working class was more readily seen by Lagrange as the relief from, and recompense for, oppressive and restrictive working conditions. But, even so, it was clear that leisure was also being made to carry the weight of a new social, political and moral vision. For instance, leisure was thought to be able to bring into being a new egalitarian society (e.g. by the mixing of social groups in sporting activities). Leisure could also encourage and promote higher standards of hygiene, and discourage undesirable and unhealthy activities (such as heavy drinking and idling in bars or cafés) and could therefore lead to the nurturing of more active and productive citizens. Not least, leisure could create the conditions, in personalist terms, for the 'blossoming' of each individual into a fully critical, socially responsible, and sensitive human being. Léon Blum himself saw this as the essence of Lagrange's leisure and cultural policy, which he characterised as 'humane socialism'. Lagrange's vision of high ideals being realised through the privileged means of modern leisure can be seen in the following statement made in 1932, on the occasion of an international conference of the youth hostelling movement:

> We want the youth hostels to grow and multiply, not only so as to offer cheap hotels to the new generations of young people, but so that in each youth hostel there will be created a centre of collective life, where the young intellectual and the young worker, the young typist and the young peasant-girl, will be able to forge the moral unity of the youth of our country and the world, without which there is no hope of salvation. Our common ambition is to save the spiritual values of the world, and for that we are counting on youth, the gold reserve of nations, because youth has profound feelings of friendship and love.[32]

As already indicated, members of the popular culture movement in France in the 1930s were at pains to stress that the new 'style of life' they were promoting – that of the 'cultural leisure' of healthy, youthful activities, sustained by an idealistic vision – was not to be identified with the apparently similar life-style promoted by the Fascists in Germany. According to the French 'popular educators', their whole aim was to create fulfilled and aware individuals in the masses, whereas fascism tried to create mass individuals without the capacity for individual reflection and critical intelligence. In the same way, later sympathisers with the 1930s popular culture movement stressed that it had had no truck with fascism even if the 'style' of the movement had been appropriated by the Vichy government during the Second World War:

> The first concern of the Vichy government was to try and annex youth to its cause. In its policy announcements, it proclaimed very loudly that it rejected everything that the Third Republic represented: its laws, its men, its institutions. In many spheres the technicians of the Vichy government made every effort to take over all the successful achievements of preceding governments and present them to the French as original policies, whereas it was, in reality, a case of gross deception. And this is what happened with all matters relating to sport. Everything that previously bore the label 'Popular' became 'National'. The projects of Léo Lagrange were stolen from him (and his stamp removed), and were carried out with the vast financial resources which were at the disposal of the French State at that time . . . . The labels were simply swapped over, and their essential spirit tampered with. The notion of art for art's sake, the joy of living, human dignity – all this disappeared, as did the idea that sports' arenas and youth hostels should be the focus of extensive fraternisation. It then became simply a case of forming, in the totalitarian manner, strong and docile young people, of manning the 'Jeunes du Maréchal', of 'redeeming our errors', and of slavishly participating in the new order. Fortunately, the majority of French youth rebelled against these directives, which ran counter to their beliefs, their instinct and their traditions. Even within Vichy's own organisations there very quickly arose centres of resistance.[33]

This is a very good example of how the word 'popular' is so frequently to be found at the centre of social and political matters. Usually it is a case of opposing camps fighting over the word, each appropriating it for its own purposes and each claiming a monopoly over its meanings. In this instance, it is rather a case of the word itself being suppressed and another put in its place. 'Populaire' has definite connotations of 'national', but clearly at this historical juncture it was identified almost exclusively with the socialist policies of the Popular Front, and the Vichy government obviously did not regard it as evoking the idea of the Nation that it had in mind. This passage, however, has another important dimension, for we see here how important it was to the popular culture movement to put forward its own version of the past. It insisted on the continuity of the popular culture struggle between 1936 and the Resistance, and rejected any suggestion that it was at all implicated in Fascist movements in the 1930s or during the war. The notion of popular culture itself had to be protected from any such possible hint of contamination if it were to survive the Vichy period and be put forward as the untainted fruit of the Resistance and the Liberation.

It is probably in the works of Benigno Cacérès that one is best able to see the extent to which the popular culture movement regarded itself as carrying out an uninterrupted struggle from 1936 onwards. Cacérès was a master carpenter before he was drawn into the Uriage group during the Resistance. In this group he met among others Emmanuel Mounier and Joffre Dumazedier. At the time of the Liberation Dumazedier and Cacérès played a central role in setting up the popular culture movement Peuple et Culture in Annecy, from where it soon moved to Paris to become the leading national organisation of popular culture and popular education.[34] In a whole series of works Cacérès has time and again recounted the story of the popular culture movement from the nineteenth century to the present. But it is the story from 1936 which has above all preoccupied him. In such a text as *Allons au-devant de la vie: la naissance du temps des loisirs en 1936* (1981), ['Life lies ahead of us: the birth of leisure time in 1936'],[35] one can see how the time of the Popular Front is set out as a mythical and utopian moment for 'popular culture', both in the sense of the popular education movement and in the sense of the actual leisure and cultural activities of the working class. The occupation of factories is celebrated as a joyous 'fête du peuple', in which workers at last found in the workplace the unity, happiness and creativity which had always been impossible there, given the alienating nature of the surroundings and the work routine. Cacérès finds in Léo Lagrange's leisure and cultural policies the essence of the idealism of the Popular Front. Not only does he quote approvingly Lagrange's stated ambitions: 'to give the popular masses the means to play sport, to travel, and to know the joys of culture', but he also describes in detail the impact on the everyday life of the working class of the Popular Front's policy of twelve days' paid annual holiday. Cacérès calls this 'the transformation of the working-class condition by the integration of leisure into daily life'.[36] Cacérès evokes the fond memory of that first experience of paid freedom and describes some of the most characteristic activities in which the working class then engaged. At this point of sudden liberation from enforced labour, Cacérès celebrates the joys of domestic tasks not yet called do-it-yourself ('Everyone had a shelf to put up, a door to repair, a kitchen to paint').[37] Men went off fishing, families visited relatives in the country and came back and built rabbit hutches. Couples dug their allotment gardens together. Even more symbolic of the new leisure style was the way in which people took to their bicycles and went off to discover the countryside (or, in the vocabulary of the popular culture movement, to 'conquer' the countryside, since everything in this new world of leisure was seen as a heroic victory over past repressions and exclusions).[38] Cacérès is particularly enthusiastic about the youth hostelling movement and he sees it as representing the true spirit of popular leisure during the period (even though he does also admit that the French working class did not take too readily to wearing short trousers!).

Youth hostelling symbolised a new life of healthy, jolly camaraderie, a coming together of social groups and a mixing of the sexes. It was also, of course, an explicit rejection of urban mass culture. Not only did it take people out of unhealthy factories, cafés and towns, but, according to Cacérès, it also offered them a life-line to an authentic popular culture which had virtually died by the end of the nineteenth century. For instance, Cacérès sees youth hostelling as having given young people the opportunity to renew contact with older traditions of popular song, and as having revitalised these traditions by adding new popular songs to the repertory. This is clearly an example of the archaicising tendency of the popular culture movement, a tendency which, however, it would be fair to say is not in general very dominant. Indeed, particularly in the postwar period, the popular culture movement was resolutely progressive and tended to believe wholeheartedly in the need to modernise all sectors of French life. But this preference for old songs which Cacérès calls 'truly popular', was a way of rejecting the supposedly falsely popular songs of 1930s mass culture.[39] Cacérès is happy to pick out those contemporary singers whom he deemed to be of high quality, and who in his view either expressed the 'popular soul'

(Edith Piaf) or succeeded in capturing the new optimistic mood of the era (Charles Trenet). However, these are seen by Cacérès as definite exceptions. Not only does he criticise the supposedly poor quality of the popular songs of mass culture, but he also charges them with political complacency:

> At the cinema or on the wireless the stars were singing songs for the general public which had sickly sweet tunes and vulgar words to match. In these years which saw the rise of fascism over our borders, and in which war was being waged in Spain, the stars were singing 'Tout va très bien Madame la marquise' ['Everything is going very well, Madame la marquise']. The song encouraged the majority of people to dream vicariously of the impossible. In reaction against this state of mind, the young in the youth-hostelling movement rediscovered the texts of old songs from France and elsewhere which were truly popular. They copied these songs down in their notebooks, not even knowing where they originated. In unexpected ways the young were rediscovering the old folklore which encompassed social songs, ballads and love songs. Modern song, with all its techniques of mechanical recording, has a far briefer life than the old songs which were only transmitted by memory. The youth hostellers proved it.[40]

Even though Cacérès, as a former master craftsman and member of a trade-guild, has often emphasised the historic roots of working-class culture, he has perhaps spent even more time singing the praises of high culture. In fact, he is best known in France as the autodidact who made good. In his early life Cacérès had had a deep desire to have access to the world of culture and learning, and he always retained his attitude of reverence towards this world, seeing it as the only one which could offer people a personal 'plenitude'. His book *L'Espoir au coeur* (1967) ['Hope in the heart'][41] describes his desire to enter this world of culture. It is supposedly a novel but is, in fact, a personal memoir of his experiences during the Resistance period, when he was a member of the Resistance group based in the Ecole des Cadres ['leadership school'] at Uriage. The Ecole des Cadres was housed in a large manor house called 'la Thébaïde' situated deep in the countryside near Grenoble. Cacérès was enchanted and enthralled by this manor house and saw it as a cultural Garden of Eden, the kind of place from which he, as an uneducated worker, had previously been excluded, but to which he was now being freely admitted. Here, in a majestic and noble setting, he was to come into intimate contact with educated and cultivated men, surrounded by grandiose architecture, luxurious interiors, beautiful paintings, classical music, and, perhaps most important of all, books. To have access to an old, scholarly library was for Cacérès to gain entry into an inner sanctum of culture, and he proceeded to read voraciously. Books always symbolised for Cacérès the essence of culture. He himself wanted to absorb this essence, and because he attributed such significance to the 'riches' that books could bring, he also believed it was of utmost importance to make these riches available to everyone else. In fact, his job in the Resistance was precisely to take culture to other Resistance fighters, in order to keep up their morale and reinforce their resolve. This he did by reading passages from French literature around the camp-fire, passages that communicated the noble mission of French culture. This was seen as a project of 'sharing' culture ['le partage culturel']. It was a project that was to be carried on at the time of the Liberation, when Dumazedier, Cacérès and others set up the popular culture and education movement *Peuple et Culture*.

At the time of the Liberation the dominant consideration was the need to create a unified nation. Citizens were called on to demonstrate solidarity in the national effort, in order to carry out the task of reconstruction. Given the widespread acceptance of this need for solidarity, the word 'peuple' took on predominantly the meaning of 'the French people as a whole'. This produced an extremely ambiguous element in the cultural discourse of the Left. While fighting for the nation as a whole ['le peuple'], the Socialists and the Communists also had in mind, of course, the need to further the special interests of the working class ['le peuple'], particularly after the war, when they wanted to ensure that reconstruction incorporated the task of creating a just and equal society. After 1947 the optimistic and willing alliances which had been forged during the Resistance and at the time of Liberation fell apart, and it was no longer as easy to maintain that the French nation was indeed a unified 'peuple'. The discourse of the popular culture movement, however, retained this ambiguity throughout the postwar period, for it constantly tried to marry the two ambitions of improving the lot of the working class, and creating a unified nation. Peuple et Culture did this by regarding the new culture to be created as a 'culture commune' ['a common culture'] which would be shared by all social groups. This common culture was also graced with the title of a 'truly popular culture'. This new popular culture embodied the ideal of a culture in which the future technocratic values would be successfully integrated with the old classical cultural values to produce a new 'humanist' culture, progressive and modern, but deeply rooted in the past.[42] Cacérès actually defined culture at one point as 'the assimilation of the past by men turned towards the future'.[43]

In his *Histoire de l'éducation populaire* (1964) ['History of popular education'], Cacérès devoted a separate chapter to 'Popular Culture at the Liberation'. In this chapter, he described how the movement of popular culture and popular education, with its history stretching back through the nineteenth century, carried on the work of the Resistance and, before that, of the Popular Front. He pointed out that the Resistance had formed the future 'militants of cultural action', who in postwar France were to continue the mission of taking culture to the people, whether as employees of the State or as members of separate cultural organisations such as Peuple et Culture. In fact, Peuple et Culture saw itself, as much as anything else, as a movement designed to equip this new breed of 'animateurs' with all the skills necessary to initiate people into the exciting new culture that lay ahead. As the title of Cacérès's book makes clear, almost no distinction at all was made between popular education and popular culture. Indeed, Cacérès was quite happy to identify 'popular culture' with 'éducation permanente' (adult education, or 'continuing education' in modern parlance). He regarded the period of the Liberation as an era of 'cultural renewal', a time of unprecedented cultural activity and creativity, when intellectuals and artists in all fields were keen to participate in democratic cultural action, and were eager to produce works for all members of society. He stressed that such cultural activity was particularly strong among film and theatre people:

It was in this climate that the new institutions of popular culture were to be launched. They had been conceived when the spirit of the Resistance was still alive, and they wanted all men to participate fraternally in cultural life. At a time when the structures of our country were not yet reestablished, and amidst difficult conditions, everything was there to be created, and everything became truly possible. I can remember the hard winter of 1944, when men with empty stomachs gathered around simple, wooden tables in the old building at 5, rue des Beaux-Arts, to plan artistic projects which did indeed become a reality, and which have had a deep influence on our country. Jean-Marie Serreau, the theatre 'animateur', was there, the man who introduced Brecht into France; Pierre-Aimé Touchard, who was later to become director of the Comédie-Française; Louis Pauwels, presently director of the journal *Planète*; Joffre Dumazedier, sociologist of leisure; André Bazin, who was to go on and found the *Cahiers du cinéma*, and distinguish himself as a cinema critic; Paul Flamand, director of the Seuil publishing house. Several theatre people were also there: Simone Jollivet, Charles Dullin, Jean Vilar, Jean-Louis Barrault, and a few distinguished people of whom no one had then heard, like the Bellec brothers who were to become les Frères Jacques. Around the figure of Delarue the journal *Travail et Culture* took up the old dream of art for everyone, and tried to give it concrete form.

The working-class and intellectual members of these gatherings participated in a multiplicity of theatrical and cinematic activities, in theatre-clubs and ciné-clubs. Actors went to perform in factories. The Sorbonne welcomed a new popular public, come to listen to lectures such as that of the Abbé Morel on Picasso, which became a famous talking-point.[44]

With the help of all these willing intellectuals and creative artists, and with the full support of the State in creating the necessary cultural infrastructure (this was the brief period during which Jean Guéhenno was in charge of a section of the Ministry of Education devoted to 'popular education'), Cacérès believed that the Liberation was heralding the new dawn for popular culture in France. The time was very near when 'the people' would be truly 'cultured' – in Cacérès's own words: 'Tomorrow a cultured people' ['Demain un peuple cultivé'].[45]

The vast utopian hopes of this period were often based on what now seem to be, in retrospect, extremely modest innovations. Nothing shows this more clearly than the significance Cacérès attached to the travelling library – 'bibliobus' – which for him, was 'a revolutionary concept':

The travelling libraries were designed to bring free reading matter to the inhabitants of departments by means of local correspondents. Thanks to the quality of the cultural work carried out in departmental lending libraries, the success of this enterprise enabled 'animateurs' in the popular education movement to rely on a solid network of book distribution outlets, on the basis of which cultural activity ['animation culturelle'] in the form of reading clubs . . . was to become a commonly employed method today. The travelling library is a revolutionary concept. Before its existence, reading in France had been based on the principle of the reader having to seek out books . . . whereas the travelling library takes the book to the reader and, in particular, to those readers who were manual workers, and who never found their way to libraries, which were always situated a long way from their usual routes and in areas where they felt like strangers. By bringing the books to the reader, a whole new popular public was reached in a very real way. One of the most important institutions of the popular education movement at the time of the Liberation had been launched.[46]

Cacérès put enormous emphasis on the need to provide cultural facilities, and on the need to make these facilities accessible to working-class people. But he was also aware that the targeted public needed, in turn, to want to be cultivated or educated. It was for this reason that he took his own case to be exemplary, and he advised the popular education movement that it must focus on the person 'who, on his own, tries to cultivate himself', in other words, the autodidact.[47] Cacérès found extreme pathos in his own case and in that of other working-class autodidacts. Above all, he stressed the heroic efforts of autodidacts to learn without having at their command any of the methods and approaches they really needed in order to achieve their cherished ambition of being truly cultured. He saw the popular culture and education movement as a scientific movement, whose aim was precisely to develop specific and appropriate pedagogic techniques which would lead the uncultured and the uneducated into the world of culture and education.

Cacérès evoked the pathos of his own case in his autobiographical 'novel' *La Rencontre des hommes* (1950) ['The meeting of men'].[48] Here he described how one winter's day, when it was not possible to work on the building site, instead of just going home, or spending time in the cinema, he decided to venture into the local library. He stressed how intimidating this first experience was. He felt completely exposed, embarrassed and ashamed in his workman's clothes and his heavy shoes. He described a similar experience when he was daring enough to go into a town-centre bookshop. However, he did not only experience shame in those places in which he felt an outsider. When he was taking his library books back to the library from his working-class 'quartier', he was so afraid of looking conspicuous as he walked through the working-class streets that he carried his books in a shoe-box. In this text, Cacérès showed that the autodidact type who was keen to 'cultivate' himself inevitably found himself at odds with his working-class life, both at leisure and at work. Weekends were described by Cacérès as simply a means of forgetting the working week that had just passed, and of putting off the dreadful thought of work starting again on Monday. He clearly found a fundamental emptiness and pointlessness in the limited range of working-class leisure activities on offer: 'bal, cinéma, foire, fête', ['dance, cinema, fair, fête']. Such activities were empty 'illusion'. Cacérès could only see worth in the solitary, reflective world of reading and in the quest for knowledge and culture. But such was the grindingly monotonous and tiring nature of the work done during the week that, according to Cacérès, working-class people simply did not have the freedom of mind required either to embark on this quest for culture or to tolerate the necessary degree of solitude. In fact, Cacérès believed that it was almost impossible to reconcile culture with manual work. Although he often praised craft values, stressed the degree of skill required in much manual work, and spoke lovingly of the craftsman's contact with materials, Cacérès refused to idealise the work of the modern tradesman, which he saw as becoming more and more mechanised and routinised. Less and less was it possible for workers to find any creative pleasure in their jobs, and more and more were they being forced to become robots. There seems little doubt that Cacérès believed that he himself found his personal 'salvation' by leaving his situation as a worker, acquiring culture, and then devoting himself to taking culture to the workers. But this hardly resolved the general problem (that Cacérès himself had recognised), of how one brought together the worlds of work and culture when they seemed to be so irreconcilable. The popular culture and education movement did, of course, see itself as attempting to resolve this crucial issue in practical terms by devising all manner of pedagogical and cultural initiatives. However, it would seem, in retrospect, that the significance that the popular culture movement attached to the autodidact type was itself a fundamental error, and a sign of some of the anachronistic assumptions of the movement.

Progressive intellectuals who addressed the question of culture and the working class in the postwar years, and indeed right up to the middle or even late 1960s, were convinced that the solution to what they saw as working-class cultural underdevelopment was the massive provision of cultural facilities placed at the disposal of the working class. As I have already stated, this belief in the need to provide such cultural resources was based on a corresponding belief in the cultural needs of the workers themselves, who were considered to be in a state of cultural deprivation and cultural frustration. It was not surprising, therefore, that a 'successful' working-class autodidact like Cacérès should have been picked out and held up as exemplary, since he symbolised all the cultural and educational ideals of the popular culture and education movement. At the end of *La Rencontre des hommes*, Cacérès rejected quite violently what he saw as the complacent suggestion that 'everyone is cultured in his way', a view which he believed only left the workers in their initial state of cultural deprivation. He then repeated his deeply held view that other workers would gain just as much pleasure and joy as he had from 'learning about history, listening to a concert, going to the theatre, visiting a museum or a cathedral, and reading books – the greatest and deepest happiness I have known'.[49]

Cacérès was far from alone in believing that culture was the only true salvation for the deprived workers. In fact, it would be fair to say that from the end of the war until the mid-1960s, there was an enormous outpouring of writings which all expressed this same view. The whole of the radically minded French intelligentsia seems to have joined together to bemoan the 'low level' of cultural activity in the working class. A typical example of this is Janine Larrue's study *Loisirs ouvriers chez les métallurgistes toulousains* (1965) ['Working-class leisure activities among Toulouse metal-workers'].[50] This study shows very well how the utopian, 'triumphalist' perspectives of a future society in which all the workers would be cultured, went together almost inevitably with an extremely pessimistic and 'miserabilist' description of actual working-class leisure and cultural activities. Like so many sociologists working in the field of working-class culture at this time, Larrue was not only influenced by the assumptions of the popular culture movement (which clearly she was to a very significant degree), but she was obviously also influenced by the ideas of the sociologist of work Georges Friedmann, who played a key role in French intellectual life in the postwar years.[51] In *Le Travail en miettes: spécialisation et loisirs* (1956) ['Work in fragments: specialisation and leisure'],[52] among other works, Friedmann painted a very depressing picture of an industrial working class deeply alienated by modern techniques of production. Friedmann was particularly concerned with the effects of increasing automation on the nature of work, and with the resulting impact on the psychology of the worker. According to Friedmann, traditional forms of work had had the potential for offering deep satisfaction to the worker (contact with natural materials, possibility for individual creativity, control over the making of a whole product, the chance to work at a natural rhythm and so forth). Modern mechanised production, however, denied the worker all these possible satisfactions and reduced him to a mere robot in the repeated performance of a limited number of very simple tasks. Given such a situation, Friedmann saw it as all the more necessary to develop the capacity for human accomplishment and fulfilment in 'free time and active leisure', since dissatisfaction with modern industrial work, in his view, led to an alienated personality. If one experienced work as a void, a source of boredom, or as an inescapable burden, then it was not likely, according to Friedmann, that one would use free time in 'active leisure' and in the development of the self. It became far more likely that one would seek to repress the consciousness of one's misfortune either by developing violently aggressive tendencies in one's leisure, or by escaping into the 'passive leisure' of mere amusement and fun. Friedmann believed that only a 'humanist education' could truly counteract the vicious effects of modern industrial work, an education which would allow the workers to profit from 'the precious values of culture, and the great works of the universal heritage'.[53]

Janine Larrue's analysis of the leisure activities of Toulouse metal-workers in the late 1950s fits in directly with Friedmann's perspectives. For Larrue, as well as for Friedmann, dehumanised forms of labour resulted in dehumanised forms of leisure. She above all stressed the lethargy of workers. According to Larrue, it was not only their physical fatigue which prevented them from using leisure time in a fruitful and creative way, but a profound mental state of passivity and resignation also kept them in their situation of 'cultural underdevelopment'.[54] In addition to the dehumanising effects of work, Larrue listed a whole number of other features of working-class life which, in her view, kept the workers in this dismal condition: lack of money, lack of education, lack of adequate lodgings, lack of extended social relationships, claustration in a small family unit. Although Larrue understood that these reasons for 'cultural underdevelopment' were deeply embedded into the social and economic system, she none the less gave the overriding impression that it was the workers themselves she was indicting and not the system. This was clearly not her intention, but it seems fair to say that those intellectuals who give such a 'miserabilist' account of working-class life seem always ultimately to lack a genuine empathy with, and understanding of, the way of life of working-class people.

An honourable exception to this, and a book to which it is, perhaps surprisingly, a relief to turn, is the study done by J. Frisch-Gautier and P. Louchet on pigeon-fancying: *La Colombophilie chez les mineurs du Nord* (1961) ['Pigeon-fancying among miners in the Nord region of France'].[55] Like other sociological works of this time which were devoted to the study of working-class work and leisure, this volume was deeply influenced by Georges Friedmann, who in fact provided the preface. The study covers the period after the war until 1960, at which point, although television had reached 50 per cent of homes in the mining community of Bruay-en-Artois, the authors stressed that it had not seriously challenged the dominance of the hobby of pigeon-fancying in this area. Frisch-Gautier and Louchet tell us that in 1952 out of 40 leisure clubs there were 4 devoted to pigeon-fancying, accounting for 1,000 to 1,200 members, which was about twice as many people as were to be found in either the fishing or the bowls clubs. Following Friedmann, Frisch-Gautier and Louchet felt the need to go over the same arguments concerning the alienating nature of labour and its alleged repercussions on leisure activities. Notions of leisure as escape from work, or as compensation or even 'revenge' for unsatisfying work, directed much of the material in this study. However, and more interestingly, one does also detect a definite attempt on the part of the authors to go beyond the perspectives laid down by Friedmann. Louchet tells us that he was himself an ardent pigeon-fancier, and this no doubt helps to explain the more sympathetic account he was able to offer of a working-class 'hobby'. In fact, what the authors give us is a lyrical, sensitive and highly 'valorised' account of pigeon-fancying. It can stand as a model of an insider view of popular culture, for it brings to bear a full awareness of the aesthetic and even existential significance that the activity had for the actual participants.

The willingness of the authors to devote a section of their study to 'the attractions of pigeon-fancying'[56] was itself a testimony to their desire to give positive status and value to what could so easily have been dismissed as the typically pointless activity of working-class men, alienated by modern conditions of labour and unable to use their leisure time to develop themselves into fully responsible and aware citizens. It is noticeable that, in their wish to give a positive account of pigeon-fancying, the authors immediately emphasised the pleasures and emotions to be gained from the physical contact with the bird, and stressed all the different aspects of 'game' and 'play' involved in the sport of pigeon-racing. It is true that, even in this section, the authors' frame of reference was still to an important degree determined by Friedmann's notions of leisure as compensation. However, the enthusiasm and the involvement of the authors were such that the activity itself was allowed to have its own justification. Pigeon-fancying was recognised as possessing its own richly textured world, and as offering the possibility of profound experiences which could to some degree be explained by being related to the nature of the work done by the miners, but whose full significance was in no way exhausted by this explanation. For instance, the authors evoked in poetic terms the special qualities of calm, whiteness and airiness that were to be found in the pigeon-loft, and although a direct comparison was being made with conditions in the mine, this in no way seemed to encroach on the experience of the pigeon-loft, in the sense of clouding or embittering it, or in the sense of reducing it to some trivial form of escapist activity. On the contrary, the miners' entry into the loft was described as an authentically liberating and even transcendent moment.

It is important to stress how rare an occasion this is in the writings of French intellectuals and academics on the subject of the culture of the working class. In this passage the authors not only accord the workers their dignity and autonomy, but they also acknowledge that the chosen and preferred leisure activities of the workers have their own intrinsic value.

3

CULTURE AND THE WORKING CLASS AND WORKING-CLASS CULTURE

The postwar preoccupation of French intellectuals with the question of culture and the working class was particularly intense in the late 1950s and early 1960s, a time when the first effects of the new Americanised consumer society were being felt, but when consumerism itself was in fact slow to develop in France, in comparison with, for example, England. This made France into a kind of battleground, in which intellectuals 'of good will' fought for the souls of working-class people, and fended off what they saw as the corrupting influences of the developing mass media and the new consumerism. Janine Larrue demonstrated this attitude in her study of Toulouse metal-workers (see pp. 64–6), where she objected to the importance that workers themselves placed on acquiring new consumer goods and on improving their own standard of living:

> They have a distorted image of leisure, more or less linked to the present state of society. They regard leisure as being exactly the same thing as diversion, and for the most part, associate it with those forms of entertainment for which one has to pay. Their dreams of leisure are inseparable from dreams of a more comfortable life: whoever does not have a car would like one; and whoever already has one wants a nicer one than he already has . . . . It is not desires that are lacking. In fact, with such a basic outlook there is no reason why desires should not be indefinitely aroused. But they all derive from the same model, which some of our interviewees call 'modern life', and others 'progress', but which, for our part, we would relate directly to the commercialisation of leisure.[1]

The workers were criticised by Larrue for seeing leisure only as a time for amusement, for wanting to improve their standard of living in material terms (reduced here to the quest for status symbols), and for being lured into believing in the capitalist 'myths' of modernity and progress. Throughout her study Larrue delivered a crushing indictment of the workers' 'passivity', which she detected in all their leisure and cultural activities. She loaded onto them an enormous burden of guilt and responsibility for their escapism, their readiness to consume rubbish, their unerring bad taste, and their refusal to aspire to a more challenging, meaningful and worthwhile culture:

> The most facile pastimes are far more likely to lead to escapism. It is a short step from tiredness to diversion, as it is from diversion to the taste for facility – another important psychological characteristic, whose influence on leisure, as we have described it, is indisputable. One only has to think, most notably, of the success of magazines, detective novels, and daily newspapers with their sensational or trivial stories, or radio programmes with their diet of light entertainment and games. One thinks also of the predilection for the cinema (and in particular for comedy, adventure and detective films), and for love stories; the attraction to musicals and especially light opera. All these distractions demand no thought, but appeal only to the imagination. They hold the spectators in thrall, as picture books and adventure novels do with children. But these are adults who say that if they pick up a book they just have to read it in one go, and that 'they cannot put it down'. All of which means that any effort of thought is abandoned.[2]

Larrue considered the mass culture that was actually consumed by the workers to be unequivocally harmful. In fact, she did not see mass culture as 'cultural' at all, 'if one admits that culture implies intellectual awareness and an openness to cultural values'. Mass culture was, in fact, 'alien to culture'.[3] This attitude fitted in with a common characterisation of French workers as being in a state of 'un-culture' ('non-culture').[4]

Although I am stressing the degree to which such attitudes towards working-class culture or 'un-culture' were prevalent in the 1950s and 1960s, it would be wrong to think that they were no longer current. In Jacques Frémontier's *La Vie en bleu: voyage en culture ouvrière* ['Life in overalls: a journey into working-class culture'], which was published in 1980,[5] a remarkably similar image emerges. Frémontier paints an unrelieved picture of gloom, as he visits the desolate modern housing estates to interview contemporary working-class people. He finds them still locked in what he regards as the age-old working-class attitudes of fatalism. Workers are depicted as accepting their miserable destiny and as having almost no means at their disposal 'to desire, do, speak, or know' (the titles of the first four parts of Frémontier's book). Frémontier shows us a frustrated, hemmed-in and repressed group of people cast into a hell of 'non-culture' and virtual non-existence by their sparse resources and by the 'terrorising gaze' of dominant culture.[6] Frémontier does not even allow for the transcendence of this miserable life through the political culture of the Communists and the union militants, which he also describes as a narrow and dehumanising culture. This attitude contrasts strikingly with Larrue's treatment of political activity. For Larrue the 'earnestness of the militant' was one of the worthwhile options open to the average worker bogged down in the lethargic consumption of mass culture (another option was the 'curiosity of mind of the autodidact').[7] In fact, Larrue ended her study by pointing out precisely that, in contrast to the passive, uncritical nature of the average worker's use of leisure time, the union militants had an active, selective view of leisure. They did not abuse their free time by simply doing whatever took their fancy, but used it as a genuine opportunity for 'liberation and advancement'.[8]

In 1960, Daniel Mothé published in the review *Socialisme ou barbarie* a lengthy article entitled 'Les ouvriers et la culture' ['Workers and culture'].[9] Mothé's article is a most violent and vigorous assault on all those views I have so far outlined which diagnosed the workers as being culturally under-developed and which advocated a policy of taking culture to the workers, in order that they could find in culture the personal fulfilment which they were unable to find in their alienating forms of work and in their impoverished forms of leisure. In addition to attacking the popular culture movement, Mothé, however, also attacked existing working-class political parties, and particularly the Communist Party, for their outdated, bureaucratic and undemocratic structures and procedures. What Mothé wanted was a truly revolutionary working-class movement, which based itself on modern realities and could claim a close knowledge of, and relationship with, the people. The Communist Party was said to be in no way able to represent a truly revolutionary working-class movement, because its hierarchical and bureaucratic structure made it remote from the people and repressed any genuine critical debate among the people. This attack on 'obsolete communism' is not the least of the links that can, in fact, be found between Mothé's article and the kind of alternative revolutionary discourse which was to become very familiar in 1968. Mothé's article could even be regarded as forming a watershed between the early postwar period of cultural optimism and hopes for cultural 'unanimity', and the later period, which was to be characterised by extreme forms of cultural 'contestation' deriving from an exacerbated sense of the evils of 'bourgeois culture'.[10] Another general interest of Mothé's article is that, in a polemical vein, it foreshadowed many of the major preoccupations of Pierre Bourdieu's sociological analyses of culture, which are the subject of the following chapter.

Mothé may have called for a new revolutionary perspective, but his initial account of the workers' relationship to mass culture was remarkably similar to the analysis I have so far outlined. Mothé followed Friedmann and his disciples in depicting the modern industrial worker as being alienated by routinised, mechanised forms of labour, and as being unable to find any outlet for creativity and initiative in his work. He also described the worker in his leisure as being a prey to mass culture, although his angry characterisation of mass culture as a bourgeois conspiracy designed to keep the workers down went far beyond what one would have found in the discourse of the popular culture movement and, as already suggested, is far more reminiscent of 1968 attacks on consumer society:

> First of all, cultural production is an industry which is in the hands of bourgeois industrialists who produce a very special commodity because it is destined to forge the consciousness of the workers. It is a commodity produced by capitalists, which is made not only with economic aims in mind but also with social ambitions. It is a moral commodity; it is a commodity which must not only be sold, but must also fulfil its educational objective – namely to make those citizens who consume it into citizens who are subjugated to this society . . . .
>
> The workers are offered a specially selected range of goods in the market-place. They are offered the kind of knowledge that can give them a position in society, knowledge that

71

diverts them from their jobs, and it is with the bits and pieces that they pick up and buy that they form their global view of the world.[11]

In Mothé's eyes, moreover, the culture that was diffused by popular culture organisations was no better than the mass culture propagated by the bosses. It was all 'culture populaire':

> Popular culture today is the culture which is consumed daily in great quantities by manual and clerical workers. It is offered at bargain prices, marketed and propagated, not only by the bosses, but also by religious sects and working-class organisations.[12]

Popular educators were just as much part of the new entertainment industry ['industrie de distraction'] as were the purveyors of mass culture, since the culture they were diffusing was, according to Mothé, a consumer product just like any other. Culture performed exactly the same function for its consumers as did other products, in that it served primarily as a 'mark of distinction'.[13] To 'cultivate oneself' was to seek to 'distinguish oneself' from other working-class people. We see here how Mothé focused upon a theme that was to become so central to Bourdieu in his treatment of popular culture. Mothé revealed the deceptive mechanisms of distinction and insisted that the worker who sought to distinguish himself through consumer products or culture was embarked on an illusory quest. Firstly, it was an illusion because nothing that a worker did in his leisure could, according to Mothé, mask the fact that he was a subjugated and alienated person in his work. But, apart from this, it was also an illusion for the worker to seek to distinguish himself, because the worker did not realise that, given the totally relative nature of the system of distinction, he was fated always to try and distinguish himself by the appropriation of those goods which the bourgeois himself had already discarded. What is more, such goods no longer performed the role of distinguishing signs for the bourgeois precisely because the worker had now gained access to them. The worker would never succeed, therefore, in putting himself on an equal footing with those who objectively had more money and power than he had, even in the supposedly free and democratic area of modern leisure and culture. According to Mothé, the popular culture movement, in its ambition to diffuse culture to the workers, was in fact making that culture a less rare, less distinguished and less desirable product for the bourgeois. In gaining access to bourgeois culture, the worker was likely to find that the rules of the game had been changed and that what he had struggled to acquire no longer carried distinction in educated bourgeois circles. For Mothé, this helped to explain the rule of fashion in French intellectual and cultural life, for by means of a rapid turnover of modish preoccupations French intellectuals sought to make sure that they were in possession of a culture which remained inaccessible to people at large:

In former times the bourgeoisie aped the nobles, and tried to sit at their tables and become initiated into their conversation and their language. Today one could say that the same thing applies to that section of the proletariat which tries to become initiated into culture. But a contradiction does arise at this point. If in the past culture has been a mark of distinction, at the present day, on the other hand, in so far as culture has become popularised and has been disseminated among the lower levels of society, it no longer possesses the distinguishing value that it formerly had. For example, to talk about existentialism in a drawing-room (even if the subject in itself is tiresome) only has any interest if during the discussion everyone can prove that he is a member of the elite, that is to say, if he can show that he is capable of saying something on the subject. As soon as the question of existentialism has been fully aired, and it has become one of the favourite talking-points of office girls and shopgirls, then at this juncture it is no longer appropriate for the bourgeoisie to continue to discuss it. The topics of conversation must be changed. It is to be noted that the same situation applies to words. Culture surrounds itself with ramparts, so that it can all the better maintain its private nature. The private property of culture is surrounded by a host of obstacles, and one of the most important of these is language. Words have their fashions like clothes. They come in and out of fashion, and only have real status when they do not go beyond a certain circle of people. As soon as they have become popular, they are rejected by the culture-makers, who then begin to use other words. Culture has thus become a commodity, which is created by specialists [writers, philosophers]. It is consumed 'brand new' by the bourgeoisie and intellectual circles, and is afterwards taken over by the lowest levels of society who help themselves to the cast-offs. Fashion in culture is more or less the same as fashion in cars. The new models are bought by the rich, and the old and second-hand cars by the proletariat.[14]

Not only could the worker not achieve the distinction he sought through culture, but, according to Mothé, he duped himself when he thought that his aspiration to culture could liberate him from his working-class condition. All it could do was displace him sufficiently to make him into an even more alienated figure, rejected and mocked by other workers for his earnest pretentions and boring single-mindedness. Mothé drew a scathing portrait of working-class autodidact types. One such 'cultured worker' whose particular expertise lay in anything to do with the navy, was considered by the others to be a 'walking dictionary' ['le petit Larousse'], because of his devotion to amassing facts and words.[15] Another 'cultured worker' had dedicated his life to seeing every available play and to attending every available lecture on every possible subject, but, unfortunately, he could never remember what he had heard and could only give the most garbled accounts of all the areas of knowledge and culture upon which he had touched. Mothé was clearly contemptuous of such types, whom he regarded as pathetic and deluded victims. He obviously believed that they came nowhere near to controlling and understanding the knowledge and culture to which they aspired and which was served up to them. Another worker eager to become cultured was described as being deeply involved in the popular culture movement, and as spending all his free time going to the theatre and going on cultural trips, where he was to be found lecturing the other workers on the cultural sights, and reciting to them speeches he had learned by heart from Corneille and Hugo. Such a figure was considered by Mothé to be in reality doubly alienated, for he was shown to be profoundly at odds both with the factory job he was required to do during the week and with the other workers with whom he spent so much of his life.

Mothé was unrelenting in his criticism of the popular culture movement, which he attacked for its 'cultural Stakhanovism', and, more intemperately, for its allegedly fascistic aims and methods. It was 'Stakhanovist' because the worker was subjected by the popular culture movement to a cruelly punishing schedule of cultural consumption:

Since the working class is obliged to wrest culture away from the bourgeoisie, it has to do it with all the fierceness of a battle. Culture must, therefore, be avidly seized during the little leisure available to the workers. They have to make the most of their leisure and stuff themselves with culture. They have to make the most of the town where they live and see as many plays as possible. They have to make the most of the hours spent travelling and admire the landscape, learn about its geological structure and its history. Finally, in the evening, after a day crammed with culture, they have to savour a period of cultural relaxation, play cultural games, sing songs of bygone days and then, alas, go off to bed.[16]

Mothé concluded that these were the same methods the bosses used to make the workers more productive, and that they were also the methods used by the Fascists in Germany in the 1930s, when culture and leisure movements regimented the workers in their free time and inculcated into them the ideas of the then dominant culture. This totally unwarranted aspersion of fascism, directed at the popular culture movement, does no credit at all to Mothé's arguments, but the best that can be said for it is that it was not followed up by Mothé in this article and remained there simply as an unjustified jibe. None the less, one could say that it did also herald the future 'gauchiste' discourse of 1968, in which reformist, let alone conservative ideology and activity would regularly be branded as fascistic. Mothé hit the target far more accurately when he concentrated on the popular culture movement's heroic view of itself as seizing culture from the bourgeois to hand it over to the workers: 'To visit Chartres cathedral is presented to the workers as a first step towards total emancipation.'[17] Mothé's own view was more than clear. If a worker truly wanted to be emancipated, he should have no truck with bourgeois culture. Mothé was more than ready to demystify culture and to divest it of the special aura that it had for popular educators. He even dared to say the unsayable and question the value judgements implicit in the discourse on 'cultural levels' and 'cultural contents': 'Why spend one's time at the theatre, rather than listening to music, or looking at art, climbing mountains, racing pigeons, attending church or going fishing. Why?'[18]

Although Mothé was indeed suggesting that all these activities were just as good as each other, his main point was that none of them could provide the worker with the general awareness that he needed of his true position in society. Mothé attacked what he called a fragmentary culture ['culture parcellaire'],[19] just as Friedmann and his followers had attacked the fragmentary nature of modern work ['travail parcellaire']. For Mothé the only culture really worth having for the worker was a 'political culture'. Only a political culture deserved to be called 'popular culture':

> Popular culture is not the vulgarisation of all existing knowledge. Popular culture is the knowledge of things which bear a direct relationship to the life of the people. And if there is no popular culture, it is because all culture in general fails to address itself to the real problems of society.[20]

In this passage Mothé was levelling his criticism at both the popular culture movement and the French Communist Party (PCF) – at the former for its uncritical attempt to diffuse all types of knowledge to the working class which it could not assimilate or use; at the latter for its retreat into bureaucracy and arcane theory. In contrast to those who fostered, or who were duped by, misguided and illusory ideas on culture, Mothé offered a portrait of a working man whose response to cultural issues he seems to have regarded as exemplary. Such a worker was certainly not the sort who was tempted to become an apostle of bourgeois culture and spend all his time trying to persuade the working class to absorb this alien culture. In fact, Mothé was convinced that workers who were passionate about culture were not 'the most conscious, the most open, the most intelligent workers'. Equally he was convinced that 'uncultured workers' ['ouvriers incultes'] were not the most reactionary.[21] The worker he put forward in opposition to the autodidacts of good will was in Mothé's eyes a genuine rebel. He had a highly developed critical sense and an attitude of extreme mistrust and hostility towards all forms of existing authority. He regarded culture with total suspicion and, apart from a few Marxist classics, he was happy to consume the mass culture that was on offer. Mothé clearly approved of this, since he believed that politically conscious workers bore witness to their exploitation by a total opposition to the dominant high culture:

> M. is an intelligent and combative worker. He is never going to read Racine or Corneille; he is never going to go to the T.N.P. [the National Popular Theatre]; he is never going to read Sartre, nor listen to Mozart. None the less, M. is a

worker who has a global view of the world, a worker who, despite his lack of knowledge, has a far more relevant overall view of things than the majority of culture vultures. He is not as crushed by culture. He has gained his knowledge of things from his relationships with his comrades in the factory, from political struggle and strikes.[22]

At the end of his article, Mothé delivered a violent critique of the PCF [the French Communist Party], and moved towards his notion of a genuine political culture, which would not only be a 'popular culture' but also a 'revolutionary culture'.[23] According to Mothé, the political culture of the PCF was moribund and had no appeal for most workers. If a new revolutionary working-class movement was to be created, it could not be created on the basis of the PCF, which was too bureaucratic, too hierarchical, too interested in theory and too embedded in the revolutionary traditions of the past. The political culture of the PCF was, in fact, as remote from the workers as high culture, and it performed the same role, namely that of distinguishing militants from other workers:

> However abstract their political culture might appear, it has a justification for the militants: namely, that of allowing them to appropriate a culture which formerly had only been the possession of intellectuals and bosses. Militants take as much satisfaction in discussing collective bargaining, as some others do in talking about *Le Cid*. This political culture raises them up to the level of the dominant class, and often even makes them appear to be a part of it. In any case, it gives them the unquestionable feeling of being set apart from other workers.[24]

According to Mothé, the politics of the PCF were contradicted at every turn by 'the reality of daily life'. In fact, so remote was the PCF from everyday life that it had no hope of remaining a revolutionary working-class party. Such a party needed to operate on the basis of an intimate relationship with the people, and not, as the PCF did, on the basis of rigid hierarchies, according to which those below simply followed the dictates and dogmas issued from above. A revolutionary culture had to be one which dealt directly with the problems of the people, and had to allow the people themselves to participate in solving these problems. For Mothé, such a revolutionary culture was a 'living culture' ['culture vivante'], and it could only be attained by the suppression of the division that capitalist society made between culture and 'real life'. Here again we find yet another call for culture to be equated with the everyday, but it also went together with a call to reject the strategy of those who wished to import bourgeois culture into working-class life. In Mothé's view, a revolutionary strategy had to insist on the destruction of bourgeois culture and on its replacement by a truly revolutionary culture:

> The ideas of the Left regarding culture are no different from those of the bourgeoisie, and they can be reduced to the one absurd and pious wish that the workers should become cultured. To which one can only reply that the workers should destroy the existing cultural habits and forms by destroying the class society itself. This struggle will prove to be a far greater enrichment of human culture than all the projects designed to 'educate the people', even if it has to end up by destroying all the monuments and museums, which, in any case, now only serve to camouflage the general mindlessness of society.[25]

A major aim of Mothé was to dissociate the revolutionary cause from the French Communist Party, to link up with earlier traditions of revolutionary syndicalism, and to hand the revolution back to the people themselves. However, other commentators were far from agreeing that this was the way to achieve a truly popular culture. In fact, Mothé could be said to have been trying to go even further than the PCF in politicising every aspect of daily life, a strategy which has itself been thought to be one of the main reasons for the inexorable decline in working-class support for the PCF.

In René Kaës's study, *Images de la culture chez les ouvriers français* (1968) ['French workers and their images of culture'],[26] the author responded explicitly to Mothé's article. While recognising some validity in Mothé's charge that culture could mystify and enslave the worker rather than liberate him, Kaës refused to go along with Mothé's outline programme of making the working class more politicised and more militant. In Kaës' view only a small number of militants wanted a purely political culture. As for the rest of the working class, they wanted by and large to be integrated into capitalist society and to profit from what increased consumption could bring them. Kaës' investigations led him to observe that working-class people suffered from a sense of humiliation and isolation due to their inability to participate fully in the culture that was open to other social groups. Their strongest desire was, therefore, to share in this culture and not to have a culture that was rooted in their own working-class condition. Above all, workers wanted to avoid or break out of 'worker-centrist' attitudes and to participate in 'an enviable culture beyond the limits of the group'.[27] According to Kaës, working-class people themselves, since at least the 1930s, had shunned notions of 'proletarian culture' and had desired to share in the 'global culture'.[28] Kaës tried, none the less, to give a sympathetic account of Marcel Martinet's classic text *Culture prolétarienne* (1935) ['Proletarian culture'], and showed the importance in the history of the working-class movement of the desire to develop a specific, self-emancipatory, revolutionary movement of education and culture.[29] However, Kaës concluded that all such projects had been marked by the austerity of the militant, unswerving in his opposition to the lures of capitalism, and inflexible in his belief that true dignity lay in 'a refusal to get on' in capitalist society ['le refus de parvenir'].[30] As has already been indicated, Kaës believed that the severe morality of the militant had long ceased to be attractive to the French working class. It is clear that Kaës himself also found it unattractive, and his hostility to the austerity of the militant went together with a critique of the traditional puritanism of the French working class, which Kaës saw as responsible for inhibiting full working-class participation in the global culture.

What one can no doubt see in Kaës's study are the timid signs of a postindustrial analysis of French cultural life. However, the sociologist Alain Touraine was perhaps the first to popularise American notions of the postindustrial society, and Kaës seems to be echoing some of the themes Touraine set out almost ten years before. In 1959, a special number of the periodical *Esprit* was devoted to the topic of 'le loisir' ['leisure'], and such figures as Dumazedier, Larrue and Kaës expounded their views on the nature and role of leisure (and particularly working-class leisure) in modern mass society. Touraine's contribution to this collective volume stands out as offering a very different approach for the time, but one which was later to become very familiar.[31] According to Touraine, 'working-class culture' had long been on the decline. What is more, all cultural activity was becoming less and less linked to social class. Touraine regarded it as a great mistake to try and turn the clock back and attempt to root people more solidly in their traditional social contexts. He believed that all people were becoming members of one vast mass society, and that to be an 'active' member of mass society one had to have access to, and be in tune with, the culture that was provided at a national level. To encourage people to be attached to a culture linked to work and social class was, in fact, to encourage a backward-looking attitude which was inappropriate in a modern mass culture. According to Touraine, modern mass culture put everyone in the position of a consumer who was free to take what he wanted and make of it what he wanted. Although he tried to give a balanced account of 'popular leisure', refusing either to stigmatise it as 'an instrument of domination in the hands of the governing class' or to exalt it as 'the symbol of growing social equality', Touraine, none the less, tended towards a very favourable view of mass culture. The aspect he found most hopeful about it was its capacity to encourage individualism. The 'means' of diffusing culture may be 'massive', he said, but there was now an increased capacity for people to respond to culture and to participate in cultural activities in more individualised ways. In terms of how this affected France in particular, Touraine believed that it challenged and called into question all those traditional ways in which culture in France had been 'organised'. Touraine seems mainly to have had in mind the whole late nineteenth-century project of imposing on culture a secular republican ethos ['la morale laïque'] as well as the more recent attempts of the PCF to impose its own notions of socialist realism on culture. However, Touraine was not thinking of popular culture organisations, for he clearly believed that these organisations were encouraging a modern, open, destratified notion of culture:

> We are seeing the weakening of all those forms of cultural expression that are tied to one specific social category or group. Nothing is more evident than the decline of traditional 'working-class culture'. Well-informed educationalists such as those in Peuple et Culture have contributed to the replacement of the idea of working-class literature (or working-class culture) by the far more realistic and, in today's terms, far more useful idea of a participation of the workers in the totality of culture.[32]

This was, indeed, the view that Peuple et Culture had of itself, but it is one which can hardly be accepted without reservation, since, as I have already indicated, popular culture organisations could equally be seen as diffusing the culture of a dominant class, and as keeping people away from a less obviously controlled area of culture (mass culture), in order to marshal them into a culture regarded as morally and aesthetically superior by 'animateurs' in the movement. But if Touraine had a somewhat optimistic view of the popular culture movement's dedication to an open culture, he himself was clearly enthusiastic about the new possibilities offered by the mass media. For instance, the popular culture movement sought to control the television viewer's response to what he saw by engaging in a programme of education to teach people how to understand and how to use the medium. The popular culture movement wanted the viewer to be vigilant as to the values that television was trying to convey, and it tried to direct the viewer towards what it regarded as morally, educationally and aesthetically of superior worth. Touraine, on the other hand, saw television as a way for individuals to liberate themselves from the oppressive interference of such initiatives and join in the exciting new culture beyond their own local sphere:

> Those who are 'home-centered' and who own a radio, a television, a record-player, magazines, are bypassing the social hierarchy of their community, in order to make direct contact with broader social realities and values.[33]

Touraine believed that the fight for the democratisation of culture in France had always brought with it the risk of 'cultural dogmatism'. Those on the Left who had for so long wanted to democratise culture had also wanted to inculcate their own values. But the paradoxical result of people gaining access to culture was that, once they had achieved this, they could cut themselves off from the social and political organisations which had fought for this access, and proceed to seek their own individual enjoyment without caring about the 'objectives, utopias and myths' which had motivated such organisations in their fight for cultural democratisation. According to Touraine, the development of modern leisure in France signalled 'a decomposition of traditional culture', by which he did not mean 'folk culture' but 'working-class culture', including militant working-class culture.[34]

The organisation which in modern times has most claimed to speak for the French working class is, of course, the French Communist Party. The decline of the PCF since its high point after the Liberation is one of the most spectacular features of contemporary French life. In the 1970s and 1980s there took place a massive rejection of the Party by intellectuals and workers alike, and there also developed an enormous industry devoted to publishing denunciations of the Party's political and cultural policies throughout the postwar years. It is true that in more recent years the Party has succeeded in modernising its cultural attitudes and it can now claim to compete with anyone in its openness to fashionable developments in all areas of mass culture. It is also true to say that the Party has always attached an exceptional importance to the project of democratising culture, and it is well known that those municipalities controlled by the Communists have tended to have an extremely dynamic cultural policy. All this having been said, it is none the less still difficult to disguise the fact that for long the PCF carried out a lamentable policy of attacking, censoring and repressing anything that did not accord with its narrow cultural precepts.

In her study *Au service du parti: le parti communiste, les intellectuels et la culture (1944–1956)* (1983) ['In the service of the Party: the Communist Party, intellectuals and culture (1944–1956)'],[35] Jeannine Verdès-Leroux gives a detailed analysis of the Party's cultural policies and practices in the period just after the war and during the Cold War, when it still exerted an enormously powerful control over French intellectual and cultural life. At the beginning of her book she says that what she has learned about the PCF during her research has put her forever on her guard against 'dogmatic utopians who, in the name of the "working class", or in the name of the people, are ready to destroy a civilisation, or make a society go backwards, including "the working class"'.[36] Verdès-Leroux's book offers an unsparing critique of communist cultural *dirigisme* and of the primitive socialist realist aesthetics which controlled French communist thinking on culture and which were taken to such extreme lengths at this time. But her criticism is also aimed at the whole intellectual class that abdicated its critical role and allowed itself to be captured, humiliated and bullied by the communists throughout this period. She is highly scornful of all those intellectuals who betrayed their true role as defenders of culture and intellectuality, and she sees the worst offenders as being those such as Paul Nizan who allowed themselves to become locked into the Manichean 'ouvriériste' perspective of the Communists, according to which everything that could be characterised as belonging to the working class was good, and everything that was said to be bourgeois was bad. Verdès-Leroux is unwilling to accept that 'culture' is 'bourgeois culture', and has no time for those intellectuals who are the first to deny culture and to conspire in its destruction. Generations of cultured, left-wing, middle-class intellectuals displayed these masochistic tendencies, because, being drawn to the Communist Party and its 'ouvriériste' mythology, they felt the need to despise and destroy the bourgeois elements in themselves as well as in all that surrounded them.

There is little doubt that left-wing intellectuals have for long periods been virtually paralysed by the myth of the people so sedulously promoted by the PCF and have stood in awe of the Party that they considered to have a kind of mystical link with the people, as well as an inalienable right to speak for it. To have been born into the working class was, in communist eyes, to be forever in a state of grace, whereas to be born a bourgeois was to be condemned to bear an ineradicable stain, and always to be suspected of being a potential traitor to the working-class cause. Intellectuals constantly sought solidarity and fraternity in 'the Party of the working class', but once in the Party they were expected to abase themselves and to atone for what the Party, in reality, never allowed them to atone for – the fact of being a bourgeois and an intellectual. By definition, no matter how hard they tried, they could not become authentically working class. None the less, the Party did seek to recruit intellectuals, particularly after the war, and tried to win them over from decadent bourgeois culture into a movement where their creativity would supposedly blossom through contact with 'the popular masses'.

Verdès-Leroux gives particularly detailed attention to the socialist realist aesthetics that dominated the Party's cultural attitudes in the years she is studying. According to Verdès-Leroux, the socialist realist aesthetics of the PCF at this period were based on the belief that cultural values were rooted in the struggle of the masses. The masses themselves were said to be the true creative force and it was thought to be the duty of all art to depict the life of the workers and to contribute to the raising of the consciousness of the workers. In other words, art should be put 'at the service of the people'. Needless to say, socialist realism in art and literature was thought to be the privileged aesthetic vehicle producing 'really popular' culture. According to Verdès-Leroux, however:

That form of literature which calls itself socialist realism is, above all, intended to glorify the Communist Party: in such literature, what one has to depict are not workers, but communist workers, not working-class struggles, but struggles led by the Party.[37]

It was the PCF's constant ambition to impose its militant ethos on all areas of culture. Verdès-Leroux highlights this ambition in the case of the 'popular songs' which the PCF tried to promote. She points to the case of Maurice Morelly whom the Party championed as *the* 'chanteur populaire', which presumably here means the singer for the working class and of the working class (and at the same time, it was no doubt hoped, the singer actually liked by the working class). But, according to Verdès-Leroux, despite the fact, or rather because of the fact, that the songs explicitly followed the Party on a whole range of contemporary political issues, Morelly apparently failed to win over 'the people'. Verdès-Leroux then turns to the case of Yves Montand, who was made to feel that his songs were not sufficiently close to party policy. In Verdès-Leroux's eyes, this only serves to demonstrate how remote the PCF was from the actual tastes of the working class and how stupid its policy was of trying to direct the working class in matters of culture and taste. She quotes Montand himself on the pressure that the Party brought to bear on him over the song 'Luna-Park':

> I never experienced total censorship, but on certain occasions I did inflict severe self-censorship on myself . . . . For example, the song 'Luna-Park', which, as you know, is an eminently popular song, evoking as it does the simple, healthy, and truly popular joy experienced by this working man, who after work goes to have a ball, as one would say nowadays, at Luna-Park . . . . Well, the argument they put to me was along the lines of: 'don't you think that this worker, rather than wasting his time at Luna-Park, should have put his energy and his efforts into serving the revolution and the working class?'[38]

Montand went on to describe the sense of guilt that he was made to feel for singing songs which he knew were good and which appealed to people (the working class included), but which were considered by the PCF to be too erotic, too frivolous, or, not least, too Americanised.

Verdès-Leroux draws a picture of the Communists as closeted

throughout these years in a subculture of their own making, consisting of socialist realist texts, hagiographical works dedicated to famous communist leaders, and Stalinist political theory, all of which they tirelessly tried to promote among the French working class. In fact, Verdès-Leroux's most characteristic approach to communist culture is to treat it as an inferior, low-grade culture, which fails to come near to satisfying the exacting standards of true intellectual and cultural life. In all her analyses she does, in fact, show herself to be close to the approach of Bourdieu. As already indicated, Verdès-Leroux criticises those genuine intellectuals who throughout the postwar period abdicated true standards of intellectuality by willingly subordinating themselves to the PCF concerning matters in which they had real competence, and in which the PCF did not. For, according to Verdès-Leroux, those who have controlled the PCF have never been part of a genuine intelligentsia, but have been a mixture of working-class autodidacts and second-rate intellectuals. In fact, Verdès-Leroux believes that it was because the Party was in the hands of second-rate intellectuals that it spent so much time castigating and humiliating genuine intellectuals inside or outside the Party. In Verdès-Leroux's opinion, the PCF at the time of the Liberation was full of people who, because of their experience in the war, had learned to see things in black and white terms, and who after the war continued to prefer militant action based on simple premises to a long and difficult apprenticeship of serious, intellectual study, which would have obliged them to face up to the changing complexity of things. These communist militants were offered prestigious positions in the PCF which they could not have hoped to match in what Verdès-Leroux calls 'the intellectual field', 'where the criteria of competition were of a completely different order'. Verdès-Leroux sees the intellectual within the PCF as burdened with a series of 'handicaps', which put him at a severe disadvantage in comparison with the genuine intellectual:

> These handicaps were: the lower middle-class origin of the majority of PCF intellectuals; a frequently interrupted education; the acquisition of cultural capital in difficult circumstances; an ambiguous relationship to this cultural capital; the obligatory attachment to values which they consider to be 'working class', but which are often in conflict with what they have acquired during their cultural apprenticeship etc. All

these handicaps mean that the communist intellectual hardly ever possesses those qualities which the classic intellectual rates as important: ease, naturalness, cleverness, brilliance, independence, curiosity about all new developments (which the classic intellectual, in fact, creates, or is quick to make his own and exploit.)[39]

In Verdès-Leroux's eyes, those working-class autodidacts who had come to the fore during the Resistance, and who were given positions in the PCF after the war, were so gratified to have reached what they considered to be such elevated and prestigious positions, that they inevitably failed to develop a genuinely critical perspective and remained firmly entrenched within an unchanging and dogmatic frame of reference. In fact, those working-class autodidacts such as Jean Guéhenno who did become genuine intellectuals outside the Party, came in for particularly violent treatment from the PCF Jean Guéhenno admitted to experiencing a life-long conflict between his working-class origins and his ultimate status as a celebrated writer and intellectual. According to Verdès-Leroux, the PCF regarded Guéhenno's 'inner distress' as a sign of weakness and class treachery. The Party preferred 'men of marble', who showed no vacillation in their commitment to their working-class origins and to the aims of the Party. Verdès-Leroux, however, obviously thinks that it is a mark of a genuine intellectual to admit to the complexities and conflicts he feels within himself, and to refuse to mask these by a discourse of double-talk. The famous 'langue de bois' [literally 'wooden tongue'], attributed to French Communists by their opponents, is considered to be precisely the language of a Party which tries to cover up complex realities by resorting to an incantatory jargon of certitudes, of which in the present context such key terms as 'working class', 'bourgeois', 'popular' and 'the people' would be prime examples.

One of the persistent strategies of the postwar PCF has been to claim to speak both for the French working class and for the French nation, a strategy greatly helped by the dual meanings of 'le peuple' and 'populaire', which can signify both the working class in particular and the nation as a whole. Although this strategy has been a constant feature of communist discourse since the war, it was, of course, particularly apparent in the very first years after the Liberation, when not only the PCF but all parties temporarily agreed to pull together to achieve common ends. A lecture given by

Louis Aragon in 1946, under the auspices of UNESCO, provides an interesting example of the way in which French Communists at this time were trying to bring together their particular concern for the working class with their more general claim to speak for the nation. The title of Aragon's lecture was 'La Culture des masses ou le titre refusé' ['The culture of the masses: rejecting the term'].[40] Aragon began by describing how Stephen Spender had suggested a title for the lecture which had become transformed by the translation into something that Aragon felt totally unable to accept:

> For the purposes of the circulars, Stephen Spender gave the lecture the following title in English (which is, as you know, his own language): 'Culture and the people', which could be translated into our language as 'la culture et le Peuple', or 'la culture et les Gens'. I would not have objected to either title, since I could, in any case, have proceeded to talk about something else. But, as it happened, the title did not pass straight from English into American, and 'Culture and the people' became something like 'Massculture' [sic] or 'Culture of the masses'. In any case, it came back into French in the form of 'Culture des masses', to which I have such serious objections that I cannot begin what I have to say without first rejecting the term.[41]

According to Aragon, the prime duty, after the experience of fascism, was to make sure that the meaning of words was not perverted in the way that it had been by the Fascists. For Aragon, this meant, in this context, refusing to use the term 'culture of the masses', because this would be to accept that culture could be separated into one culture for the elite and one for the rest, which he adamantly refused to believe:

> Above all else I want to put forward the principle that culture is one and indivisible, that it is not the sole possession of a few people who somehow draw it out of their heads. It is the common property of all people, and whether you call them masses, peoples, or nations, it is in humanity that culture has its solid roots; it is from deep within nations that it has its origins, its principle of growth and renewal.[42]

Aragon's 'democratic' discourse on culture offered a characteristic mixture of humanist and idealist notions, allied with violently anti-fascist and anti-aristocratic attitudes. At one and the same time,

Aragon appealed to the community of nations and peoples, and to the unifying notion of shared humanity, while also delivering bitter tirades against those elite social groups which had an 'aristocratic' conception of culture. In Aragon's view, a small elite had plundered the people of its culture, just as a small social group had exploited the labour of the people for its own profit. According to Aragon, it was the masses who created culture, just as he believed that it was the masses who created wealth. This was obviously Aragon's version of cultural materialism, since he regarded aristocratic culture as ethereal and parasitical, whereas the culture of the masses was considered to be 'earthy', and to be the only culture that was truly productive. In fact, rather than rejecting the term 'culture of the masses', Aragon was actually appropriating it and purifying it of its pejorative connotations. Aragon glorified the masses, for it was they, he tells us, who through their heroism and martyrdom succeeded in overcoming fascism and collaboration, and brought France through the war. Here we can see how Aragon was capitalising on the extensive communist participation in the Resistance and on the great favour in which Communists were held after the war, in order to be able to suggest that the heroic masses were the communist masses, who were in turn the nation. The elites, on the other hand, were the Fascists and collaborators who set themselves against the nation. These were false elites, in Aragon's eyes, for the true elite was one which grew out of 'the leaf-mould of intellectuals and the simple man':

> Elites are only elites in so far as they are an expression of what you could call nations, peoples, or masses. Elites are connected in life and death to the destiny and future of these 'masses', and they refuse to oppose them.[43]

According to Aragon, only peasants, workers and intellectuals stood up for the values of culture and reason during the war, and it was only with them that the destiny of France rested in safe hands. Aragon's lecture turned into a hymn of praise to Man, Europe and the Nation, but, above all, to the last of these. For what Aragon really wanted to talk about was national culture, although for him this seems to have been adequately rendered by the word 'culture' on its own:

> It is a fact that, in a country where culture is a single, unified phenomenon (in the sense that there is not one culture for the

elite, and one for the masses), it has a life and a value because of the national form it takes. It is the nation that precisely brings together elites and masses, because the nation is the mould of which we are the leaves and in which culture sets down its strong roots, and from which it draws its life and strength. It is also a fact that human culture, in all its greatness, is the sum of all national cultures, and is not created by cutting off individual cultures but by fostering the coexistence and harmony of these.[44]

At this important moment of French history Aragon was sharing in the collective desire to forge a united nation, but he was also engaged in mystifying the realities, because, while putting forward the ideal of a united nation, and a unified culture, he disguised the fact that the nation was profoundly divided. It was, after all, not true that all opponents of communism were Fascists and collaborators. A united nation on the terms laid down by the Communists was never going to become a reality in postwar France, however much the proclaimed policy of the PCF was that of forging 'popular union'. Aragon explicitly rejected 'pluralist' notions of culture in this lecture, in favour of a near-mystical idea of a national culture built on the union between the masses and intellectuals. Apart from the fact that this left out of account whole social groups with different interests and ideologies, it also skated over the brutal reality that, although they paid lip-service to the union between the masses and the intellectuals, the Communists had, in fact, no intention of admitting intellectuals into the party of the masses except on terms which divested them of their intellectuality.

One can observe the continuities in communist strategy and in communist discourse by looking at the writings and speeches of Roland Leroy, member of the Political Bureau of the PCF and secretary of the Central Committee. These writings and speeches are all from the period 1967–72 and were collected in a volume published in 1972 entitled *La Culture au présent* ['Culture in the present'].[45] Georges Marchais' preface set the tone and put forward the orthodox communist view on cultural matters. Monopoly capitalism was blamed for the cultural deprivation of the people. Only the introduction of socialism could radically change the prospects for the majority of the nation:

Out of 100 French people, 58 have never read a book, and 78 have never been to the theatre. Out of 1000 working-class children, only 34 enter higher education. How can one deny that these extremely negative features of cultural life – and the list could go on for ever – are essentially caused by the difficult living conditions of our people, by the excessive length and intensity of their working day, by the continued existence of a veritable system of social segregation in the schools, and by the cultural underequipment of the country?[46]

In his own introduction to his essays, Leroy took up the theme of access to culture for the masses. He praised the efforts of the popular culture movement since 1936, a movement in which he says Communists had always played an important role. Incidentally, he took issue with the term 'popular culture' used in this context, and suggested that it should simply be 'the diffusion of culture'. He accepted that the task of diffusing culture, undertaken by municipalities, working-class organisations and cultural associations, was a crucial one, but he also insisted that such initiatives could never replace 'a general political struggle, of which only an outcome that favours working-class and democratic forces will create the conditions for mass cultural development'.[47] According to Leroy, there was a need for a 'cultural revolution' which, however, could only take place on condition that there was a prior transformation of social relationships. Leroy said he was following Lenin in his definition of what was involved in the term 'cultural revolution'. Firstly, the working class and 'the popular masses' had to be given access to culture, and the cultural level of the whole population had to be raised by removing the obstacles which a capitalist system put in the way of such objectives. Secondly, the importance of intellectuals must be increasingly acknowledged; they had to be helped to become conscious of their responsibility to society, and they had also to be encouraged to add their specific contribution to the progress of society. Thirdly, culture should develop by a process of 'critically assimilating the cultural heritage'.[48]

For a movement that claimed to believe, as a matter of fundamental principle, in the existence of class conflict, and in the necessity of class struggle to bring about the future good society, French communism has always given an excessively large place in its cultural discourse to notions of unity and continuity. Although claiming to be working towards a 'cultural revolution', Leroy did not in any way envisage a break with the past, but simply 'a critical assimilation of the cultural heritage'. So long as French

Communists claimed to speak for the nation, it was, of course, impossible for them to spurn, let alone seek to destroy, the historic culture of France. In the same way, although Communists have claimed to believe in class struggle, in their discourse they have, none the less, constantly resorted to universalist concepts of 'Man'. Thus, we find Leroy agreeing with the following definition of culture, based primarily on notions of unity and continuity, and on idealist concepts of humanity:

> As far as we are concerned, culture is still what Paul Langevin said it was: 'One could say that culture ['culture générale'] is what enables the individual to feel his solidarity with other people: people of other times and other places, as well as people of his own generation, those that have gone before, and those that will come afterwards. To be cultured is to have been involved in all manner of human activities and to continue to be involved in activities other than those which relate to one's work and that enable one to enter into contact and communion with other people.'[49]

Leroy's championing of a rather vague and idealist, even senti-mental, humanist discourse coincided with the events of May 1968, when the students called into question precisely those idealist abstractions of Man and Culture which underpinned communist cultural discourse. What is more, the students invoked a more radical and violent notion of cultural revolution, as well as also claiming to speak directly for the people. It is not surprising, therefore, that the French Communists reacted scathingly to the students' notion of cultural revolution, which they considered to be nothing but cultural nihilism. On behalf of the working class, Leroy rejected the student call for a thoroughly politicised culture, and reaffirmed the view that workers did not need a political culture devised specially for them, but simply needed to be given the means of gaining access to the whole of contemporary culture. Leroy saw the students of 1968 as attempting to resuscitate the Russian *Proletkult* of the 1920s:

> One finds among the men of the *Proletkult* in Russia in the 1920s the same things that we sometimes encounter nowadays: the same rejection of the heritage of the past; the same break with national life; the same excessive use of the epithets 'proletarian', 'popular', 'revolutionary'; the same

nihilism; the same claim to bring to the working class the 'new culture' invented by ideologists from outside its ranks. For instance, Kirillov, one of the poets of the *Proletkult*, wrote the following: 'For the sake of the future, we will burn Raphaels, we will destroy museums, we will trample on the flowers of art.'

It is in the name of similar ideas that today one finds amongst us certain people who begin by daubing a fresco of Puvis de Chavannes, then go on to destroy a painting by Philippe de Champaigne, and go so far as to protest against Vilar and Béjart at Avignon, against the festival which was the object of a violent assault by Gaullists (who are afraid of anything new), and by leftists (who preach the politics of the blank sheet in cultural matters).[50]

Against the assaults of the students of 1968, the PCF continued to uphold its 'humanist' faith in Art and Culture, seeing them not as unique but none the less as privileged means by which people could attain their full humanity. Leroy's particular outrage at the treatment received by Jean Vilar in Avignon, at the hands of representatives of the 1968 cultural revolution (which I will look at in some detail – see pp. 142ff.) shows how the Communists, like those in the popular culture movement, were deeply wedded to the idea that culture had a special, even sacred, role to play in the experience of the people. Equally sacred to Leroy and the Communists were the heritage and the nation. However much it tried to present itself as a revolutionary party, the PCF in its discourse betrayed time and again its attachment to profoundly conservative notions of nationhood, history and culture.

In a series of studies, Georges Lavau has called into question the claim of the PCF to be a revolutionary party. In a long article entitled 'The PCF, the state, and the revolution: an analysis of party policies, communications and popular culture' (1975),[51] Lavau insisted that the Party was 'no longer the vanguard of the Revolution. It has become a party of management and order.' Lavau, however, conceded that in the cultural sphere the PCF had made considerable efforts to counter the dominant bourgeois ideology by carrying out a very active cultural policy of its own:

> The PCF has shown its understanding of the importance of creating its own ideological apparatus to offset the dominant ideas and the 'sens commun' of a bourgeois society by forming

its own mass organisations and assigning its own militants to them, by making special efforts to have its own press and to assure its widespread distribution; it has encouraged its intellectuals to participate in running radio and television media, it has created its own chain of publishing houses, bookstores and record shops, it has organised the distribution of political films in its own cinemas by skilfully making use of 'maisons de la culture' and 'maisons de la jeunesse', it has named streets and school buildings in its communes with names of symbolic French and foreign revolutionary heroes, it has constantly organised demonstrations to commemorate great revolutionary events such as the Paris Commune and the October Revolution.[52]

But ultimately Lavau does not seem impressed by all this cultural activity. In his view, Communists have not by and large succeeded in breaking through into a wider cultural sphere, but have ended up by creating their own self-enclosed cultural world, particularly at the working-class level. So much of the cultural activity of the Communists is said by Lavau to have been principally a way of reinforcing their own identity as a group. Lavau uses the term 'popular communism' to refer to the way that the working-class members relate to the Party, and he characterises this popular communism scathingly as 'an ideological patriotic-republican-working-class syncretism, a sentimental and shallow attachment encouraged by a warm ambiance and by frequent celebrations (the First of May, "the fête de *l'Humanité*", the "fêtes" of local communist newspapers, the annual renewal of party cards in the cells, and so on)'.[53] In fact, Lavau regards popular communism, like popular catholicism, as both a substitute folk culture and a substitute religion, remarkable for its ability to forge the solidarity of a circumscribed group through ritual and superstition.

In his book, *A Quoi sert le parti communiste français?* (1981) ['What is the French Communist Party for?'],[54] Lavau continued his critical treatment of the PCF as a party chiefly dedicated to reinforcing its own image of itself. Here Lavau focused particularly on the 'ouvriérisme' of the PCF, and on the way in which the Party has nurtured the idea of a self-enclosed working-class culture with its own history, myths and traditions. Lavau pointed to the communist notion of the militant as indicative of a movement which has admired above all else the person who identifies himself through and through with the party he is serving, and who refuses to compromise in any way with the society against which he is fighting. However, according to Lavau, the high-mindedness of the communist militant has often been simply a form of puritanism, which has not proved very appealing in the years since the war, when such moral austerity has come more and more into conflict with the enormous cultural changes that have taken place. What is more, the exclusive concentration on the working class has made the PCF very slow to respond to the cultural demands of other sections of society who see themselves as oppressed (women, regional groups, homosexuals, immigrants).

As already mentioned, Verdès-Leroux also considers that it is the austere, puritanical militant ethos of the Communists that has been largely responsible for the PCF's increasing loss of support since the war. In her treatment of the 'earnestness' of the militant, Verdès-Leroux gives a convincing suggestion as to why the PCF should have become less and less appealing to people who lived in a mass culture where 'fun morality' was to become so prevalent, and where living for the day was to become such a dominant 'philosophy':

It is militancy which brings into being and develops this kind of extreme earnestness . . . which is based on a Manichean view of the world and justifies itself by constructing a millenarian plan. Everything conspires to lead the militant to refrain from laughing and joking (he only allows himself the noisy celebrations that follow upon political victories). First of all one must not laugh, because Henri Martin is in prison, or because there is a war in Korea. And in a more grandiose vein, the task of working for a better future does not leave enough time to enjoy oneself today. Militancy invents the deferred laugh. If one adds together all the moral references thrown around by the Communist Party there is no room left for hedonist values: whether it is the references to the French Revolution, to the Soviet ethos (glorifying the working-class shocktrooper, the collective farm worker, the Red Army hero . . .); or whether it is the references to the Resistance and the sacrifices it demanded. What is more, the extreme efforts made to create the future society (with its 'shining peaks') lead them to turn the present into a time of renunciation, austerity and vigilance.[55]

94

Verdès-Leroux identifies the austere militant ethos exclusively with the Communists, whereas Lavau concedes that it is, in fact, an ethos which has been embraced by all radical sections of the French Left. There is no doubt that socialist theorists of culture have traditionally refused to consider individual 'pleasure' as constituting one of the valid aims of culture. On the other hand, it is one of the notable contributions of the events of May 1968 that the question of pleasure was so often put at the centre of cultural debate, although one has to recognise that 1968 also saw the revitalisation of notions of militancy that advocated in an extreme way the necessity of dedicating the self to the revolutionary cause.[56]

4

POPULAR CULTURE AS BARBARIC CULTURE: THE SOCIOLOGY OF PIERRE BOURDIEU

In the period since the war the most sustained intellectual effort in France to engage with notions of culture, popular culture and working-class culture has without doubt been that of the sociologist Pierre Bourdieu, particularly in his massive volume *La Distinction: critique sociale du jugement* (1979) [*Distinction: A social critique of the judgement of taste*).[1] This work has already become a classic text on the subject of popular culture and working-class culture. Much of the substance of the text had, however, already appeared in Bourdieu's earlier works. In fact, the main lines of his arguments can perhaps be seen more clearly in these earlier works. In particular, these earlier texts show to what extent Bourdieu's work has been a response to those French debates on culture and popular culture which had been taking place at least since 1936 and which became particularly active in the period from the Liberation to the mid-1960s, when the cultural ideals of the popular culture movement gradually took concrete form in State policies of cultural development.

In *L'Amour de l'art: les musées d'art européens et leur public* (1966), ['The love of art: European art galleries and their public'][2] which he co-wrote with Alain Darbel, Bourdieu tackled the question of 'the social conditions of cultural practice' by looking at which social groups visited art galleries, and by examining the social, economic and cultural factors which facilitated or hindered this cultural practice. According to Bourdieu, there was a very close correlation between the level of educational attainment and the propensity to engage in traditional and highly regarded cultural practices such as visiting an art gallery. Formal education was said by Bourdieu to play the decisive role in developing not only the habit of cultural practice, but also the disposition towards cultural practice (that is, both the desire or aspiration to engage in cultural practice, and also the belief in the importance of so doing). In addition, formal education was needed if people were to be able to understand the culture to which they aspired, and in which they wished to participate. But if formal education, according to Bourdieu, played the truly decisive role, one should by no means underestimate the power of the family to perform a similar function, or rather those families which had a high cultural level. In fact, so important was the family in developing the cultural disposition, and in handing down 'cultural capital', that, for instance, children from families with a long-standing high cultural level continued throughout their lives to have the edge in cultural matters over those who may have attained a similar educational level, and occupied a similar social position, but who came from families with less cultural capital. According to Bourdieu, working-class families have no 'cultural capital' to hand down to their children (that is, of course, 'legitimate' cultural capital). Nor do working-class families develop the cultural disposition in their children. Working-class people do not engage in legitimate cultural activities, and are in no position to understand or appreciate legitimate culture. They are either intimidated or humiliated by a culture that is alien and incomprehensible to them, or they are profoundly indifferent to it. In Bourdieu's terms, cultural dispossession leads to a dispossession of the consciousness of dispossession. That is to say, working-class people are not only deprived of culture, without knowing they are deprived of it, but, more significantly, are deprived of the desire for culture, since they do not see it or recognise it as a value to which to aspire.

It is for this reason that Bourdieu attacked the notion of 'cultural needs', which underpinned so much of the 'cultural action' of the popular culture movement. In Bourdieu's view, cultural needs are themselves created by the school system. It has, however, been one of Bourdieu's main tasks in his sociological studies to show that the school system has worked against the interests of working-class children and not in their favour, as superficial democratic rhetoric would like one to think. Bourdieu believes that the school system has failed to take into account and to compensate for initial social inequalities, and has indeed compounded these inequalities. In cultural matters advantages and disadvantages are cumulative. Those who set off with a cultural disposition and with cultural capital continue to add to their cultural capital, whereas those who begin without either become less and less able to develop the 'cultural attitude' and, relatively speaking, become even more bereft of 'cultural goods'. But if the school system has failed to develop the cultural disposition in working-class children, this was not, in Bourdieu's view, a reason for abandoning the task to the popular culture movement, which he considered to be in no position at all to carry through such a vast undertaking. In fact, Bourdieu considered the cultural and educational ideas of the popular culture movement to be naïve and mistaken in the extreme, not least because, however much they claimed to 'prepare' the working class for cultural practice, they did in fact rely heavily on the notion of 'cultural innocence', that is to say, the belief that confrontation with a work of art had, by itself, the capacity to convert a person to cultural practice. Bourdieu is adamant that 'the school system [is] alone capable of creating the "cultivated attitude"'.[3] He insists that if people have failed to develop the cultural disposition at school, then the system has failed to do its job, and more time and more appropriate methods need to be applied in order to develop the cultural disposition in working-class children, and in order to equip them with all that they need to understand and enjoy the culture which remains the preserve of the middle and the upper classes.

Although Bourdieu attacked the popular culture movement for its naïve and misguided ideas, he by no means called into question its ambition to 'democratise the access to culture'. He was, rather, concerned to give a 'scientific' definition of what the social conditions of cultural practice actually were, in order that policy on cultural democratisation could be more realistic and more effective. As many others have done, Bourdieu pointed to the fact that attendance figures at art galleries and theatres indicated beyond any doubt that, however much such cultural institutions directed their policy at attracting working-class people, the overwhelming majority of those actually turning up were those middle-class people who were already highly cultured. For Bourdieu, this served to confirm his belief that only the school system, and not the marginal activities of a separate cultural movement, was in a position to offer the long and disciplined preparation that was needed to inspire working-class children with the cultural disposition and provide them with the necessary tools with which to understand and appreciate culture. If Bourdieu did not call into question the ambition to democratise the access to culture, neither did he appear to challenge the ideal of culture which, in his view, society held up as a model to which all should aspire. As far as *L'Amour de l'art* goes, Bourdieu was concerned to give what he considered to be an accurate description of cultural practice in modern France, which necessarily involved an acknowledgement of the supreme importance attached to legitimate culture by the dominant classes and by the State itself, particularly in its educational institutions. Indeed, Bourdieu characterised these institutions as being 'charged with the task of organising the cult of culture'.[4] Those who had already been inculcated with a 'devotion to culture' by their families would clearly prosper in such an educational system, whereas those who had not (that is, those from the working class) would be gradually eliminated from the system, since they had failed to develop the cultural disposition which, in Bourdieu's view, it was precisely the task of the school system to develop. For Bourdieu, however, the creation of the cultural disposition is not the same as the inculcation of cultural values. When a person has been successful in the educational system, and ends up at ease in the world of culture, he is, in fact, in a position to call it into question:

> Only those people are free to transcend academic constraints who have themselves successfully assimilated academic culture, and who have internalised the liberated attitude towards academic culture which is to be found throughout an educational system that is so deeply imbued with the values of the dominant classes that it quite readily adopts the views of those in fashionable circles who depreciate academic practices. The academic opposition between, on the one hand, a classical, stereotyped and, as Max Weber would say, a routinised culture, and, on the other hand, an authentic culture which has freed itself from school discourses, only has a meaning for a tiny minority of cultured people, because the full possession of academic culture is the precondition for going beyond school culture and acquiring a free culture, that is to say, a culture which has thrown off the shackles of its academic origins, and which is regarded by the bourgeoisie and the educational system as the highest of values.[5]

Authentic culture is, for Bourdieu, that whole free area of culture which encompasses the culture of the school but also goes beyond it. Bourdieu has, in fact, often stressed that such new cultural forms as jazz and cinema, which he characterises as being 'on the way to cultural legitimation', are in the main appropriated by those very people who are in a position to appropriate legitimate cultural goods. This, of course, only serves to reinforce even further his view that it is education which is primarily responsible for developing the cultural disposition.

Although Bourdieu likes to keep his ideological positions well under control in his sociological work, it seems clear that his treatment of cultural matters has been significantly determined by his own attitudes. One of the principal ways this can be seen in *L'Amour de l'art* is in his assault on what he called the 'charismatic ideology' of cultural practice.[6] By this, Bourdieu had in mind the 'aristocratic' relationship to culture – that of the connoisseur who was thought to have a natural, unforced, intuitive appreciation of cultural forms. But in Bourdieu's view, what was thought to be a purely natural and intuitive appreciation of culture was, in fact, simply the result of a certain privileged social background. The connoisseur has assimilated high culture in a natural and easy manner through the normal processes of upper-class family life. The connoisseur is able to appreciate culture not because of a natural cultural disposition, but because he has had a long and intimate familiarity with it. Bourdieu believes that the connoisseur has *learned* how to appreciate culture, but the process of learning has been effectively masked, and the upper-class cultural disposition appears to be an innate 'gift'.[7]

It is obviously Bourdieu's profound belief that the aristocratic conception of culture dominates the cultural field in France. It is also clear that his own ideological project is to elaborate in his sociological works a truly democratic notion of culture, which he hopes will provide the scientific basis for a truly democratic cultural policy. Bourdieu believes that if the mass of people are ever going to develop the cultural disposition, and be in a position to amass their own share of cultural capital, then they must be taught how to do this. Since the families of most people are not able to perform this function, it must obviously be the duty of the educational system to do it for them. Bourdieu has enormous faith in the democratising role of education, and he is very hostile to those who uphold and represent an aristocratic notion of culture and education, and who belittle or despise the learning and cultivation that are the products of the schooling process. Since this aristocratic notion of culture is, however, the dominant one, it actually works in varying degrees against all other categories of people who cannot claim 'natural' taste, and who are, therefore, destined to be regarded as cultural parvenus. For instance, it not only works against those autodidacts who, however hard they try to gain access to culture, never succeed in learning the cultural codes. It also works against those who have been successful in the educational system and have learned the cultural codes, but who, in the eyes of the connoisseurs, betray too many traces of how hard they have had to struggle in order to become cultured. Since, in the aristocratic view, to be cultured is to have a natural and easy relationship to culture, then even the most successful in the educational system can be discounted by these criteria.

The meritocrat clearly has his own bone to pick with the connoisseur, and Bourdieu himself obviously falls into the category of someone from relatively humble origins who is supremely successful in educational and cultural terms, but who still feels that the ultimate accolade of 'the cultured man' can be refused him by those who hold to a purely aristocratic notion of culture as an inherited gift. But, in Bourdieu's view, this would no doubt be to put an inappropriately personal slant on his analysis, which he insists on seeing as purely scientific and objective. According to Bourdieu, other social groups suffer far more than do the successful meritocrats from a system which sets up as cultural models those who appear to have acquired their culture in an effortless and natural way. Bourdieu often uses the term 'bonne volonté culturelle' ['cultural goodwill'] to describe the attitude of the lower-middle class type who has only achieved moderate success in the educational system, but who is ever eager to make up for this by constantly trying to appropriate the culture which has so far eluded him, and which seems to him an essential qualification for his own success and prestige. In Bourdieu's terms, such a type has a high level of 'cultural aspiration', rather than a high level of cultural attainment.

However, the social group that suffers most from the aristocratic notion of culture and from its 'charismatic ideology' of cultural taste is, of course, the working class. Using terms and arguments drawn from Kantian aesthetics, which also serve as the basis for the analysis of popular taste in La Distinction, Bourdieu actually describes the taste of the working class as 'barbaric' ['le goût barbare'],[8] that is, as being on every point opposed to the taste of the truly cultured. According to this view, popular taste has no understanding of the aesthetics of contemplation and disinterestedness; it is a completely utilitarian and functional taste; it sees art as reality and not convention; it responds on the level of sensation and emotion, and not on the level of spiritual abstraction. Totally deprived of the codes necessary to understand high culture, working-class people constantly import their extrinsic criteria into the appreciation of art, and interpret art in terms of their daily practical concerns. On the rare occasions that working-class people actually go to art galleries, it is for them, according to Bourdieu, a particularly disconcerting experience. They only have the capacity to offer the most rudimentary responses to the pictures themselves, and they have no way of organising their perceptions, or the knowledge they may pick up. They cannot remember the names of artists or paintings, nor can they fit them into any stylistic or historical order. What Bourdieu, in fact, is attacking here is the way in which the ideology of 'cultural innocence' has misled all those involved in the popular culture movement and the world of 'cultural animation'. In Bourdieu's opinion, popular educators and 'animateurs' have been great believers in the idea that people simply needed to be faced with works of art for a spontaneous cultural conversion to take place. Bourdieu's view of popular educators and 'animateurs' is that they have been, in general, hostile to mainstream education and have wanted to set up for themselves an alternative educational and cultural system. Bourdieu criticises them for claiming that the working class was hostile to 'educational action', and accuses them of 'the class ethnocentrism characteristic of populist ideology'.[9] In his view, they were simply projecting onto the working class their own attitudes to culture and education. Bourdieu believes that it is cultured people who reject educational aids in their visits to art galleries, whereas working-class people are only too willing to accept any help they are offered in a situation in which they feel totally at sea. In fact, according to Bourdieu, it is because working-class people feel disoriented in art galleries that they stay away from them:

> It is certainly not going too far to think that what contributes, in large measure, to keeping people away from museums is the profound feeling of unworthiness and incompetence which haunts the less cultured visitors, who, faced with the sacred world of legitimate culture, appear to be crushed by a sense of awe.[10]

When working-class people did enter an art gallery, Bourdieu believed that their whole behaviour demonstrated that the gallery was experienced by them as something sacred which kept them at a distance. They showed exaggerated respect, deference and humility. The art gallery was perceived as a religious shrine, in which silence had to be observed and objects were not to be touched. Bourdieu clearly saw the traditional art gallery as symbolic of the aristocratic notion of culture, according to which the aesthetic experience was considered to be close to a mystical revelation, available only to the aristocratic few on whom 'grace' had been conferred in the form of the gift of true appreciation and understanding. Those popular educators who wanted to take culture to the people (or people to culture) were, in Bourdieu's eyes, guilty of the same 'sacralising' view of art, for they believed that not only a privileged few but all could become devotees of the religion of culture; all could be transfigured and illuminated by direct contact with the sacred relics of culture, and all could attain the blessed state of cultural salvation ['salut culturel'].[11]

In contrast to this, Bourdieu showed a decided preference for a new democratic, desacralised art gallery, which would not only be more open, welcoming and congenial, but which would be ready to provide the educational aids to understanding and appreciation which the traditional art gallery seems on principle to have refused to supply. Over the period covered by his survey of attendance at art galleries (late 1950s and early 1960s), Bourdieu considered that French galleries were stuck in old, aristocratic ways, whereas he believed that in other European countries, and in the United States, great progress had already been made in creating institutions which were more accessible and which were far more aware of the need to provide appropriate educational information:

Numerous techniques of making art galleries more accessible are employed by galleries in other countries. In the Rijksmuseum there are explanatory boards to help the visitors. In the Fitzwilliam Museum at Cambridge, old ladies, doing their knitting at little desks, have replaced the sleepy and severe attendants who follow every step of the solitary visitor to provincial galleries in France. The little folding stools that visitors to the National Gallery in London carry around with them also help to transform the atmosphere of a visit to the gallery, because they suggest a walk round the park, rather than a solemn visit to church. Why not also provide some music, which would give visitors the feeling that they can say a few words without disturbing the religious silence? Why not strengthen the educational services (in the galleries of the USA these are almost always more important than the conservation department)? And why not equip the galleries with libraries, concert halls, bookshops and gift shops that sell prints, jewels and folk objects? Why not make the gallery more welcoming by installing bars, lounges and restaurants, which would enable the visitors to spend a whole day at the gallery?[12]

A passage such as this amply shows that in *L'Amour de l'art* Bourdieu wanted to see the emergence of a cultural policy that would offer genuinely democratic access to a desacralised world of culture. However, Bourdieu believed, of course, that the most efficient way of increasing participation in cultural activities was to increase the amount and the nature of the schooling that children received in mainstream education. This was, in fact, according to Bourdieu, a prior condition of any increased cultural activity among people at large, whether it was visiting art galleries, going to the theatre or to a concert, reading, or tuning into cultural programmes on TV and radio. Bourdieu's aim, as he described it, was 'to define scientifically the social and cultural conditions of attendance at art galleries and, more generally, of all forms of cultured leisure ["loisir cultivé"]'.[13] To reaffirm what was said earlier, it must be stressed that Bourdieu did not, of course, believe access to be the crucial problem. Just as it would be naïve in the extreme to think that putting the prices down in an art gallery would bring the working class pouring in, so it would be naïve to think that more sophisticated strategies of taking culture to the disadvantaged classes would be any more successful:

As if they believed that it is only the physical inaccessibility of the paintings that prevents the great majority of people from wanting to see them, and savour them. Those in charge of galleries and the 'animateurs' seem to think that if one cannot bring the people to the works, then it is enough to take the works to the people. The exhibitions of paintings at the Renault factories or the theatrical productions put on for workers at Villeurbanne are experiments which prove nothing, since they remove the very object of the experiment by treating as already solved the very problem which they claim to be solving, namely the question of the conditions of cultural practice as a positive and regular activity. But at least these experiments have the effect of convincing those who undertake them of the legitimacy of their enterprise.[14]

In the study *Un Art moyen: essai sur les usages sociaux de la photographie* (1965) ['A Middling Art: an essay on the social uses of photography'],[15] Bourdieu gave a more extensive analysis of the cultural taste of different social groups, and devoted one particular section to 'le goût barbare' ['barbaric taste'], that is to say, the aesthetic and cultural taste of 'the popular classes'.[16] According to Bourdieu, photography has an 'ambiguous' status as an art, chiefly because it appears to be a largely mechanical activity, in which the creative intervention of the artist is seen as minimal. In Bourdieu's view, it was certainly not part of legitimate culture, and barely seemed to qualify for the category of an art which was 'on the way to cultural legitimation', such as cinema and jazz. However, this ambiguous status only served to highlight those strategies in the global culture whereby some cultural practices were granted prestige and others were not, and whereby some practitioners of culture were considered as having true aesthetic taste and others as having barbaric taste. Bourdieu's account of 'popular taste' in *Un Art moyen* was based upon the reactions of a sample group of peasants and workers to a selection of photographs presented to them for their comments. In the reactions of these members of 'the popular classes', Bourdieu found a confirmation of the opposition between the functionalist, utilitarian, and naturalistic aesthetics of the popular classes, and the disinterested aesthetics of pure form of the cultured classes. In Bourdieu's opinion, it is realist painting which, in fact, embodies the ideal of working-class aesthetics, because not only does it fulfil the requirement of faithful imitation, but it also displays the labour involved in achieving the imitation – a practical consideration which is central to the aesthetic taste of the working class. However, if photography does not represent the ideal of working-class aesthetics, it none the less goes a long way in this direction.

It is important for working-class taste that the thing being photographed is considered to be worth photographing. In addition, it is important that it is clear why it is being photographed, and for what social purposes it will be used. According to Bourdieu, one of the fundamental aesthetic criteria of 'popular naturalism' is that 'a beautiful image is nothing but the image of a beautiful thing, or much more rarely the beautiful image of a beautiful thing'.[17] In fact, working-class aesthetic judgements are ultimately inseparable from ethical judgements in their insistence that everything represented in art should be faithful to life and should have a reason and a justification for being represented. When peasants are photographed, they insist on dressing up and adopting formal poses. According to Bourdieu, this demonstrates their view that for a photograph to be worth taking it must be a special occasion, and must be treated with due respect and dignity.

According to Kantian aesthetics, which Bourdieu considers to be the aesthetics of the cultured classes, true art is a gratuitous and non-functional activity, which, ideally, should lend itself only to the disinterested contemplation of pure form. The 'barbaric' taste of the working classes is evident in their refusal to consider the aesthetic shaping of form as being in itself a worthwhile activity. It is also evident in the virtually exclusive significance working-class people attach to the subject or content of art. The members of the working-class sample in Bourdieu's survey were, therefore, happiest when they could fit the photographs they had been shown into recognisable categories, that is, when the image was of something that was in itself considered to be of value, and that was also considered to be worth photographing, and, in addition, when it was obvious what useful social purpose the photograph could perform. Working-class people have no concept of any possible 'universality' that the image might have (another criterion of Kantian aesthetics), and only take into account what possible purpose it might serve for certain people in certain circumstances. Bourdieu gave several examples of the disorientation experienced by working-class people when they were faced with relatively abstract images of such things as waves, pebbles and tree bark, which they could not see the point of photographing, and which they regarded as offering no emotional, moral or didactic interest. Bourdieu pointed out that this was precisely Kant's definition of barbaric or popular taste, namely that a higher form of disinterested contemplation was replaced by an 'interested' form of consumption.

Elsewhere, Bourdieu has stressed how powerful is the activity of naming things,[18] and one feels that by following Kant's characterisation of popular taste as barbaric, Bourdieu may, in reality, have done as much as Kant to perpetuate the idea that popular culture is a grossly inferior and degraded form of culture. Of course, Bourdieu would say he was doing nothing of the kind. As always, he claims to be carrying out a purely scientific and impartial exercise:

> What may appear to the aesthete to be an anti-aesthetic is, in fact, still an aesthetic, since, whether it is formulated in a sophisticated way or not, it none the less presupposes a lived experience in which the sense of beauty has its place. The judgement of taste that Kant analyses, presupposes another form of lived experience, which, like the working-class experience of the beautiful, is socially conditioned, and which, in any case, is never independent of those social conditions which make 'people of taste' possible. It follows from this that one has to acknowledge the claim of popular taste to an aesthetic dimension even if this claim is inspired, at least in part, by an awareness of the aesthetics of high culture.[19]

Bourdieu wished to show here that no taste could pretend to escape from social conditioning, and that the pure taste of the cultured classes was as much the result of social conditions as was the barbaric taste of the working class. What is more, the working-class aesthetic experience is said to have its own validity, and to play its own role within working-class life, and Bourdieu suggested that it should be respected for these reasons. Therefore, on the one hand, Bourdieu was trying to deal fairly with the matter of cultured taste and popular taste while, on the other hand, he was also making moderate claims for the value of working-class culture in its own right. However, since it has been Bourdieu's ultimate ideological aim to show the evils of a cultural system in which a supposedly legitimate culture relegates the working class to a situation of 'barbarism', he has not usually chosen to characterise working-class culture as itself having intrinsic value. Since he believes that the cultured classes have superior power (economic, social and cultural), he has put most emphasis on describing the ways in which popular taste is viewed from the vantage point of the cultured classes and from within the system of dominant, legitimate culture. He has also emphasised the ways in which working-class people internalise the values of the cultured classes, in the shape of

107

feelings of fear, humiliation, incomprehension and a general sense of inferiority. Even in such an area as photography, which is not part of legitimate culture, and where one might, therefore, expect that working-class people would not be a prey to feelings of social and cultural inferiority, Bourdieu has claimed that they are still aware of superior practices and attitudes, and sense that their own practices and attitudes are despised.

Long before he published *La Distinction*, Bourdieu had been marshalling his evidence to demonstrate the social basis of taste and culture. He had also already shown the importance which he attached to strategies of differentiation in the cultural field:

> Photography offers a privileged opportunity to observe the logic of *the search for difference through difference,* or in other words, the logic of the snobbery which experiences cultural practices not in themselves and for themselves, but rather as a form of relationship between the groups who give themselves up to these practices.[20]

In *Un Art moyen*, one could already see how Bourdieu used the term 'repoussoir' ['foil'] to describe the role played by the working class in the global system of culture. Not only was working-class culture the degraded and barbaric reverse image of high culture, but it was also the point of reference which all social groups above the working class used to determine their cultural attitudes, that is, by refusing or rejecting any cultural practices that smacked of vulgarity. For instance, Bourdieu quoted the example of a petit-bourgeois type who poured scorn on the photographic practices of the working class, and demonstrated his 'cultural goodwill' by showing a superior concern for the aesthetics of photography. As always, Bourdieu defined 'cultural goodwill' as the characteristic cultural attitude of those lower middle-class people who were deprived of real cultural status and yet who were keen to acquire it with all the means at their disposal:

> The significance that lower middle class people confer upon the practice of photography conveys or betrays the relationship that the middle classes have to culture, that is to say, on the one hand to the upper classes who are the privileged possessors of those cultural practices held to be the most noble, and on the other hand to the working classes from whom they intend at all events to distinguish themselves,

by demonstrating, through those practices that are open to them, their cultural goodwill. It is in this way that the members of photography clubs endeavour to ennoble themselves culturally by attempting to ennoble photography itself, which is for them an accessible and appropriate substitute for the noble arts.[21]

The same logic of differentiation operates right up the social hierarchy until one reaches the upper classes, where, according to Bourdieu, one meets with a general rejection of such a widespread activity as photography. Bourdieu evoked the superior scorn of the cultivated classes faced with all those tourists running around, 'doing' the sites of Europe and taking as many photographs as they could. The upper-class way was, of course, to abandon oneself to contemplation and demonstrate one's capacity for aesthetic detachment, as opposed to those who engaged in the far more materialistic activity of 'anxious accumulation of memories'.[22] In a chapter entitled 'Différences et distinctions', which he contributed to the collective volume *Le Partage des bénéfices: expansion et inégalités en France* (1966) ['Sharing the profits: expansion and inequalities in France'],[23] Bourdieu said that this mania for tourist photography was seen by the cultured classes as a form of 'indiscriminate and voracious consumption',[24] and, therefore, as totally opposed to their more spiritualised and selective responses. In this essay, Bourdieu also spoke of 'the dialectics of divulgation and distinction',[25] by which he meant that process by which cultural practices lost their ability to confer distinction on the practitioners, as they became more widely available and hence less rare. Rarity for Bourdieu is the essential condition of distinction. Therefore, those who wish to display their distinction either reject a cultural practice once it has become common, and move on to other activities, or they show their superiority over the general run of people by adopting a different way of engaging in the cultural practice. This essay is particularly interesting because it showed Bourdieu attempting to deal with the changing social, economic and cultural situation of postwar France, whereas so much of his work, and not least *La Distinction*, gives the impression that he is treating the cultural system as relatively static.

In this essay Bourdieu described a dynamic world of population movements, migration into the cities, erosion of traditional class mentalities, and gradual incorporation of agricultural workers and industrial workers into modern urban life with its new patterns of consumption. However, Bourdieu did not believe that these changes heralded a new period of cultural democracy, nor did he think that they closed the gap between the culture of the under-privileged classes and the culture of the middle and upper classes. In fact, as the working class managed to satisfy its 'primary' needs, and acquired a whole range of goods which previously had only been owned by members of higher social groups, then, according to the logic of differentiation, these higher social groups, in their quest for distinction, became less concerned with the objects in themselves, and sought different ways of using them. According to Bourdieu, this logic could be seen operating in relation to the mass media, which offered the most widely available forms of culture, and which, allegedly, provided the conditions for cultural democracy. On the basis of the situation in 1965, Bourdieu asserted categorically that television and radio by no means heralded a new age of cultural democracy, as was often optimistically thought:

> Although the ownership of radio or television sets increases as one rises up the social hierarchy (first degree inequality), and although they are used in a very different way by social classes, since the 'cultural' level of the programmes listened to depends closely on the level of education of the audience (second degree inequality), the members of the middle classes can express misdirected cultural goodwill by choosing to listen out of preference to dramatic and scientific programmes or light opera (as opposed to the light entertainment and songs openly preferred by manual and even clerical workers), whereas executives and senior managers reveal a desire to keep their distance from vulgar practices like watching television by refusing to partake of them, or by demonstrating a cool and reserved interest in them (third degree inequality). One notes, in fact, that in January 1965 the proportion of owners of television sets, despite significant differences in income, is barely higher among executives and senior managers (59.3%) and among heads of industry and commerce (53.5%) than among middle management (52.4%). One also notes that the ownership of a record-player (much rarer) almost always excludes the ownership of a television set, and that senior managers, when they own a television set, use it selectively.[26]

It is this 'dialectic of divulgation and distinction' which is at the centre of Bourdieu's major work on class, culture and taste, *La Distinction*. Bourdieu presented this work as an account of 'the objective relations between groups', and as a scientific work which went beyond the partial accounts of conflicting and antagonistic participants. But behind the enormous effort of objectivity and impartiality there do lie definite ideological and personal *partis pris*. Firstly, the work is a monumental testimony to Bourdieu's belief in the rightness of the sociological way of looking at the world, that is to say, of seeing all human activity as being socially determined. Secondly, and however much this is masked by its 'scientific' procedures, the work is fundamentally a Rousseauist and Proudhonesque exposure and refusal of the cultural game as played by the rules laid down by the powerful and cultured classes.[27] Bourdieu has spoken elsewhere of his contempt for the way in which fashion rules French intellectual and cultural life, and he has shown his clear preference for the values of assiduous scholarship over the ephemeral 'brilliance' of cultural journalism.[28] His scientific stance may well be in part a way of making sure that he is not, like Rousseau, forever cast in the role of eccentric or boor. None the less, he makes it plain that, as with Rousseau, his initial starting-point is a refusal to play the cultural game, allied with a willingness to approach culture from the standpoint of the uncivilised barbarian. For, according to Bourdieu, one already has to have, in the eyes of the cultured classes, a barbaric attitude to culture, if one is ready to analyse it in terms of the social conditions that make it possible. In Bourdieu's view, dominant culture is characterised by its 'denial of the social',[29] for, on the one hand, the cultured classes believe that the capacity to appreciate and understand culture is a natural, god-given gift, and, on the other hand, they consider art to be a higher form of abstract play. This is why Rousseau was such a disturbing figure, because he refused to treat culture in this way, and insisted on seeing it in terms of truth and error, and as a matter of life and death. Bourdieu would no doubt deny that his work is, like Rousseau's, an open denunciation of the prevailing cultural system, but it seems fairly clear that when, at the end of *La Distinction*, he allows himself an extremely rare moment of personal intervention, there is, in fact, an exact coincidence between his sociological commitment to explain the world in terms of its actual, social and material conditions, and his determination to expose the injustices of the cultural system:

111

and barbarism, Bourdieu cannot totally escape the charge that he himself is merely replicating the view of the dominant classes. However, very occasionally one finds in *La Distinction* passages in which Bourdieu systematically and deliberately balances the opposing claims of popular culture and dominant culture, as if he did believe that popular practices had as much validity and coherence as those of the dominant classes. A key example is the section on food in *La Distinction*, where Bourdieu sets out the opposition between form and substance, which he takes to exemplify the polarity between high culture and popular culture.[32]

'Two representations of human excellence' are here juxtaposed and confronted with each other, and although Bourdieu claims not to arbitrate between them, it is for once the values of popular culture which surely emerge as the superior values over those of the supposedly dominant culture. This is a rare example of Bourdieu tipping the scales of description in favour of popular culture, while giving the impression that he is presenting the case in terms of two equally balanced forces. What is far more usual is that, when Bourdieu is trying to perform this delicate balancing act, he in fact almost always concludes by affirming that, since the scales are in reality unequally weighted in favour of legitimate culture, popular culture cannot attain a state of autonomy in relation to legitimate culture, let alone achieve any superiority over it.[33] At one point, Bourdieu expressed the view that it was, in fact, specifically in the cultural field that working-class people were most dependent and most dominated, whereas he seemed more willing to concede that in other aspects of their lives they could attain fully dignified and even rebellious ways of being and doing, although here again he could not resist concluding on a more sceptical note:

> It is not . . . in the area of culture that one should look for a distance, or a self-distancing, from the dominant class and its values, other than a purely negative one, by default. There is, of course, everything which belongs to the art of living, a wisdom taught by necessity, suffering and humiliation and deposited in an inherited language, dense even in its stereotypes, a sense of revelry and festivity, of self-expression and practical solidarity with others (evoked by the adjective 'bon vivant' with which the working classes identify), in short, everything that is engendered by the realistic (but not resigned) hedonism and sceptical (but not cynical) materialism

which constitute both a form of adaptation to the conditions of existence and a defence against them; there is the efficacity and vivacity of a speech which, freed from the censorship and constraints of quasi-written and therefore decontextualised speech, bases its ellipses, short cuts and metaphors on common reference to shared situations, experiences and traditions. There is also everything concerned with politics, with the tradition of trade-union struggles, which might provide the one genuine principle of a counter-culture, but where, in fact, the effects of cultural domination never cease to operate.[34]

Bourdieu seems to be engaged in a battle between his heart and his head. When he allows himself to drop his cover of scientific impartiality, he shows not only that he is emotionally drawn to the life-style of the working class, but that he is also drawn to the moral values that he sees it as embodying. Equally, he often shows his distaste for the life-style of the dominant classes, and for the immoral way in which he believes they use their power against the underprivileged classes. However, he sees himself as too much of a realist to give in to what he would regard as the sentimental, idealised, and ultimately erroneous view of the working class that has often had currency in French left-wing intellectual circles, and that has been embodied in numerous forms of populism. In fact, in *La Distinction* Bourdieu is to be found attacking intellectual populists for projecting their own conceptions onto the working-class, and for nurturing romantic notions about the revolutionary potential of this class. By contrast, Bourdieu himself refuses such a populist attitude and constantly insists on the degree to which the working class internalises the values of a society in which it is objectively the dominated class, and in which it is recognised as such, both by itself as well as by the dominant classes. He uses the term 'class ethos', or more usually 'class habitus', to describe the mentality or world-view of a social group. In the case of the working class, its habitus is considered by Bourdieu to be defined essentially by the notion of 'making a virtue out of necessity'. In fact, this maxim is, according to Bourdieu, applicable to all social groups, since in his view, 'taste is almost always the product of economic conditions identical to those in which it functions'.[35] But in the case of the working class, he regards this maxim as particularly appropriate:

The fundamental proposition that the habitus is a virtue made of necessity is never more clearly illustrated than in the case of the working classes, since necessity includes for them all that is usually meant by the word, that is, an inescapable deprivation of necessary goods. Necessity imposes a taste for necessity which implies a form of adaptation to and consequently acceptance of the necessary, a resignation to the inevitable, a deep-seated disposition which is in no way incompatible with a revolutionary intention, although it confers on it a modality which is not that of intellectual or artistic revolts.[36]

The whole style of life of working-class people is, therefore, marked by their objective situation, which is that of a 'submission to necessity'.[37] However, the working class is not only subject to material deprivation, for it also experiences deprivation across the whole cultural field, where here also it makes a virtue out of necessity by actually internalising this cultural deprivation, and in so doing comes to accept it: 'It would be easy to enumerate the features of the life-style of the dominated classes, which, through the sense of incompetence, failure or cultural unworthiness, imply a form of recognition of the dominant values.'[38] The working-class habitus is described by Bourdieu as 'an extraordinary *realism*',[39] according to which the working class, knowing it cannot attain things and values outside its closed world, does not even aspire to them and, in fact, makes a virtue out of not aspiring to them and not having them. It is difficult not to see Bourdieu here quite simply as criticising the narrowness and the prejudices of a working-class life-style, which have, it is true, been forced upon them by social and economic conditions, but which the working class has interiorised and made of them its own vision of the world. When Bourdieu says that 'the universe of possibles is closed' to the working class,[40] he is pointing not only to the objective obstacles in the path of working-class people, but also to their subjective 'deep disposition' which discourages them from attempting to transcend their dominated condition and indeed accustoms and adjusts them to it.

In the chapter 'La transmission de l'héritage culturel' ['The Transmission of the cultural heritage'] in the volume *Le Partage des bénéfices* ['Sharing the profits'],[41] Bourdieu focused on the large part played by this dominated mentality in working-class attitudes to education. Basing his remarks on the clear statistical evidence that working-class children went to those educational institutions with lower academic prestige, left school early, and largely failed to go on to higher education, Bourdieu concluded that the majority of working-class parents 'mistake reality for their desires':

> In this domain, as elsewhere, the form and content of aspi-
> rations and demands are defined by the objective conditions,
> which exclude the possibility of a desire for the impossible.
> For example, to say about classical studies in the lycée 'it
> isn't for us', is to say more than 'it's beyond our means'.
> It is, rather, an expression of internalised necessity, couched
> one might say in the imperative-indicative, since it expresses
> both an impossibility and a prohibition.[42]

It is also in this essay that Bourdieu asserted that 'the specific aim [of the educational system] is to transmit to the majority of people, by training and practice, the attitudes and aptitudes which make the cultured man'.[43] Therefore, in Bourdieu's view, when the working-class person rejects educational opportunities, he is rejecting the only way he has at his disposal of attaining the status of the cultured man, which not only the educational system but also society at large puts forward as the ultimate criterion of what it means to be fully human. The working class, serving as it does as a 'foil' for all those who are cultured, or who aspire to be cultured, is 'the nature against which culture is constructed . . . nothing other than what is "popular", "low", "vulgar", "common"'.[44]

Bourdieu believes that there are totally clear-cut distinctions separating the life-style, taste and culture of different social groups, and in addition, that there is a profound internal coherence linking the life-style, taste and culture of each specific group. Consequently, what might appear to be diverse practices and preferences can in reality be shown to share common features, and indeed to be based on the shared disposition of the group. Thus we find Bourdieu characterising the opposed tastes of the two fractions of the dominant class (that is, intellectuals and employers) in the following way:

> The antagonism between the life-styles corresponding to the
> opposing poles of the field of the dominant class is clear-
> cut, total, and the opposition between the teachers and the
> employers (particularly between the lower and middle ranks
> of the two categories) is comparable to the gap between two
> 'cultures' in the anthropological sense. On one side, reading,

and reading poetry, philosophical and political works, *Le Monde*, and the (generally leftish) literary or artistic magazines; on the other, hunting or betting, and, when there is reading, reading *France-Soir* or *l'Aurore*, *Auto-Journal* or *Lectures pour tous . . .* etc.[45]

It is, in fact, only in the higher social groups, according to Bourdieu, that this infinite and antagonistic game of cultural difference and distinction takes place, with each group constantly fighting for symbolic supremacy over the other. To all intents and purposes, working-class culture is considered to be out of the game, except in so far as it serves as the primitive point of reference, symbolising all that is non-cultural and non-human. Bourdieu will have no truck with what he sees as 'the myths of cultural homogenisation',[46] which would have us believe that in the modern mass-consumer society all citizens have relatively equal access to goods and facilities, that class barriers have been broken down and class differences evened out. For Bourdieu, culture is still a class-related phenomenon, and this is nowhere more evident than in the 'un-culture' of the working class. Whatever the working class does, it always bears the distinguishing marks, or rather the 'stigmata', of its subordinate and despised condition:

The brand which Marx speaks of is nothing other than lifestyle, through which the most deprived immediately betray themselves, even in their use of spare time; in so doing they inevitably serve as a foil to every distinction and contribute, purely negatively, to the dialectic of pretension and distinction which fuels the incessant changing of taste. Not content with virtually lacking all the knowledge or manners which are valued in the markets of academic examination or polite conversation nor with only possessing skills which have no value there, they are the people 'who don't know how to live', who sacrifice most to material foods, and to the heaviest, grossest and most fattening of them, bread, potatoes, fats, and the most vulgar, such as wine; who spend least on clothing and cosmetics, appearance and beauty; those who 'don't know how to relax', 'who always have to be doing something', who set off in their Renault 5 or Simca 1000 to join the great traffic jams of the holiday exodus, who picnic beside major roads, cram their tents into overcrowded camp sites, fling themselves into the prefabricated leisure activities designed for them by the engineers of cultural mass production; those who by all these uninspired 'choices' confirm class racism, if it needed to be confirmed, in its conviction that they only get what they deserve.[47]

According to Bourdieu, intellectual discourse on popular culture almost always moves between the two poles of devaluation and rehabilitation.[48] If one defines the working class principally in terms of its being in a state of deprivation, then one is devaluing it. If one seeks to rehabilitate the working class, then one will choose to say, for instance, that what it has and does is as good as anything else, and so forth. Bourdieu believes that intellectuals should not be trapped between these two alternatives, but should find another way of posing the problem. For Bourdieu, the solution lies in pursuing the scholar's scientific task of showing the logic of the cultural system and not taking sides. Whether one accepts the scientific nature of Bourdieu's discourse or not, it is clear that Bourdieu adopts this scientific posture because he believes that intellectual discourse upon the working class has so far been more about the intellectuals themselves than about the working class it purports to observe.

> If we have not at all analysed ourselves socially, we are going to project our fantasies, our images, our repressions, our guilts etc., upon the working classes, who do not give a damn about them. One needs to realise that in the sociology of the working classes it is basically a question of the sociology of intellectuals.[49]

In Bourdieu's view, there is a need for intellectuals to be fully aware of their own personal position in relation to what they are discussing. Indeed, this reflexivity is seen by him, in general, as the first duty of the intellectual. If intellectuals have this awareness, and have become conscious of their own 'interest' in what they are discussing, then, according to Bourdieu, they are more likely to know the limitations of their own point of view. They are far less likely, for instance, to be guilty of the kinds of populism that have marked the French intellectuals' treatment of the working class and its culture.

One might have expected Bourdieu, who is prone to scorning the irresponsible and unscientific discourse of intellectuals, to attach little importance to their words. However, he is, in fact, ready to grant the utmost significance to what they say, since he believes that words play a major role in the crucial political struggle to impose particular versions of reality in a given society. According to Bourdieu, 'the struggle between classifications is a fundamental element of the struggle between classes'.[50] In other words, opposing and conflicting social groups are always involved in a battle of words, which is nothing less than the struggle to decide who has the authority to determine what is reality, and who has the authority to speak about, or in the name of, this reality. Thus, Bourdieu believes that when intellectuals speak about 'the people' and about 'popular culture', they are, in fact, dealing with questions that are essentially political ('When one says "popular culture", one should know that one is talking about politics').[51] The very act of naming and labelling is considered by Bourdieu to be a powerful political gesture, since this act of naming creates a political reality. As far as 'popular culture' is concerned, Bourdieu even goes so far as to suggest that the term already embodies all the political and cultural preconceptions of the dominant class: '"popular culture" – a veritable juxtaposition of words by which one imposes, whether one wants to or not, the dominant definition of culture'.[52] Bourdieu, therefore, believes that crucial political issues are at stake when intellectuals define something as 'popular culture', for by naming it they are, in fact, producing a certain reality. Since Bourdieu wants his scientific brand of sociology to make a useful contribution to the creation of a political democracy, he feels he must challenge the words with which others falsely categorise social reality, and by which they betray their false representations of social reality:

> The social world is the site of verbal struggles, which owe their seriousness – and sometimes their violence – to the fact that, to a large extent, words make things, and that to change words, and more generally to change representations . . . is already to change things. Politics is essentially a matter of words. That is why the struggle to understand reality scientifically must always begin with a struggle against words. Now, in order to transmit knowledge, one must frequently resort to the very words that one had to destroy, in order to conquer and construct this knowledge. It is easy to see that the use of inverted commas contributes little, when it is a case of emphasising a major change of epistemological status.[53]

Although Bourdieu is not, in fact, here speaking specifically about popular culture, I did note earlier that the term popular culture can hardly be used in French without it being put in inverted commas. These inverted commas clearly signal reservations and ambiguities about its usage. For some writers the use of inverted commas seems simply to signal the lack of one agreed meaning among a number of possible meanings. Bourdieu's reservations seem principally to be political ones, namely that, in his view, the term tends to carry the populist fantasies of left-wing French intellectuals. Hence one finds the following important passage in *La Distinction*, a small part of which has already just been quoted:

> Those who believe in the existence of a 'popular culture', a paradoxical notion which imposes, willy-nilly, the dominant definition of culture, must expect to find – if they were to go and look – only the scattered fragments of an old erudite culture (such as folk medicine), selected and reinterpreted in terms of the fundamental principles of the class habitus and integrated into the unitary world view it engenders, and not the counter-culture they call for, a culture truly raised in opposition to the dominant culture and consciously claimed as a symbol of status or a declaration of separate existence.[54]

As already indicated, Bourdieu seems above all intent on dis-abusing left-wing intellectuals of their naïve and romantic notions of the working class, and this perhaps goes some way to explaining his stress on popular culture as a culture of deprivation, and not, for instance, as a culture of resistance or rebellion. If, as Bourdieu claims, the struggle for the meaning of words is a political strug-gle between different social groups, then one can conclude that Bourdieu is attempting to wrest the meaning of popular culture away from those who had 'romantic' notions of the revolution-ary potential of the working class, and these, most recently and most notoriously, were the student 'revolutionaries' of 1968. In an essay in *Choses dites* (1987) ['Things said'], entitled 'Les usages du "peuple"' ['The uses of "the people"'], Bourdieu says that 'the people' and 'the popular' are among the most significant categories fought over by competing intellectuals.[55] (Others would be, for instance, 'the State, society . . . the workers, the nation, . . . the French, the Party . . .'.)[56] According to Bourdieu, intellectuals who feel authorised to speak of or for the people, gain different degrees of prestige and power within their own intellectual fields by so doing. For instance if, as intellectuals, they operate in the political field, they can derive a considerable degree of prestige and power, whereas if they operate in the literary field, they will gain little from speaking of or for the people, since in Bourdieu's view the literary field does not attach significant value to 'the popular'. Bourdieu, therefore, regards intellectual discourse on the people and the popular as being largely determined by the position that intellectuals hold in the 'field of cultural production'. Firstly, he believes it is the tendency of intellectuals to fight for dominance in, and even sole control of, their own intellectual field, and this is shown by their primary need to separate themselves off from the laymen. Intellectuals tend to despise what is popular and brand it as 'illegitimate', because it evokes a world which is out of their reach and which has no need of them. However, those intellectuals who attempt to give a positive account of the people and the popular are, according to Bourdieu, those who, objectively, occupy a domi-nated position in the fields of cultural production, and who use the rehabilitation of the popular as a way of ennobling themselves. When Bourdieu says this, he does not mean to attribute cynical motives to such intellectuals, but he sees it as an inevitable part of the logic of the cultural and intellectual struggle for dominance, that those intellectuals and writers who fail to become members of the dominant class of intellectuals should turn against this class and adopt a populist stance of anti-intellectualism. In stressing the 'objective' reasons why certain intellectuals speak of and for the people, Bourdieu believes he is avoiding the two usual approaches to the question of the people and the popular, both of which he regards as erroneous, that is, on the one hand, an exclusively negative view ('class ethnocentrism'), and, on the other hand, an exclusively positive view (populism).

Bourdieu does not believe that this apparent impasse created by two opposing points of view, which reflect each other and cancel each other out, can be resolved by simply listening to what the people themselves have to say. To believe that what comes out of the mouth of the people is truly 'popular', and is the truth about the 'people', is, according to Bourdieu, to follow the dubious example of the 'pharisees of "the people's cause"'.[57] Bourdieu points out that what the people themselves say is more than likely to be the result of what they have picked up from a rag-bag of educational, cultural and religious sources, rather than being the authentic discourse of the people which populists would like to think it is. According to Bourdieu, those who attempt to rehabilitate 'popular culture' are misguided, if they believe the solution lies in accepting and proclaiming as a badge of one's identity what is customarily seen as a stigma. Bourdieu clearly believes that 'resistance' cannot be true resistance if it is simply a call for the recognition of those values which, objectively, are responsible for keeping one in a dominated situation. Equally, he is unwilling to regard those people as guilty of 'submission' to the system, who try to lose those traits that brand them as 'vulgar', and who seek to acquire other traits which will make them appear less vulgar and more distinguished. Bourdieu affirms quite categorically that 'Resistance can be alienating and submission can be liberating'.[58] For instance, he quotes the example of a person who tries to lose a 'vulgar' accent. Bourdieu is not prepared to see this as a betrayal of the people or as an act of submission to the system. This is clearly because he refuses to conceive of the people and their culture as having some quintessentially superior qualities. It is also because Bourdieu has a highly developed sense of the *realpolitik* of social and cultural life. In Bourdieu's eyes, social and cultural life is a power game in which individuals, if they are not going to agree to occupy a totally inferior and dominated position, must fight to acquire the means by which they will gain respect and power.

Bourdieu makes this quite plain in another context concerning the acquisition and use of language. In *Ce que parler veut dire: l'économie des échanges linguistiques* (1982) ['What speaking means: the economy of linguistic exchange'],[59] Bourdieu applied his notion of distinction to the linguistic field, and also gave concrete examples from this field of how vulgar or popular speech differed from and served as a foil for educated, bourgeois speech. But he also made clear how he conceived of the social and cultural world as one of conflict and struggle, of self-assertion and self-effacement. In the following quotation one can see how the notion of 'linguistic competence' could be said to be analogous to the 'cultural competence' which is Bourdieu's underlying concern (although not his term) in his other discussions on cultural and educational matters:

The competence sufficient to produce sentences capable of being understood may be totally insufficient to produce sentences capable of being *listened to*, sentences calculated to be acknowledged as *acceptable* in all those situations in which one might have occasion to speak. Here again, social acceptability is not limited to grammatical correctness alone. In reality, speakers deprived of legitimate competence find themselves excluded from the social worlds in which this is required, or they are condemned to silence. Thus, what is rare is not the ability to speak, which, falling within the sphere of biological inheritance, is *universal and therefore essentially non-distinguishing*, but the necessary competence to speak the legitimate language, which, since it depends on social inheritance, translates social distinctions into the strictly symbolic logic of differential gaps, or in a word, of distinction.[60]

This passage once again makes it clear that Bourdieu's central interests are cultural power and cultural legitimacy. In Bourdieu's view, to be in possession and control of 'legitimate culture' is to occupy a position of power over those other people who are not in possession of it and who because of this are excluded from 'the social worlds in which this is required', and are thereby constantly made to feel a sense of their own inferiority.

For many people, Bourdieu's view of the role of culture in modern society is not only very pessimistic but also rather outdated. Bourdieu's analysis of social and cultural snobberies might seem to have been above all appropriate to the period up to the early 1960s, at which time 'keeping up with the Joneses' could still be thought to have been a key aspect of social and cultural life. This was a time when people were keen to be part of the modern Americanised consumer society, and constantly looked over their shoulders to see if they were managing to compete successfully with neighbours in the race for goods and the new consumer life-style. It was also a time when there was still a relatively unified and stable notion of an acknowledged high culture (classical music, great literature, grand masters, etc.), which people considered it necessary to know about, or at least to want to know about, if they were to think of themselves, and be thought of, as successful members of society. Without accepting some of the extreme illusions of the postindustrial analyses of modern society (classlessness etc.), one has still to recognise that there have been profound social and cultural changes. Bourdieu's analysis of 'distinction' in modern society would be seriously challenged if one were to suggest that there is now, in fact, no 'legitimate culture' that dominates or 'tyrannises' the cultural field. The contemporary definition of 'legitimate culture' has certainly gone beyond the narrow limits set upon it in the 1950s and early 1960s. For instance, those arts that Bourdieu designated as being 'on the way to legitimation' (jazz, cinema) could now be said to be well and truly within the domain of legitimate culture, and one might say the same for photography, and even pop music. However, if there is still a case for insisting that there continues to be a distinct high cultural field which excludes such areas as cinema, jazz, popular music and photography, in favour of the classical canon of literature, music and painting, it has perhaps become difficult to claim that the 'culturally dispossessed' still derive in any important sense a feeling of inferiority by dint of their not being in possession of this high cultural domain.

There is no doubt that Bourdieu has had a profound influence on French debates on culture and popular culture. There has, however, also been a definite reaction against his ideas.[61] No doubt this reaction is part of a general retreat among French intellectuals from embattled, ideological ways of viewing the social world. It is also part of a rejection of the very project of sociology itself. If sociology, as practised by such as Bourdieu, is a discipline which claims to lay bare those mechanisms that condition the behaviour and attitudes of people, then in recent years there have been many who have wanted to reject it, in favour of a far more optimistic approach which emphasises people's ability to respond actively and freely to social forces. However even-handed and balanced Bourdieu has tried to be, many of his critics have persisted in seeing his work as irredeemably deterministic and pessimistic. Of all the critical and hostile responses to Bourdieu's work none is perhaps more interesting than that of his former co-author Jean-Claude Passeron,[62] who, having for long apparently shared Bourdieu's sociological views, seems finally to have rebelled against them. Some early signs of Passeron's differences with Bourdieu can perhaps be seen in the introduction that he provided for the French translation of Richard Hoggart's *The Uses of Literacy: Aspects of working-class life with special reference to publications and entertainments* (1957). The French translation was published in 1970 as *La Culture du pauvre: étude sur le style de vie des classes populaires en Angleterre* ['The Culture of the poor: a study of the life-style of the working classes in England']. The French title itself is a little odd, but 'culture of the poor' was no doubt arrived at in part as a way of avoiding the vexed term 'culture populaire'.

Passeron regarded Hoggart's *The Uses of Literacy* as an extremely valuable account of working-class life and culture precisely because

it offered an example of a good-humoured, sympathetic and knowl-
edgeable study by an intellectual who had himself been a member
of the working class he described. According to Passeron, this was
a feat not likely to have been achieved by French intellectuals
themselves:

> all the qualities of this book derive perhaps from an initial act
> of daring, doubtless more probable, sociologically speaking,
> in Britain than in France, where the relationship of intellec-
> tuals to the working class, including those of them who come
> from this class or the lower echelons of the petite-bourgeoisie,
> is more controlled by the rules of good taste and good tone
> and thereby more 'intellectualised', and it needs to be said,
> all the more shameful for it. The discussion on the realities of
> class is certainly prevalent in numerous fractions of the French
> intellectual milieu, but it is not altogether wrong to suppose
> that its theoretical and abstract tone serves also to keep at bay a
> whole set of realities at once simple and scandalous – or worse
> than scandalous, vulgar. The whole empirical force of these
> realities is evident when a description at once ethnographic
> and autobiographical such as Richard Hoggart's brings them
> into focus directly, above literary artifice and scholarly exer-
> cises. If *The Uses of Literacy* impresses the reader at once as
> one of those books in which in all its simplicity and truth there
> shines out everything which by different means is repressed
> by university sociologists (those specialists in sublimation and
> displacement) and by populist and even revolutionary intellec-
> tuals (those virtuosos of counter-suggestion and projection),
> this is because the author has succeeded despite all the defence
> mechanisms which protect the intellectual of working-class
> origins from his own social origins, in finding through a study
> of himself at once sociological and self-analytical, the difficult
> way by which to effect the return of the repressed.[63]

This passage shows that Passeron was still, in important respects,
working within a framework very similar to that of Bourdieu,
who has always liked to highlight the illusions nurtured by the
intelligentsia concerning the working class and its culture. Passeron
sees *The Uses of Literacy* as being in part 'a protest . . . against the
superior, populist, apocalyptic or foolishly optimistic stereotypes
which stand between the life of the working class and its observers,
who are necessarily intellectual or bourgeois'.[64] Like Bourdieu,

Passeron sees the sociology of working-class culture as being in reality a matter of the sociology of intellectuals. Where, however, Passeron seems to differ significantly from Bourdieu is in the importance he attributed to Hoggart's empathetic evocation of working-class life and culture. Passeron clearly responded to what he considered to be Hoggart's ultimately optimistic portrait of a class which still valued 'the hedonistic communion of the family community',[65] and which had its own strategies for coping with change and for resisting the onslaught of external forces. For instance, Passeron was particularly impressed by what he saw as Hoggart's refusal to join in the lamentations of the intelligentsia over the coming of mass society and the repercussions this had allegedly had on traditional working-class life and culture:

> Most valuable of all from the point of view of social science, Richard Hoggart breaks with those images of popular behaviour determined by the observers' membership of the intelligentsia. Too numerous to mention are the themes of sociology-fiction which have piled up until today; they constitute a vulgate of the ills and dramas of 'mass civilisation'. These owe what credibility they possess to the social and psychological functions which they perform for intellectuals, themselves the producers and principal consumers of this literature. The analysis, alternatively or simultaneously pejorative or fascinated, of the 'conditioning', 'brutalisation' and 'penetration' of the masses by the mass media is a well enough known orthodoxy with its sects, schisms, and theological debates. *The Uses of Literacy* is among those rare works which, whilst not denying the magnitude of the transformations that the new type of leisure and the new means of communication have effected amongst the general public, does attempt a balanced assessment. This leads the author, without any great theoretical fanfares, to pose some questions as pertinent for theory as for the empirical analysis of the transformations in popular culture and the receptivity of the different class levels to the ideological solicitations contained in the messages of the cultural industry and directed at them.[66]

It is not here a question of deciding whether Passeron was giving an accurate and comprehensive account of Hoggart's work. In fact, he does seem to have stressed positive and optimistic aspects of

Hoggart's portrayal to the exclusion of more critical ones. For instance, Passeron seems to have missed what Hoggart said about the limited, parochial mentality of the working class. Indeed, Hoggart's account of the working class's preference for its own way of life ['a deep refusal to be committed outside the small known area of life'][67] is very close to Bourdieu's fundamental idea that the working class becomes complicitous in its own subjugation. What is more, the notion of the 'taste of necessity', which is central to Bourdieu's characterisation of the working class is also crucial to Hoggart's account, although it is not of course called this. So much of Hoggart's description of the working class highlights its cosy acceptance of the objective limitations that constrain every dimension of its life [e.g. 'The mistrust of cafés has been reinforced by the knowledge that they can hardly be afforded anyway'].[68] But although Passeron may have given a somewhat partial account of *The Uses of Literacy*, it is none the less important to recognise that this partiality itself reveals something significant about French intellectual treatment of popular culture. In comparison with the French treatment of working-class culture, Passeron saw Hoggart's work as offering a refreshingly optimistic picture. He saw it as avoiding the twin excesses of populism and contempt for the people, and as a genuinely human document which granted the working class its own autonomy and dignity.

There is no explicit attack on Bourdieu in Passeron's introduction to the French translation of *The Uses of Literacy*. One feels, however, that Passeron was using the Hoggart work in order to formulate his sense of dissatisfaction with the French sociological and intellectual community, and not least with Bourdieu himself. In 1985 Passeron, together with Claude Grignon, published *A Propos des cultures populaires* ['Concerning popular cultures'],[69] which appears to be a frontal attack on Bourdieu's treatment of working-class culture. The central issue of this text is the question of how to find a way of avoiding either a 'triumphalist' or a 'miserabilist' approach when treating working-class life and culture. According to Grignon and Passeron, Bourdieu clearly adopted the miserabilist approach by accepting the rule of cultural legitimacy, and by consigning working-class culture to a position of constant inferiority. It is not that Grignon and Passeron deny the reality of issues of cultural legitimacy, power and dominance, but they insist that to stress these exclusively is to leave out of one's account other, more positive aspects of popular culture. They do not believe in absolute cultural

127

relativism, or in other words that there is an absolute 'symmetry' between dominant culture and popular culture. But in order to give an account of popular culture which accords it its full validity and autonomy, they stress that the dominated groups are not always conscious of their subjugation and, indeed, that their experience of themselves as a community and as a culture is actually achieved in those moments when they 'forget' that they are dominated:

> It is the forgetting of domination not the resistance to it that opens up to the working classes the privileged site for those of their cultural activities which are least marked by the symbolic effects of domination. If the parenthesis of Sundays, the insular activities of doing odd jobs in the home, or the relaxed habits of sociability among equals allow one best to grasp the cultural world of city and working-class life in its symbolic coherence . . . it is because these conditions open up a world removed from confrontation, moments of respite, sites of otherness. It is not by chance that the rich harvest of working-class 'values' and 'traits' garnered by Hoggart's ethnographic description was made possible by his decision to go prospecting in the local, family world of the working-class 'home'. That such expressions of working-class culture as 'having a quiet life' and 'keeping oneself to oneself' do not constitute a political or ideological threat to the dominant classes is another story, which however cannot replace the necessary task of description which falls to sociology (and in any case many of the most aggressive attitudes of militant culture can be seen in the light of historical analysis to have been just as innocuous for the dominant classes).[70]

Grignon and Passeron, therefore, take issue not only with Bourdieu's miserabilist account but also with the triumphalist perspective of those who constantly look upon popular culture as a 'culture of resistance'. Both these approaches have the similar effect of portraying the working class as always being in a state of 'unequal confrontation'. But Passeron insists that popular cultures are neither fixed in a perpetual state of deferential awareness of legitimate culture, nor are they mobilised day and night in a permanent attitude of revolutionary confrontation. Passeron points out that popular cultures are also frequently 'at rest', and that in such a condition they exist in a relative state of autonomy, and that it is this state of autonomy that the sociologist should also examine, and not just situations of domination or rebellion. The obsession with domination or rebellion is, according to Passeron, an obsession of intellectuals and is not shared by the people themselves. So, for instance, when the people are able to live, and forget that they are dominated, this tends to be interpreted by intellectuals as a proof of their alienation, or of their fundamental acceptance of domination.

In a very general sense, one can see that Grignon and Passeron are attempting to transcend the thoroughly politicised and ideological perceptions of social and cultural life that are endemic in French society, and which became extremely accentuated around the late 1960s and early 1970s. One can see, therefore, how the translation of Hoggart's book in 1970 contributed to an emerging tendency to abandon intensely political and ideological perceptions of the working classes (seeing them as either passive victims or as potential revolutionary heroes) and move towards seeing them on their own terms within their local communities and in their everyday lives. Such writers as Michel de Certeau and Pierre Mayol, whose work I looked at in the first chapter, clearly shared in this general abandonment of an acute political consciousness, when they sought to find value in apparently more modest and circumscribed ways of life. More than this, Grignon and Passeron, like De Certeau and Mayol, insist, in explicit opposition to Bourdieu, that the working classes have their own autonomous and creative styles of life, which are not just the negative or second-rate versions of the styles of dominant culture, and which are not reducible to functionality and utility. On this point as well, reading Hoggart may have helped these French intellectuals to develop a more positive perception of popular culture ['To live in the working classes is even now to belong to an all-pervading culture, one in some ways as formal and stylized as any that is attributed to, say, the upper classes'].[71] In his rejection of Bourdieu, Grignon is even willing to follow the linguistician Labov, who inverts the notions of dominated and dominant culture, in order to make the point that, viewed from the angle of popular culture, high culture can also be shown to be characterised by absences, lacks and deficiencies.[72] In reality, Hoggart could also have provided Grignon with similar examples: 'A working-class man would come to grief over the right way to move through a seven-course dinner: an upper middle-class man among working-class people would just as surely reveal his foreign background by the way he made conversation . . . used his hands and feet, ordered drinks or tried to stand drinks.'[73] Grignon

5

CULTURE, THE STATE
AND 1968

In the preceding chapter I pointed out how, in the mid-1960s, Pierre Bourdieu had called into question the ambition of militants in the popular culture and popular education movement to achieve cultural democratisation through their various strategies of 'cultural action'. For Bourdieu, it was only the mainstream education system itself that could offer the mass of people a meaningful chance of becoming initiated into high culture. However, I also pointed out that, if Bourdieu accused the cultural militants of being naïve and wrong-headed in their attempts to take culture to the people (or the people to culture), he did not, on the other hand, call into question the desirability of the State and other bodies providing cultural opportunities that would parallel and reinforce the long process of cultural education that took place throughout the years at school and university. In fact, it is of course true to say that by the early 1960s the project to 'democratise culture' (that is, to make high culture more accessible to people at large), had already been taken up by the State as one of its major strategies:

In 1959 cultural action became an affair of State! The democratic campaign had triumphed, since the decree of 24th of July 1959 defined the task of the new Ministry of Cultural Affairs in the following way: 'To make accessible to the largest number of French people possible the major artistic works of humanity, and above all those of France; to ensure the widest possible audience for our national heritage, and provide favourable conditions for the creation of artistic and intellectual works which will enrich this heritage.'[1]

131

Those cultural militants who had begun by operating inside the popular education and popular culture movement, in such organisations as Peuple et Culture, were subsequently called upon by the State to help in the rational planning and efficient implementation of a State cultural policy designed to provide access to high culture on a scale previously unknown.[2]

It is Evelyne Ritaine in her study *Les Stratèges de la culture* (1983), ['The cultural strategists'] who has most lucidly told the story of how the heroic mission to diffuse culture, which had been taken up at the time of the Liberation by such groups as Peuple et Culture, soon became transformed into a State profession. Cultural militants such as Joffre Dumazedier and Benigno Cacérès, who had initially considered themselves to be marginal and even outsider figures in French cultural life, and who had spent their early years fighting on behalf of the working class's right of access to culture, were to find themselves brought into the State's centralised process of formulating and implementing a policy for the 'cultural development' of France. In Ritaine's view (and it is an opinion shared by other commentators), the cultural action of the popular education movement had always been underpinned by a humanist discourse made up of a somewhat vague mix of personalist and socialist ideas. This was a discourse which in its 'unanimism' lent itself easily to the State's purpose of using culture as one of its chosen ways of achieving unity and consensus, and of humanising economic development. In the early postwar years, the ambitions for cultural democratisation were informed by an acute awareness of the gap that separated the privileged elite from the mass of people, as well as by a deep sense of the injustice of a political system that had no interest in providing cultural opportunities for the majority of its citizens. When, however, those cultural militants who had been working for cultural democratisation, appealed to the State to take responsibility for the increased provision of cultural facilities, and found that the State agreed to do so, they themselves were in danger of being left with nothing but the bureaucratic task of ensuring that the new public service sector of culture was being run efficiently.[3] In adopting the perspectives of the State, and, indeed, in agreeing to work on its behalf, there was the distinct risk that the cultural militants would come to share its quantitative approach to cultural questions.[4]

It was particularly at the time when General de Gaulle came to power in 1959 as President of the Fifth Republic, that the cultural militants were brought in to help implement the active Gaullist cultural policy headed by André Malraux at the Ministry of Cultural Affairs.[5] This Gaullist cultural policy has been most commonly identified with the grandiose plan to construct Maisons de la Culture in regional centres throughout France. The cultural militants who had been working in such associations as Peuple et Culture, and who had been part of the 'popular theatre movement'[6] (or the movement of 'theatrical decentralisation', as it is often called), were brought in at this time to help in the planning of these prestigious 'homes of culture'. Some of them, as for example Gabriel Monnet at Bourges, were indeed put in charge of individual Maisons de la Culture.[7] At this point, the State took over the ambitions and the rhetoric of cultural democratisation, already formulated in the associations, and developed a whole new politics of cultural development which was envisaged as a crucial element in the overall objective of creating a modern, technocratic, economically efficient France. Malraux carried forward key notions of the cultural democratisation campaign, but he put by far the greatest stress on the need to make the most distinguished examples of high culture accessible to as many people as possible. Within this project, the distinguished works of the French cultural heritage were to be given special attention. Malraux had an intensely idealised, and even mystical, notion of what role culture should play in modern society. Essentially, he took culture to be the spiritual replacement for lost religion. He thought of the Maisons de la Culture as the new cathedrals to which people would come, having left behind them the materialistic, ephemeral preoccupations of their daily lives, in order to encounter works of art dealing with the great questions of life and death.[8] Malraux was vehement in his criticism of the mass culture purveyed by cinema and television, since he saw it as appealing only to the basest aspects of humanity.[9] In opposition to these modern mass cultural forms, Malraux held up theatre as the appropriate focus of his cultural policy. In his view, it was theatre of the highest calibre that could offer the ideal experience of human communion and spiritual transcendence. In his insistence that only culture of the most distinguished and most demanding kind should be offered to those people coming to the Maisons de la Culture, Malraux was deliberately setting out to make sure that there would be no suggestion of amateurism, nor any hint that culture was being watered down at the provincial level. His constant concern was that people should not be fobbed off with a third-rate culture ['une culture au rabais'].[10] The idea of such an inferior culture was inseparably connected in Malraux's mind with activities promoted by local cultural associations.[11] In fact, throughout Malraux's policy for the Maisons de la Culture one detects an absolute horror of anything smacking of the local and the provincial. He wanted to bring national and international standards to the provinces, and he emphasised that there should be virtually no local input in the Maisons de la Culture, at the level of policy-making or performance.[12]

It is at this point of opposition between the national and the local that one can see important ambiguities and conflicts within Malraux's policy of cultural democratisation. His concern was to provide a prestigious cultural service which would make distinguished works of art accessible to a vastly increased number of people. But, as Jean-Jack Queyranne has amply shown, the Maisons de la Culture under Malraux's regime signally failed to find the audiences that they were supposedly set up to attract. In his account of why this particular 'populist gesture' was not successful, Queyranne marshalled together all the many criticisms levelled at the Maisons de la Culture, and at Gaullist cultural policy, during and after the events of 1968. It is, of course, well known that the Maisons de la Culture, along with other State cultural institutions, came in for special attack during the 'cultural revolution' of that year. As well as the assault from outside their walls (and from inside when these institutions were occupied), the Maisons de la Culture also underwent an internal crisis among their personnel. This crisis resulted from the loss of purpose and direction that beset the 'animateurs' when they realised that the working-class people, whom the Maisons de la Culture had principally hoped to reach, constituted in reality only a very small proportion of the public attending these institutions. This discovery of the 'non-public'[13] had a traumatic effect on all those cultural militants who had carried with them into their new careers in the State cultural service the old idealistic and populist ambition of creating a culture in which intellectuals and workers would come together, and in which workers would be initiated into the riches of high culture.

Writing his thesis on the Maisons de la Culture in the early to mid-1970s, and deeply influenced by the perspectives opened up by the events of 1968, Jean-Jack Queyranne set out the many reasons why, in his view, the Maisons de la Culture did not succeed in becoming a cultural forum for all the people. The monumentality of the architecture of the Maisons de la Culture was itself, in Queyranne's opinion, an important dissuasive factor.[14] In order to symbolise the importance that the French State was now going to give to culture, and to the diffusion of the national and international high cultural heritage, it was obviously deemed appropriate to construct imposing buildings of great prestige. But, for Queyranne, such structures only served to intimidate the majority of people, who soon came to regard them as places which were not designed to encourage them to come in, and which, in any case, were offering a type of culture that was too remote and highbrow for them. According to Queyranne, it was only too obvious to people that the Maisons de la Culture were State institutions intent on imposing high culture upon them. The mass of people responded by feeling either intimidated or indifferent. Queyranne concluded that the elitist and 'authoritarian' notions of culture that were put into practice in the Maisons de la Culture, together with the dissuasive monumentality of their architecture, meant that these institutions ended up by contributing almost nothing to a genuine process of cultural democratisation. In Queyranne's words, those who planned the Maisons de la Culture had failed to think through in any real way the problems of what a real 'popular culture' might be.[15] The Maisons de la Culture were simply prestigious State institutions which had been dropped into the middle of a city, and which had little or no connection with the actual lives of the majority of the inhabitants. In fact, the Maisons de la Culture catered only for those few people who were already educated and cultivated: students, teachers, academics, professionals and technocrats.[16] For Queyranne, therefore, the Maisons de la Culture had institutionalised a remote and elitist notion of culture, and had failed to engage with the mass of people in their everyday lives.

At the time of the events of 1968, State cultural institutions, including the Maisons de la Culture, were singled out for special attack by students and other diverse supporters of the 'cultural revolution'. What is more, those militants who had worked in the campaign for cultural democratisation since the Liberation, also became principal targets for the scorn and abuse of a new brand of cultural activist who emerged in 1968. The reverential attitude to high culture, and the humanist ideals of the early militants were pitilessly mocked by this new generation of cultural revolutionaries, who drew their inspiration from Marxism, Surrealism and Situationism. The cultural militants of the earlier generation, who had worked within the popular education movement, or within the popular theatre movement, and who then later found themselves representing the State in its cultural institutions, were put in the impossible situation of defending a cultural policy (and cultural notions and practices), of which they themselves had also, in fact, become suddenly critical. When the directors of the théâtres populaires and the Maisons de la Culture met in Villeurbanne near Lyon in May 1968, to discuss what ought to be done in the face of the crisis that they were encountering, they came up with a signed document which explained their views on the inadequacies of current cultural policy and practice, and which sketched out the lines along which, in their opinion, a more democratic culture ought to be encouraged to develop. Essentially, they admitted to having had forced upon them the full realisation of the inappropriateness and futility of their existing methods of carrying through a project of cultural democratisation. This project, they had come to see, was nothing more than 'the reassuring task of sharing out the cultural heritage in a more equitable fashion'.[17] Confessing their faults before the tribunal of the French cultural revolution, they admitted to having been responsible for perpetuating an exclusively 'bourgeois' notion of culture. They also acknowledged that they were the old men whose time had already passed:

The mere 'diffusion' of works of art, even when supplemented by a little 'animation' has come to seem less and less capable of producing a real encounter between these works and the vast numbers of men and women who are struggling with all their might to survive in society, but who, in many respects, remain excluded from it. While obliged to participate in the production of material goods, they are deprived of the means of contributing to the way in which society is run. In fact, the gap between groups has been getting progressively wider – that is, between those who are excluded and the rest of us who one way or another have been becoming more and more complicitous in their exclusion. All of a sudden the student revolt and the workers' strike have revealed this situation for what it is in a particularly stark fashion, even though many of us had more or less come to acknowledge it . . . . The violent events have now put an end to our prevarications, and our timid thoughts. Now we cannot ignore the true situation, and no one can: the split which has now occurred in our culture is a deep one, and it is a split between economic and social groups, as well as between generations. And in both cases it is . . . our own attitude to culture which has been challenged in the most radical way. Whatever the purity of our intentions, in reality our attitude appears to a considerable number of our fellow citizens to reflect the preference of a privileged few for a culture that is hereditary and particularist – that is to say, for a bourgeois culture.[18]

This admission of cultural sins marked a particularly poignant moment for a generation of militants who since the Liberation had invested so much idealism in the project of cultural democ-ratisation, only to end up by agreeing to pour scorn on what they had previously prized so highly.[19]

In the course of her account of the way in which the State had incorporated the popular culture movement into its own cultural service, Evelyne Ritaine drew up an identikit portrait of the type of people who had become cultural militants, and who had carried out the idealistic, humanist project of cultural action from the time of the Popular Front, through the periods of Resistance and Liberation, and on into the postwar era. Basing her account on particular figures such as Benigno Cacérès, Jean Guéhenno and Joffre Dumazedier,[20] she suggested that, because of their humble social origins, and the particular nature of their educational experi-ences, these autodidacts and working-class scholarship boy types had developed an excessively reverential view of culture. They had begun by feeling deprived of culture; they had aspired to possess it, and eventually had acceded to it by dint of their abilities and efforts. According to Ritaine, they were people who had themselves staked everything on culture. Consequently, they greatly exaggerated the need of others for it. What is more, they were the least likely to call culture into question, and were ultimately to prove very happy to go along with the State's definitions of culture, and with the uses to which the State wanted culture to be put.

Ritaine's picture of those who were to enter upon the mod-ern career of 'animateur' after 1968, was different in some key ways from her portrait of the older-style cultural militants such as Dumazedier and Cacérès. According to Ritaine, the kind of person who chose a career as an 'animateur' after 1968 was someone from the middle class who had been relatively unsuccessful in the academic field, and who had, therefore, been unable to prove himself in one of the traditional professions.[21] Such a person turned to the new career position of 'animateur' in order to stake out his own professional terrain, which he did by constructing values and practices which were in direct opposition to those of traditional scholarly culture. In insisting on such an interpretation of the world of cultural action, Ritaine showed herself to be fully the disciple of Bourdieu, for, like him, she took for granted that there was a fixed criterion of distinction in the intellectual and cultural sphere. Anyone who did not succeed according to this fixed criterion of distinction, was, therefore, depicted as having to devise strategies of compensation and even revenge, in order to make up for their sense of relative failure and inferiority. In addition, Ritaine, like Bourdieu, had a very clear view of who was part of the true intelligentsia, and who was not. For instance, she was sure that anyone who was a genuine intellectual would have had nothing to do with the world of cultural action in the first place. For Ritaine, the project of cultural democratisation was simply the last in line of a whole tradition of 'populist gestures' whereby intellectuals tried to 'meet the people'.[22] This utopian dream of the future union between intellectuals and the people underlay the whole historical ambition of achieving a cultural democracy, and, according to Ritaine, every militant was inspired to carry on the campaign as a result of the memory of his own (or the story of someone else's) exalting, if momentary, experience of communion with the people:

> In this idealist vision of history, the pedagogical techniques of militant action are always capable of improvement. One only has to find a better way of 'going to meet the people', of 'making oneself like the people'; one only has to step out of the magic circle of 'high culture' in order to respond to 'popular needs'; one only has to find effective 'approach techniques' . . . . And so the euphoria of a few people nurtures the utopias of others: from one tale of lived experience to another, the myth takes on a resonance and is further amplified. Every militant believes that, for a few hours or a few days, he has 'joined up with the people', and he has left a vibrant record of this reunion. Personal testimonies are followed by new aspirations, and the mythical moments of cultural action are those in which intellectuals seem to have finally come together with the people.[23]

According to Ritaine, the cultural militants' desire to 'meet the people' showed them to be the self-deluding victims of a mythical discourse which had long since lost any reality. Ritaine even went so far as to claim that true intellectuals had given up the utopian aspiration to achieve communion with the people some time before, and at least by the end of the war. These true intellectuals may have continued to use populist rhetoric, but, in Ritaine's view, they certainly did not take it literally:

> The cultural militants were the only ones who were trapped into believing populist discourse. Political strategy only re-quired one to proclaim the need for cultural unity and cultural participation. The intelligentsia itself, aware of what was necessary in the cultural field, was quite happy to make purely verbal pronouncements. The militants, on the other hand, felt the need to act. Their dreams led them to believe that it was really a question of meeting the People. They were so worried and uncertain as to their own social positions, that they actually tried to meet the People. This was obviously a naïve gesture, and it was naïve because it was utopian.[24]

In fact, Ritaine did go on to concede that, whatever the naïvety of such an ambition, the desire to 'meet the people' had undeniably been one of the truly humanising forces in history. But this positive interpretation comes very late in Ritaine's book, and does little to alter one's sense that, yet again, the weight of high culture and scholarly culture has succeeded in crushing anything that seems to fall short of the alleged paramountcy of its standards. In any case, what is most misleading in Ritaine's assessment is her claim that in postwar France true intellectuals had not been duped into believing in the 'populist gesture' of taking culture to the people, or of creating a 'popular culture'. It would seem quite inaccurate to claim that in the postwar period true intellectuals did not share hopes for a 'common culture', or 'a popular culture', and did not actively work towards the creation of such a culture. One only has to remember the enduring vitality of myths of the people for such a pre-eminent intellectual figure as Sartre, and to recall the importance he attached to his own populist gestures, to realise that true intellectuals have indeed shared with 'second-rate' intellectuals similar cultural and political dreams and ambitions.

From *Qu'est-ce-que la littérature?* [*What is Literature?*] in 1948 to his involvement with the Maoist *La Cause du Peuple*[25] after 1968,

Sartre showed that he believed the central issue for intellectuals and writers to be how to unite with the people, and how to create a new culture that would be a genuinely popular culture. One hardly needs to stress that Sartre was, of course, a long way from fulfilling such goals, but it is important, nevertheless, to emphasise that, if 'populist gestures' in postwar France are to be characterised as incorrigibly naïve, then it is a naïvety that has not been the monopoly of 'second-rate' intellectuals in the world of cultural action. The following passage from Sartre's *On a raison de se révolter* (1974) ['One is right to rebel'], demonstrates how Sartre persisted in his dream of a new form of popular culture, which, somewhat improbably, he hoped would eventually incorporate such works as his own monumental and complex work on Flaubert, *L'Idiot de la Famille*:

> I consider this work to be a socialist work, in the sense that, if it is successful, it should contribute to furthering the understanding of human beings from a socialist point of view. In this respect, it seems to me that I am working for the socialist society of the future. I hope I am right in thinking that bourgeois writers are part of a long-term project, and that they could be part of another culture, a popular culture, providing that ways are found of mediating their works.[26]

The example of Sartre should also remind one that, contrary to what Bourdieu and Ritaine might suggest, true intellectuals have themselves not always believed in the absolute primacy of their own intellectual culture. Indeed, Sartre's populism constantly led him to depreciate himself, and the intelligentsia as a whole:

> Workers and peasants, when they rebel, are totally moral, because they exploit nobody. That is why intellectuals have nothing to teach them. It is undoubtedly true that intellectuals have revealed the existence of exploitation and oppression, but only in an abstract way, as if they were simply the logical outcome of bourgeois morality. As for understanding what is meant by refusing to obey authority, intellectuals can only learn this from the people, and by joining with the people in their political struggle.[27]

The growth of a specifically French form of Maoism offers one of the most striking instances of the revival of populist mythology at the time of 1968, and in the years subsequent to these events. During this French version of the cultural revolution, many students, intellectuals, writers and artists came to regard their existences as only being justified if they put themselves completely 'at the service of the people'. Indeed, many of them ended up by being convinced that, as educated bourgeois, they were worth nothing, and that they could only attain humanity by subordinating themselves to the people, or even by throwing off all vestiges of their former social selves and fusing with the people. In Michèle Manceaux's *Les Maos en France*, one finds the political autobiographies of those who, in their desire to break down the barriers between intellectuals and workers, chose to live the anonymous life of the masses, and themselves went to work in the factories. These Maoists gloried in their new situation of being just one small element within an enormous collectivity. They thought they had, in fact, finally broken away from purely verbal gestures of solidarity with the people, and had actually succeeded in living the life of the people.[28] Such Maoists took their determination to 'serve the people' to an extreme point, and, in so doing, believed they were successfully destroying in themselves the last traces of bourgeois selfishness and individualism:

> In every act of your daily life, in every area of your social activity, you must ask yourself the question: whom should one serve? Are you living, fighting, working for your own interests, or the interests of a small handful of people? On the other hand, are you living, fighting, working for the interests of the great mass of people? Are you serving the people, or the opposite of the people, that is to say, the enemies of the people – the bourgeoisie?[29]

Maoism was certainly one of the most startling expressions of populism in 1968. However, in this eclectically inspired cultural revolution, it was, in fact, a rather different creed – that of Situationism – which has prior claims to being considered the source of its revolutionary mythology.[30] A very characteristic text of the Situationists, entitled *De la misère en milieu étudiant* ['The wretchedness of being a student'], was issued as a pamphlet by the Situationist International in November 1966.[31] It gives a very good idea of some of those central concerns of the Situationists which were to be taken up so passionately in 1968. Not least, it allows one to see how violent was the Situationist assault on high culture, and on the culture promoted by the State:

> Students compensate for the genuine wretchedness of their daily lives by turning to the realm of the imaginary, and to their principal opium – cultural commodities. In the world of the cultural spectacle students take up their natural position as respectful disciples. Students are near the site of cultural production, but never quite get there – they are forbidden entry into the inner sanctum – and so they discover 'modern culture' as admiring spectators. In a period when *art is dead*, it is mainly students who continue to attend theatres and 'ciné-clubs', and it is they who are the avid consumers of the corpse of art, frozen and packed in cellophane in the supermarkets of culture . . . . If the 'maisons de la culture' did not exist, students would have invented them. Students are living proof of the most banal analyses of the American sociology of marketing: one only has to see how subject they are to the laws of conspicuous consumption, and how they constantly claim that there are differences between products which are all equally worthless (Perec or Robbe-Grillet, Godard or Lelouch).[32]

According to the Situationists, the existence of modern man was nothing but a living death in a society in which all vital and spontaneous experiences had been eliminated in favour of second-hand, vicarious 'spectacles'. Perhaps the chief targets of the Situationist assault were the modern visual media of television and cinema. But, as one can see from the above quotation, the Situationists also looked upon all forms of high culture as simply 'merchandise', marketed and displayed in such supermarkets of culture as the Maisons de la Culture for avid customers to come and ogle, and then passively consume. Jean-Jacques Lebel took up this supermarket image as the central thread in his *Procès du festival d'Avignon* (1968), ['The Avignon Festival in the dock'].[33] In this text Lebel made a direct attack on those old men of good will in the popular culture and popular theatre movements, who had allowed themselves to become absorbed into a cultural industry which was indistinguishable from any other form of commercial enterprise. One anonymous tract that Lebel cited in his volume singled out for ironic treatment 'the technocrats of popular culture' and 'the mass educators . . . with their good consciences' – by which was clearly meant the cultural militants in the popular culture and popular theatre movements.[34] Another item in the Lebel volume explained the opposition to the Festival as deriving from a general recognition of the failure of the State's cultural policy:

> One can understand why there is silence surrounding what is really going on at the Avignon Festival (neither press nor TV mentions it, or if they do, they give false information): what is happening is, in fact, the realisation that the cultural policy, which has been conducted with so much hullabaloo under Malraux, has failed. The Maisons de la Culture had become the alibi for the regime. There is now a rejection of the cultural industry which in Avignon is totally inseparable from the tourist trade.[35]

In Lebel's eyes, Jean Vilar, as organiser of the Avignon Festival, was simply the managing director of an enterprise controlled by professionals and technicians of culture, whose job was to fabricate products that would not only tempt the culture-vulture customers to buy, but would also help to condition these customers to their place in capitalist society.[36] The 'popular culture' diffused by the cultural militants, and by such as Vilar in the popular theatre movement, was condemned outright by Lebel and other 'enragés' and Situationists as 'bourgeois culture'. As one tract put it:

> THE BOURGEOISIE IS HANDING US: BREAD CIRCUSES AND COPS.
> With our taxes:
> THE BOURGEOISIE IS DOLING OUT CHARITY
> Popular grub
> Popular Culture
> Popular repression!
> THE BOURGEOIS STATE PREVENTS US FROM THINKING AND ACTING.
>   THANK YOU.
> WE MUST PARTICIPATE . . .[37]

According to Lebel, the Avignon Festival could not claim to be 'a free and popular festival', because it did not represent those whom Lebel saw as being the 'popular' elements attending the Festival.[38] For Lebel, the crucial failure of the Festival was its inability to cope with the fringe and countercultural activities – a failure above all symbolised by the exclusion of Julian Beck's Living Theatre. The very fact that the festival organisers could not accept Beck's theatre group proved to Lebel that the old-style, liberal humanism was an empty myth. When confronted with something that went outside their experience, and that challenged their values, they simply chose to attack and repress it. Their liberalism was, therefore, 'merely verbal'[39] and a front for their support for capitalism and the State.[40]

Those who attacked Vilar and the Avignon Festival did so in the name of their own conception of what an 'authentically popular culture' ought to be.[41] In their eyes, the 'popular culture' of the cultural militants and the directors of the théâtres populaires and the Maisons de la Culture, simply embodied the illusion of a high culture shared more equitably. As against this, the 'enragés' and Situationists at Avignon believed they were calling for a revolution in the cultural sphere. In part they adopted a Marxist model of cultural revolution, since they wanted to expropriate the owners of culture, and put culture under the control of the people themselves.[42] But they also followed a Situationist idea of cultural revolution, in that they sought above all to liberate the individual's psychic forces. Such a liberation was, in the Situationists' view, absolutely imperative, if a truly creative culture were ever to come into being. This alliance of Marxism and Situationism accounted for many of the cultural ideas expressed by the 'contestataires' of 1968. On the one hand, Lebel was calling for a kind of workers' control of culture ['autogestion culturelle']. On the other hand, he was also calling for the breaking down of all forms of institutional repression, for this was a pre-requisite if the individual were to become a permanently creative being:

We are searching for modes of permanent creation, free from all censure and from all institutionalisation. These modes would be 'irrecuperable', and would neither be reserved for specialists, nor be consumed by sheep-like spectators. These modes of collective creation need no fixed scenario, no dog-matic theory, no absolutist ideology. Until capitalism has been destroyed, we cannot know what will result from a total freedom of creation and action. We know only one thing for certain: this psycho-social mutation is an integral part of the revolutionary process which, all over the world, has begun to transform the power relations between the managers and the managed, and between the possessors and the dispossessed.

We also know that when these power relations have been reversed, it will be possible to envisage the end of the reign of 'having', and the beginning of the reign of 'being'.[43]

The revolutionary project of the Situationists was designed to call into question not only bourgeois and State notions of popular culture (as symbolised, for instance, by the Avignon Festival), but also the sclerotic ideas on culture held by the French Communist Party. The communist opposition to the events of May 1968 had demonstrated to the new revolutionaries that the Communists were no longer true and fit representatives of the 'cause of the people'.[44] Equally, the local communist hostility to the countercultural elements at the Avignon Festival had only served to underline the Communists' inability to understand the changes occurring in the cultural sphere.[45] With heavy irony, Lebel highlighted what he saw as the dismal cultural populism of the PCF by showing it as offering to the workers the lowest common denominator of culture – namely, the culture of mass entertainment:

> The brilliant strategists of the Party showed that they were not insensitive to popular culture – that is to say, the true kind of popular culture! – particularly when it was a question of 'winning over the petite-bourgeoisie to the cause of the proletariat': they put on Mireille Mathieu, and, just to prove they could be avant-garde, the Red Army Choir (fancy that!).[46]

For Lebel, a truly popular culture had to be revolutionary. It had to turn its back on the culture of mass entertainment, and on the high culture promoted by the State. It needed to find new ways of meeting the people. According to Lebel, this involved a complete break with the institutional framework of culture, as well as with the traditional notion that culture was necessarily to be identified with the individual works of artists working within the established genres of art.[47] For the Situationists, a truly popular culture was one that was created spontaneously and collectively on the streets. In Lebel's eyes, the Living Theatre represented this new, revolutionary popular culture, precisely because Julian Beck refused to accept the rules of a consumer culture which closeted creativity within the walls of State institutions, and served up cultural products in the form of spectacles. According to Lebel:

> By going out onto the streets, the Living Theatre escaped from the strait jacket that had been imposed on it. It wanted

to play not only FOR but WITH people who had never set foot in the theatre. It wanted to play FREE OF CHARGE, outside the walls of the supermarket, outside the cultural precincts, outside the space allocated to it by the authorities. In the end, it wanted the festivities to transgress the prohibitive code laid down for commercial reasons. It wanted the theatre, once and for all, to cut the umbilical cord which bound it to the property-owning class. Contacts were set up with the workers; public meetings took place between artists, students, peasants and railwaymen. The process of breaking down the compartments that separated people had begun.[48]

If one leaves aside the self-dramatisation, and the revolutionary posturing, it is difficult not to notice how much of the Situationist and countercultural critique of consumer society, mass culture and high culture simply added an insolent and provocative edge to the same calls for a truly democratic and popular culture that had been issuing from the movement for cultural democratisation ever since the war. The hope of creating a shared culture; the promise of a utopian coming-together of intellectuals and the people – these were still to be found in texts such as Lebel's. One needs to remember that, throughout the postwar years, the popular culture and popular education movement had been waging a tireless campaign against the materialistic values of consumer society, against inhuman conditions at home and at work, and against the supposedly new leisure society, which it saw as threatening to destroy the civic sense by the constant promise it offered of a life of pure entertainment and fun. One also needs to remember that the popular culture and popular education movement had considered itself to be challenging an elitist culture restricted to the privileged few, and to be working for the creation of a more human and more everyday culture. A study of the democratic rhetoric of 1968 has, therefore, to take into account the fact that many of the 1968 attacks upon previous attempts at cultural democratisation were conducted in very similar terms to those that had already been employed by the popular culture and popular education movement from the time of the Liberation right up to the 1960s. This was something of which the older cultural militants must have been painfully aware, when they found themselves to be among the prime targets in 1968. The revolutionary ambitions which had been brought to the fore in this year were in reality not that distant from their own broadly socialist objectives. In fact, the cultural militants often showed themselves ready to welcome this new input of revolutionary fervour into the fight for new forms of cultural democracy, even if this welcome involved a degree of masochistic self-castigation over past errors, as in the case of the Villeurbanne declaration.

Lebel's *Procès du festival d'Avignon* is a text which helps one to see how the 'enragés' and the Situationists meted out rather rough treatment to those in the popular culture and popular theatre movements.[49] However, the one Situationist work that had, perhaps, the most general impact in 1968 was Raoul Vaneigem's *Traité de savoir-vivre à l'usage des jeunes générations* (1967), ['Treatise on how to live for the use of the young generations'].[50] It seems to have been from this text that the 1968 graffiti writers took much of their inspiration, and there seems no doubt that Lebel, for instance, was deeply influenced by it. Perhaps more than any other single source, it helps one to understand the essential form and content of the cultural revolution of May 68. Vaneigem had a nightmare vision of mass society as one in which people had been reduced to solitary and anonymous figures in the crowd,[51] repeating their mechanical, alienated gestures, as they went through their crushing and meaningless routines of work and leisure.[52] Within each individual, however, there still existed the profound desire to break out of the artificialities and oppressions of mass consumer society, and find a way of living creatively, authentically and passionately.[53] Modern consumer society was an affluent society, but material comfort and material possessions had brought boredom, lethargy and inner emptiness.[54] The new media of television and cinema had further accentuated modern man's distance from living experience, and he was condemned to see life from a distance, through an endless series of 'screens'. A total revolution was, therefore, needed, in order to break with the alienation of modern mass consumer society. It was, of course, a revolution which could have nothing to do with those existing political parties that still claimed to have revolutionary aims. All the old Socialists and Communists were deeply wedded to an ascetic ethos, and believed that the revolution could only come through painful struggle and the sacrifice of self to a greater cause.[55] In opposition to this, Vaneigem insisted that the true revolution would only ever come about as a result of a total rejection of all constraint, and through the complete liberation of the individual's anarchic desires. Pleasure was the individual's only reliable guide, and to seek to live in a condition of permanent 'fête' was the only way to achieve a revolutionary break with society as it existed.[56] To throw oneself passionately and unconditionally into love and play was the means of subverting the old society, and of ensuring that 'everyday life' became the occasion for the unleashing of unrestricted, individual desire:

> The organisation of work and the organisation of leisure are the means by which society castrates a race of tame dogs – supposedly in order to improve them. Will we one day see the strikers calling for automation and the ten-hour week, and, as a sign of their break with society, choosing to make love in the factories, the offices and the Maisons de la Culture?[57]

When Vaneigem exhorted people to make love in the Maisons de la Culture, he was, of course, demonstrating his contempt for these State institutions of culture, which he took to be an integral part of the repressive mass consumer society. Like consumer goods, the culture promoted by the Maisons de la Culture was, in Vaneigem's view, merely a sop designed to deflect people from their fundamental desire for revolutionary change.[58] For Vaneigem, traditional high culture was a corpse in a museum, the deep-frozen remains of dead passions, whereas a truly living culture needed to be the spontaneous creation of the moment.[59] Culture was no longer a living culture when it could be 'recuperated' by bureaucrats and safely housed within the walls of the museum.[60] A living, spontaneous culture was the only one that could claim to be a popular culture, because it existed in the sphere of everyday life, and because it was a culture open to every individual. Vaneigem's populist faith rested upon his belief that not only individuals but 'the people' in general possessed the revolutionary potential, and the revolutionary determination, to change their lives and change the world.[61] The creativity latent within individuals was the inflammable substance which, when ignited, would produce the true revolution of 'federated subjectivities'.[62] Vaneigem's notion of popular culture was, therefore, one in which people would come together in a spontaneous surge of creativity and celebration, breaking down all the constraints, repressions and taboos of capitalist society. What is more, in coming together in collective acts of collaboration and rebellion, individuals would be finding their own separate fulfilment. The ideas of the Situationists were among the most striking features of the graffiti and the posters that covered the walls of French institutions during 1968. These posters and graffiti brought populist themes to a pitch of intensity, as they invoked popular energy, popular creativity and popular power, and called for the union of students, intellectuals, workers and peasants as the means of bringing about the joyful destruction of capitalism.[63]

The populist images and messages carried by the posters and graffiti of May 1968 were not, of course, drawn exclusively from Situationist sources. But their provenance has, in any case, often been thought to be far less important than the sheer fact of their sudden appearance. It was Michel de Certeau who was one of the first to characterise the essential nature of the cultural revolution of 1968 as that of a gigantic explosion of popular *expression*. In *La Prise de parole* (1968), ['Starting to speak'], De Certeau depicted the events of May as the occasion when the masses emerged from their anonymity and silence, and finally spoke out against those authorities and institutions which had refused to acknowledge them and treat them as human equals.[64] Many of the militant texts of 1968 represented the State as an overwhelmingly repressive and sadistic force which crushed people with such violence that they were deprived of any freedom of speech or action. One thinks, for instance, of the Atelier populaire posters, with their images of ferocious, helmeted police with mask-like faces, wielding their batons. One thinks also of the posters showing the bandaged heads of the young with their mouths closed by a large safety-pin. The State was represented as totally intolerant of dissent, and as ready to protect its own power, and instil its own ideology, by a remorseless policy of control and indoctrination, backed up by police and military brutality. Any activity or institution funded or supported by the State was considered to be directly carrying out the orders of the State. Hence, there was a call for the people to seize back the public institutions, such as universities and the broadcasting service, and put them under popular control. The famous graffito 'When I hear the word "culture", I get out my CRS troops',[65] indicated the degree to which culture was seen as a sphere controlled and policed by the State. This was, of course, one of the most insistent themes of 1968, and it helps to account for the savagery of the attacks upon such State institutions as the Maisons de la Culture.

A text which reveals very clearly how culture came to be seen, in Althusser's term, as an ideological apparatus of State,[66] is B. Miège, J. Ion and A-N. Roux's *L'Appareil d'action culturelle* (1974) ['The apparatus of cultural action']. For the authors of this work, the whole mission of cultural democratisation had, in reality, simply been a way of inculcating and reinforcing the dominant ideology, of conditioning people to serve capitalism, and of reproducing existing social relations.[67] The State plan for cultural development was a strategy to ensure that the State bureaucracy could control the cultural field and use it for its own purposes. Culture, as promoted in the new institutions of culture, was the acceptable face of a regime, designed to mask its true economic and political nature:

> The 'animateurs' become the principal agents of these new institutions, and just as the teaching profession had been the principal instrument for spreading the myth of egalitarian democracy, so now a whole new social category is in the process of being constructed, and is already elaborating and transmitting the new ideology. This is the objective social role they are being required to play, and most of them are taken in by it, as were the majority of the secular teachers of the Third Republic. Cultural mediators, agents of change, agents of development, educators, leisure 'animateurs', educational 'animateurs' – the designations leave no room for doubt. They are, every single one of them, given the task of encouraging adaptability, openness and mobility, all of which are indispensable for the survival and development of the economic system.[68]

Since Miège, Ion and Roux believed that the State institutions of culture were designed to serve the interests of the State, they concluded that a truly free culture could only exist outside the sphere of State control and surveillance. Thus, for instance, they found some signs of a genuine, grass-roots oppositional culture in gangs of working-class youths who demonstrated a violent, instinctive class resistance to all forms of cultural promotion and organisation. Such youths refused to be corralled into official spaces and, if they came off the streets at all, they insisted on doing things in their own way.[69]

The fact that 'the bourgeois State' was constantly identified as the implacable enemy in 1968 seems to have led inevitably to a search for forms of culture that either opposed or escaped its crushing dominance. While Miège, Ion and Roux saw some indications of resistance or independence among rebellious working-class youth, they also acknowledged the existence of other 'countercultures', 'subcultures' and 'marginal cultures'.[70] However, these authors were still sufficiently wedded to their Marxist critique of society for them to believe that, in order to constitute a genuine revolutionary threat to the State, all such forms of oppositional activity needed to be integrated into the class struggle. In sticking to their hard-line Althusserian analysis of culture, and in continuing to look to the working class as the crucial catalyst of revolution, they were, however, by 1974 already beginning to occupy a rare position. Some of the most acute commentators on 1968 and its aftermath have stressed the way in which the oppositional culture that arose around 1968, although it began by stressing the conflict between the bourgeois State and the working class, was soon to widen its perspectives and focus upon a whole range of other marginal and repressed groups. For Pierre Gaudibert, this widening of perspectives was a form of 'cultural pluralism' the emergence of which was to have profound significance for the way that social, political and cultural questions were henceforward to be perceived and treated:

> Cultural pluralism, which is opposed to the ideology of cultural democratisation (as it is to Malraux's religion of Culture), does not only mark the sudden reappearance of the problem of culture and social class, and in particular of a duality much played on again since 1968 (that is, bourgeois culture/proletarian culture); it also takes on board the dualities of scholarly culture/popular culture and official culture/marginal culture. Cultural pluralism is now willing to pay attention to all the minority cultures within the national culture (ethnic, regional . . . etc.), and also to all other types of subculture or microculture (women, youth, émigrés, under-class, professions, unions, militants etc.) Finally, cultural pluralism pays attention to what has been variously called spontaneism, counterculture, underground culture.[71]

When Michel de Certeau said in *La Prise de parole* that the essential feature of May 1968 was that people, in all their number and variety, had finally come forward and spoken up, he too had had in mind this idea that society was going to have to adjust to a 'plural culture'. For De Certeau, 1968 marked the appearance into public view of other people in all their difference from those social and cultural norms represented by bourgeois society, and promoted by the State. 'Otherness' and 'difference' were, for De Certeau, the key words for understanding the new culture that was emerging. Popular culture was, therefore, now 'une autre culture'[72] – an 'other' culture, a different culture. What was other and different had always been regarded by the bourgeois State as dangerous and threatening, and had, therefore, been consistently subject to repression or annihilation. Now, according to De Certeau, the 'objects' of history were coming forward as political and human 'subjects'. They were insisting on their right to their own lives and culture in all their otherness and difference. They were also insisting that their lives and culture be accepted as fully valid, and be treated with utmost respect. As well as representing a crisis for the bourgeois State, this eruption of difference offered a challenge to the intellectual and cultivated classes, since it forced upon them the need to extend the categories of their own thinking and experience. Intellectuals would now have to learn to cope with what went on beyond their own frame of reference. They would have to find a way of acknowledging and understanding it, but not just so as to be able to relegate and consign it to 'the museum'.[73] 'Other cultures', therefore, constituted the same challenge as that presented formerly to western ethnologists and anthropologists in their quest to understand foreign cultures. Now the intellectual classes would have to stop imposing their reductive and destructive categories on the many different cultures within their own society. According to De Certeau, when people stepped forward and made themselves seen and heard, they destroyed the myths that intellectuals had constructed about them in their absence.[74] Viewed in this light, popular culture was not to be understood in relation to elite culture, high culture, dominant culture and so forth. Such approaches were themselves evidence of the way in which intellectuals persisted in bringing the unknown within the frame of reference of the known. Popular culture had to be seen as offering its own realm of difference and otherness, and had to be understood on its own terms. What is more, it now needed to be recognised that it was no longer possible to think in terms of just one 'popular culture' in opposition to dominant culture, for popular culture itself had become, in De Certeau's formula, 'a plural culture'.[75]

In 1979 there appeared a volume, edited by Geneviève Poujol and Raymond Labourie, significantly entitled *Les Cultures populaires* ['Popular cultures']. It is a volume which enables one to take a little further the story of what was understood by the notion of popular culture in French intellectual circles a decade after the events of 1968. The description of the contents of the volume that appeared on the back cover summarised three of the main definitions of popular culture that had had currency in postwar France up until the mid 1970s, and then went on to indicate which definition was going to be followed in this particular volume:

> Three principal – and at first sight divergent – meanings can be attributed to the expression 'popular culture': firstly, a campaign to take culture to the workers; secondly an emancipatory, if not revolutionary, form of cultural action; finally, the cultural affirmation of a people, or a minority social group. The plural 'popular cultures', which appears in the title of this volume, obviously gives priority to the third of these meanings. The attention given nowadays to the plurality of cultures, cultural identity, regionalism and everyday life, inevitably reveals a militant approach. However, it remains true that any action in support of popular cultures must depend on a full knowledge and a deep understanding of them.

At least one of the editors of the volume (Raymond Labourie) was keen to suggest that the most meaningful and relevant definition of popular culture in France at the time of the mid- to late 1970s was one that had moved on from the idealist and populist presuppositions of the popular culture and popular education movement, as well as one that had gone beyond the revolutionary conceptions that had emerged around 1968. He did, however, admit that there was far from being unanimity in this volume and, indeed, perhaps its most interesting feature is that it demonstrated how at this time there still existed within French intellectual circles considerable conflicts, disagreements and differences of emphasis concerning the definition of popular culture. The contributions of Dumazedier[76] and Besnard[77] showed that there was still vigorous support for the objectives of the popular culture and popular education movement, that is to say, for a programme of cultural action in which a trained and committed body of 'animateurs' would work for the full inclusion of all people, and above all of the working class, in the life of the nation. It does, however, seem true to say that 'animateurs' had by and large lost much of their zeal as cultural missionaries, and had become far more interested in 'socio-cultural' and 'socio-educative' schemes. The contributions of Besnard and Barthez[78] also made it clear that the spirit of 1968 was not going to die easily, and that many intellectuals were prepared to stick to their revolutionary, confrontational conception of popular culture as a militant culture in conflict with a dominant and repressive bourgeois culture. In

Besnard's chapter, for instance, one finds an acerbic attack on the notions of popular culture being developed by such a figure as Michel de Certeau (also a contributor to this volume).[79]

De Certeau was seen by Besnard as actively depoliticising the concept of popular culture, and as trivialising it by associating it with the 'microcultural' level of the 'everyday' activities of 'ordinary' people. In his attack on De Certeau, Besnard also had in his sights the review *Autrement* whose first number appeared in the Spring of 1975. This review, as it developed over the ensuing years, can be taken as representing the gradual shifts in Parisian left-wing intellectual circles from the politicised and confrontational notions of popular culture inherited from 1968 towards gradually more depoliticised and pluralist concepts. Besnard's attack on De Certeau and his essay 'The beauty of the dead' (which I looked at in the first chapter) was accompanied by a withering condemnation of the special issue of *Autrement* on popular culture published in November 1978,[80] where popular culture was identified with all manner of subcultural, marginal and, in Besnard's eyes, trivial activities. Against all such recent attempts to depoliticise and pluralise the idea of popular culture, Besnard insisted on retaining a much more pugnacious definition. In fact, he defined popular culture as the continuing struggle to achieve better conditions for the cultural and economic lives of underprivileged people, and to win for such groups an acceptable measure of dignity and self-respect. According to Besnard, dire consequences would ensue from failing to remember that this remained the essential definition of popular culture:

One would lapse into the kind of reductive interpretations which only associate popular culture with activities such as gardening and feeding the cows, do-it-yourself and folklore, slot machines and decorated jeans, masks and bergamasks, graffiti and ex-votos, naïve painters and chromolithographs – all of which may help to embalm the dead body of popular culture, but do not help us to discover its truth or beauty.

It is all, in fact, just evidence of the cultural vampirism of the petite-bourgeoisie, which, having no culture of its own, tries to rise from its ashes by avidly looking for resources and renewal elsewhere. The current celebration of popular culture is very worrying, for it is only serving to fuel mass culture and consumer culture. What we have is a group of windbags and gravediggers who, in the end, are seeking to recover a social energy which has deserted them.[81]

Not only was Besnard unforgiving in his attack on 'petit-bourgeois', trivialising ideas of popular culture, but he was also equally critical of the continuing influence of Bourdieu's notions of cultural dominance and cultural legitimacy, according to which popular culture was always presented as an inferior, 'handicapped' culture. In this respect at least, however, Besnard found himself in agreement with many of the other contributors in the volume, since one can see in many of the chapters a definite rejection of Bourdieu's analyses of popular culture. In fact, Geneviève Poujol (one of the editors of the volume) devoted her chapter specifically to a consideration of the question of whether popular culture was to be thought of as a handicapped culture, or as a culture that offered independent and stout resistance to the dominant culture.[82] For Poujol, the essence of popular culture was that it managed to exist in relative independence from the dominant culture – whether it did so by just carrying on with its old ways, or by creating new forms of cultural practice which differed from those of dominant culture. Poujol acknowledged that Bourdieu's 'denunciation' of the cultural hegemony of the dominant class was a very necessary step in the understanding of popular culture, but she stressed that this now needed to be complemented by an awareness of the extent to which this cultural hegemony was, in fact, far from absolute. Even so, Poujol was unwilling to propose that popular culture was 'antagonistic' in a consciously political sense. She suggested that it negotiated its resistance to dominant culture in more individual, flexible and cunning ways.

This notion of a popular culture which was not just a passive victim, nor an organised revolutionary force, but a culture of individual, active negotiation, is a concept that was to underlie much of the thinking about popular culture in France from the mid-1970s onwards. It seems to have offered leftist French intellectuals a way of salvaging a positive notion of working-class agency, once they had jettisoned their more utopian ideas of a militant popular culture created by a revolutionary proletariat. The influence of Gramsci obviously played an important part in the development of this more flexible idea of popular culture. This influence was acknowledged, for instance, by Louis-Jean Calvet in his 1976 study *La Production révolutionnaire: slogans, affiches, chansons* ['Revolutionary production:

slogans, posters, songs']. In this text Calvet was obviously trying to come to terms with the experience of 1968, and particularly to challenge its exclusive identification of popular culture with militant revolutionary culture. He quoted an article from the Maoist *La Cause du peuple* to show how the extreme Left in 1968 and after had insisted on the revolutionary essence of popular song:

> 'There is only one kind of true song. It is not the one that can be heard on the radio or TV, but it is the song that was sung by Gavroche before he was shot by the cops of Capital. It is the song that can be heard rising from the depths of the black ghettos of Harlem. It is the song that was chanted by the Bolsheviks before they went off to beat the White Russian troops. It is the song of those who fight for the people . . . . Nothing can suppress the revolutionary song because it is learned in the struggle, and a song that has its violent birth on the streets is a thousand times more important than any sickly sweet commercial tune.
>
> The new freedom fighters who are rising up every day, will find a way of seizing this weapon that the bourgeoisie has stolen from them. Tomorrow hundreds of revolutionary songs will come into bloom, written by work-worn hands, under the fire of battle, in the factory, in the shanty towns, in the demonstrations. Tomorrow one will find in the verses written by the people and for the people the sweat, the suffocation from tear gas, and the odour of spilt blood.'[83]

Against this idea of a revolutionary working class creating its own militant culture, Calvet drew on Gramsci, and on the favourite 1968 concept of 'détournement', to propose that popular culture selected and appropriated elements from the dominant culture that could be used for its own purposes.[84] This notion of a selective and cunning (mis)appropriation of what was offered by dominant culture was to be found in many of the contributions to the Poujol and Labourie volume, particularly the chapter of Michel de Certeau, where he sketched out his ideas on 'cultural practitioners' which I looked at in the first chapter. As a way of countering the idea that ordinary people lived dominated and passive lives, De Certeau insisted on the active and creative strategies that people employed:

> I am interested in the use that these 'practitioners' make of the urban environment, of the range of products sold by the

supermarket, or of the stories disseminated by their daily newspaper.[85]

In so far as the 'practitioner's' response was in some sense consciously critical and subversive, then this notion of appropriation could be seen as taking up and elaborating the 1968, Surrealist-inspired practice of 'détournement', whereby, for instance, an advertising poster would be written over, or altered in some way, so as to transform the capitalist, consumer message into a radical statement. And, indeed, in the 1979 *Les Cultures populaires* volume, Michel de Certeau retained the idea that popular culture was a culture of resistance in his chosen metaphor of ordinary people as 'poachers' in the land of dominant culture:

> I will quickly describe what I mean by the tactics of the practitioner by taking the example of reading . . . . To begin with, in consumer society, which offers a constant assault upon our visual senses, the reader is allocated a position of passivity, whereas writers are considered to be active creators. The reader is supposed to just swallow the text that has been given to him. In reality, the silent practice of reading corresponds to the way in which colonised Red Indians negotiated the culture imposed by their conquerors. The reader skims the page, he dreams, he skips sentences, he retains what is of interest to him. A word, a name, makes him digress and leave behind the given text, in order to make something else with it – or more precisely, with its fragments, its shreds. The reader is a hunter in another's land. He is a poacher in the master's forest, pursuing his lost interests and desires. Faced with the printed page, the reader exercises his activity as a reader, just as the viewer in front of his television set reads the images in his own way. Perhaps millions of people are watching the same programme at the same time, but each person creates in his own coherent and superb way something different from everyone else.[86]

When De Certeau, along with other contributors, depicted popular culture in terms of its active manipulation of dominant culture, he was, of course, looking for ways of countering the vastly influential schemes of Pierre Bourdieu. It was, for instance, obviously Bourdieu who was being targeted by the editor Geneviève Poujol, when she invoked 'the inescapable determinism' of some

157

sociological treatments of popular culture. By this she clearly had in mind the idea that Bourdieu's work consigned the working class to an irredeemable position of inferiority in all aspects of their lives. It is, however, true that at least one of the contributors, Jean-Claude Barthez, refused to join in with the general rejection of Bourdieu, and indeed reiterated the central features of Bourdieu's characterisation of popular culture. According to Barthez, popular culture remained essentially the polar opposite of dominant culture, to which it stood in a relation of dependence and subjugation. Barthez followed Bourdieu in asserting that, if one wanted working-class people to achieve full dignity and full citizenship, they had to gain control of the social, linguistic and cultural codes of dominant culture. In order to help them achieve this end, it was, according to Barthez, imperative that intellectuals continued to think of popular culture in a political way. Barthez was, however, almost alone in putting forward this view in the volume *Les Cultures populaires*. Indeed, one of the most significant and striking features of this text is the way in which many of the contributors refused to identify popular culture with 'the people' (defined as the working class), and insisted that any valid definition of popular culture had to take into account a whole range of different cultural experiences and traditions.

The volume *Les Cultures populaires* can be fairly said to mark a significant development in French intellectuals' notions of popular culture. The text appeared at the end of a decade in which there had been intense interest in folk culture and regional culture. This interest contributed enormously to the growing awareness that definitions of popular culture and dominant culture had previously been based on limited and unitary concepts. In addition, the social and cultural landscape seemed to have changed so profoundly by the late 1970s that many of the contributors to the volume took it for granted that the older conception of popular culture as the mission to take high culture to a culturally impoverished working class, was no longer remotely applicable. Finally, ten years after 1968, the contributors followed the general pattern of rejection of militant notions of culture, and turned their attentions to 'microcultural', everyday activities as the defining features of popular culture. However, what did remain relatively unchanged in the attitudes of all the contributors was the traditional intellectual hostility to the mass media and consumer culture. Virtually all the contributors emphasised that an authentic popular culture could only be said to exist in so far as people escaped from, remained indifferent to, or actively resisted the malign influence of mass culture. Thus, we find Geneviève Poujol defining the boundaries of her conceptions of popular culture by insisting that it was most definitely not to be confused with mass culture:

> It seems impossible that a French academic could confuse mass culture with popular culture, as is still [*sic*] often the case with certain Anglo-Saxon academics.[87]

This deep-rooted antagonism to mass culture has been one of the most significant aspects of French intellectual attitudes to the question of popular culture throughout the modern period. Right up to the late 1970s one finds great resistance to mass culture and the mass media at almost every level, and in almost every sphere, of French intellectual and cultural life. Geneviève Poujol's statement, just quoted, also demonstrates quite clearly how she saw this resistance to mass culture as a distinctively French phenomenon. There seems little doubt that this resistance has been in large part due to the overriding importance traditionally attached in France to the values of literary high culture. But this resistance can also be explained by the profound significance that populist myths have had for French intellectuals. These myths have constantly led intellectuals to look to popular culture for signs of revolutionary opposition to dominant culture, or, more recently, for signs of difference and separateness from it. The idea that popular culture constituted its own autonomous sphere of resistance to mass culture was a much favoured notion in 1968, and one could see this in Michel de Certeau's *La Prise de parole*:

> Would it nowadays be a very reliable approach to equate the culture of television viewers with the kind of programmes that are made for them? This would be to confuse what is the expression of a local, and undoubtedly *different* experience, with the cultural system that is imposed upon it from on high, and the tendency of which is to eliminate, or more and more to marginalise it. Here again, and particularly in the analysis of 'popular culture', one can see how the intellectual frame of reference of an elite postulates in advance the result which will justify it.[88]

The legendary hostility of the 1968 protesters to the mass media and consumer society was not a new or isolated position within the French intellectual community. Previously, the whole popular culture and popular education movement had been united in its own attempt to create a popular culture separable from mass culture. The State itself had then come along to reinforce the attitudes of the popular culture movement, by claiming that true culture was to be encountered in the Maisons de la Culture, and not in front of a television screen. A truly major shift in the attitude of French intellectuals to the mass media was, therefore, needed before they could begin to look upon mass culture in a favourable way. One of the most significant indications that this shift had started to occur by the late 1970s and the early 1980s, was the fact that intellectuals began precisely to equate popular culture with mass culture – something that Geneviève Poujol, for instance, had found totally inconceivable only a few years before,[89] and something that almost none of the intellectuals that I have looked at so far in this study would have dreamed of doing in the years from 1936 to the late 1970s.

6

MASS CULTURE, POP CULTURE AND PLURALISM

In previous chapters I have set out the various meanings of the French term 'culture populaire' which had currency from at least 1936 to the late 1970s. Throughout these years there was a long-standing refusal on the part of French intellectuals to equate popular culture with mass culture. Since the late 1970s there has, however, occurred a very significant shift, and French intellectuals have become more and more willing to apply the term 'culture populaire' to the whole range of experiences offered by mass society and the mass media. A new generation of intellectuals has emerged which has gone beyond the high cultural, moral and political resistance to mass culture that had until quite recently been such a striking feature of French intellectual and cultural life. One only needs to look at the work of a young cultural historian such as Pascal Ory to see how the definition of the cultural field has been vastly widened to include forms which would previously not have been considered as worthy of inclusion in a cultural history of France.[1] Strip cartoons, science fiction, pop music, TV programmes – all seem to be acknowledged as entering into the cultural sphere. Those arts such as cinema and jazz, which not so long before had been seen by Bourdieu as only 'on the way to cultural legitimation', are now made to seem part of the long-accepted cultural heritage. The whole discourse of cultural democratisation, with its underlying notion of a deep aspiration to culture, and its accompanying preoccupation with providing access to high culture, seems to have lost most of its relevance in a world where culture – both high and popular – is abundantly and easily available on television and cinema screens, on transistor radios and personal stereos, in bookshops, and in cultural supermarkets such as the FNAC. What was the 1968 nightmare seems to have finally

161

turned into the accepted reality of the 1990s. There is no longer the missionary zeal to promote high culture, and, indeed, high culture could be said to have lost the aura of sacredness which in the past occasioned such a deferential respect for it.[2] Now it must take its chance in the market-place along with other cultural goods of very differing kinds. There is no longer even the guilt induced by the critique of consumer culture. Indeed, the consumerist model of cultural consumption holds sway and people cannot be intimidated or cajoled into choosing those allegedly higher quality products that others think good for them. Popular culture is now said to be quite simply what is 'popular', that is to say, what is chosen and liked, not by 'the People', but by the public.

Although the word 'popular' might always seem to have had the self-evident meaning of 'what is liked by a considerable number of people', a close study of the discourse of French intellectuals on culture has, in fact, shown that there has been the most enormous resistance to using the word in this way. This has clearly been due in large part to the determination of intellectuals to project their own tastes, preferences (and even fantasies) onto other people, rather than trying to find out, or rather than accepting what people actually did like. What now seems obvious is that people have, in fact, always liked what mass culture has had to offer them, and nothing has demonstrated the gap between popular and cultivated taste throughout the twentieth century as much as the distaste and contempt shown by generations of intellectuals to mass culture. This entrenched hostility of French intellectuals to mass culture has been considerably reinforced by their longstanding attitudes of aggression towards the United States, which they have traditionally seen as the true home of capitalist mass culture in all its vulgarity and exploitativeness. The very recent developments in France, where one has seen a widespread conversion of intellectuals to mass culture and witnessed the emergence of a class of 'branché' intellectuals, 'plugged in' to all that the modern media put on offer, have inevitably brought with them an almost total reversal of attitudes to everything American.[3] The review *Autrement* has been picked out for special comment in this respect. It has been cited as offering striking evidence of the trendy French metropolitan Left's abandonment of the revolutionary ideology of 1968, in favour of an enthusiastic endorsement of the style-conscious, media-dominated, Americanophile world as witnessed in the 1980s:

Those who now sing the praises of the new individualism were formerly 68 protesters, in fact Maoists, who found it all the easier to be converted to a love of all things American because they had never had any solid links with orthodox left-wing politics. Ensconced in the cultural pages of the *Nouvel Observateur*, or clustering around the review *Autrement*, they have followed the same path as American radicals of the Jane Fonda type. They have transformed their rebellious ideas into support for the spirit of initiative, individualism, sport and travel. The image of America that they promote is made up of a vague mixture of French dreams and imaginings, glimpses of fashionable aspects of the American scene, a good deal of Parisian snobbery, and a new cosmopolitanism based on status and its material trappings, rather than on ideas (see in particular the *Autrement* issues on California and New York). This Americanophilia is the expression of that craving for open spaces, novelty and freedom of action, which is to be found among the class of young executives who want to transcend the boundaries of 'little France'. These intellectual gurus, who go in for anything and everything American, have reversed the traditional contempt of the French for all things foreign, and have succeeded in making a religion out of whatever comes from America.[4]

In such a passage we are warned against looking to fashionable and fickle Parisian media intellectuals for the evidence of a new broadly based Americanised popular culture. However, although there is no doubt justice in this criticism of a certain type of intellectual, one must also recognise that a review such as *Autrement* represents, in fact, only one small instance of a widespread enthusiasm for American mass culture that is shared by French people at large (and particularly young people) and that is far from being the preserve of a trendy Parisian in-group. Indeed, the painful, self-questioning process which has seen intellectuals of older generations (including by now the participants in 1968) finally coming to accept mass culture as the new popular culture, is a process which is, of course, foreign to younger people, who are not likely either to have begun by attributing a sacred significance to high culture, or to have felt any need to resist the attractions of the mass media. Younger French people, in general, feel no such resistance to mass culture, and for decades they have been perfectly

163

at ease with it, and indeed have considered Anglo-Saxon rock and pop music and American cinema to be their own living culture.

Teenage popular culture, like television, had from the beginning been one of the principal targets of attack for the educationalists in the popular culture movement, as also for the protesters of 1968. The literature of the popular culture movement in the late 1950s and early 1960s is littered with complaints about the worthless new world of teenage culture and its moronic 'yé-yé' music. Jacques Charpentreau, for example, expressed acerbic views on what he saw as popular musical trash. In contrast to the new pop music, he stoutly defended the virtues of the 'intellectual' and 'literary' tradition of French song, and campaigned for forms of popular music that encouraged ethical awareness and civic responsibility.[5] The student revolutionaries of 1968 were also hostile to teenage culture – a fact which in itself casts an interesting light on the distance between their cultural tastes and those of their working-class contemporaries to whom they claimed to be so near. In fact, it has been pointed out that the students in 1968 had distinctly high cultural, or rather avant-garde aesthetic preferences.[6] When Bourdieu and Passeron did a study of the cultural tastes of eighteen high-flying young students in the early 1960s, they also discovered how highbrow they were:

> For all of them reading was their chosen form of leisure activity, and their preferences focused upon the same acknowledged group of avant-garde writers: Camus, Malraux, Valéry, Kafka, Proust. Eleven of them said they particularly liked classical music and theatre – cinema and jazz always ranking second in their preferences. Of course, they indignantly rejected any idea that Johnny Hallyday could be taken as representing contemporary youth, and they put Greece at the top of those countries they would like to visit. Thus each year the top young graduates display, in their future plans, those qualities celebrated by obituaries.[7]

During the events of 1968 the assault on consumer society and the mass media inevitably included an attack on teenage pop culture. The Situationists had already prepared the ground for this hostile attitude, and Vaneigem had pointed to the new youth culture as a quintessential example of how people were manipulated into becoming passive consumers in modern society:

Already the concept of 'teenager' is leading to a situation in which the buyer is identified with the product he buys, and in which potential choice is being reduced to a set range of consumer products (records, guitar, blue jeans . . .). One is no longer as old as one's heart or one's skin, but one is as old as the things one buys.[8]

For the 'enragés' of 1968, to be interested in the hit parade was a sure sign that one had been duped into accepting the culture marketed by the mass media, and that one was not concerning oneself with more important political questions.[9] According to the 'enragés', the events of 1968 had persuaded young people to embrace a purely political culture, and bourgeois society had become fearful that the young would now turn their backs on the pop singer Sheila and look in preference to Marcuse and Che Guevara.[10]

Emile Copfermann's text on French teddy boys[11] ['les blousons noirs'] offers a very good example of how leftist intellectuals in the early 1960s treated youth culture as just one other element within capitalist mass culture. Drawing on Friedmann's critique of the alienated nature of work in capitalist society, and also on the literature emanating from the popular culture movement (which spoke for the need to create a civic awareness in the new leisure culture), Copfermann portrayed the teddy boys as a pathetic case of a group of discontented, aimless youths who had been misled into accepting the roles set out for them by the new entertainment industry, and who had found an outlet for their underlying frustrations in meaningless acts of violence. As for rock and pop music, it was said merely to reinforce the teddy boys' inability to develop a genuinely useful and critical response to their situation, since it offered only a mindless, instantaneous and undemanding form of experience:

The fact that these predigested consumer products can be so easily picked up and made use of, further adds to their considerable attraction. The feelings of the songs with their sentimental and rhythmic tunes can be shared by the listeners without their having to make any effort themselves. One only needs to have a bit of feeling in order to love; one only needs a bit of rhythm to dance. It is the fact that the majority of people find these things so easy to do that explains the whole process of how mediocrity is producing a levelling-down effect in society.[12]

For Copfermann, French young people were joining the young people of the world in one anonymous mass of consumers who were part of a 'culture' that offered purely physical and materialistic experiences:

> The entertainment industry . . . begins by gratifying people's vague aspirations. On the basis of these it provokes artificial needs and then caters for them in abundance, thereby creating its own profits and, at the same time, producing a standardised effect. The youth of towns in Germany, Italy, England and France are all beginning to look the same. From their dress to their vehicles, from their dances to their drinks – give and take a few details – they represent one anonymous mass! How many Brigitte Bardots and how many 'Chaussettes noires'.[13]

However, despite this initial intellectual contempt for teenage culture, there did develop in the late 1960s and early 1970s a certain awareness that groups of disaffected youth such as the teddy boys might actually constitute some kind of serious opposition to bourgeois society. For instance, the Situationist Raoul Vaneigem temporarily wondered if the teddy boys, despite their apparent incorporation into consumer society, had not in reality succeeded in maintaining an authentic vitality which might grow into a true revolutionary consciousness and put them at the very centre of the destruction of capitalist society:

> I am thinking of the teddy boys. Their puerile will to power has often managed to preserve almost intact their will to live. Of course, the threat of 'recuperation' looms over the teddy boy: firstly in his capacity as consumer, because he ends up desiring the objects he does not have the means to buy; secondly, in his capacity as active agent, in so much as he is bound to grow older. None the less, for the moment the sense of risk inside teddy boy gangs is so acute that there is a chance that it will resolve itself into a revolutionary consciousness. If the playful violence inherent in gangs of young delinquents were to stop being expended in often ridiculous and 'spectacular' gestures, and were instead to turn into the poetry of rebellion, then this would no doubt cause a chain

reaction, a substantial shock wave. Most people are, in fact, acutely aware of their own desire to live authentically and reject restrictions and specific social roles. All it needs is a spark and an appropriate strategy. If the teddy boys ever manage to achieve a revolutionary consciousness, by simply discovering what they are, and demanding to be more than this, they will in all probability determine where the epicentre of the future revolution will be. To federate their gangs would be the one action which would both reveal this consciousness and also allow it to express itself.[14]

Intellectuals on the Left, therefore, were only willing to grant any value to the youth culture of the late 1950s and the 1960s, when they thought it offered a radical challenge to the status quo of bourgeois capitalist society. For the most part, however, they were happy to see youth culture as simply an integral part of a trivial and materialistic mass culture. Even since Copfermann's day there seems to have been very little intellectual or academic work done in France which could remotely be compared with the sophisticated analyses of popular culture and popular music that have been, for instance, such a characteristic feature of British cultural studies, where one typically finds that a radical critique of capitalist society has gone together with an intense empathy with the music and styles of youth culture.[15] In the early to mid-1970s there was some evidence that French intellectuals were becoming interested in the subcultural styles and practices of disaffected and rebellious young people. The very first number of the review *Autrement* in Spring 1975 was, in fact, devoted to this topic, and one finds in this issue, for instance, a sympathetic treatment of the updated versions of the teddy boys.[16] However, it seems fair to say that the kind of engaged, empathetic response to youth culture that one associates with British cultural studies somehow got lost in France between the period of the political rejection of rock and pop culture around 1968, and the euphoric period of pluralist embrace of all things popular that was to arrive in the late 1970s and persist through the 1980s. In this latterday enthusiasm for pop culture, it even became common for trendy French metropolitan intellectuals to claim that they had liked Eddy Mitchell all along, and that they themselves had eagerly participated in teenage pop culture.[17] Much of the intervening period after 1968 and until the late 1970s was one in which intellectuals were fascinated by the alternative, counter-cultural trends associated with folk, hippy and regionalist culture. This period, therefore, also marked yet another long moment when urban mass youth culture was stigmatised as false and alienated – this time when judged against allegedly more natural and earthy forms of culture.[18]

Although most French intellectuals seem from the beginning to have kept a superior and contemptuous distance from youth culture and pop culture, Edgar Morin represents an interesting case of an eminent figure who not only tried to understand youth culture, but also felt positively drawn towards it, and readily admitted to the liberation it could offer him. In 1967 Morin published a study of the changing nature of a Breton village community,[19] in the course of which he gave substantial consideration to the question of how the new youth culture was contributing to social and cultural change. In a remote, rural place like Plozevet, it was not so much a case of pop culture challenging a dominant high culture, nor even an older folk culture (neither of which, according to Morin, was in any case particularly alive in Plozevet). It was, rather, a question of a new adolescent culture trying to find ways of expressing itself (and places to do so) within a context where a 'traditional' adult pattern of collective popular sociability was rapidly giving way to a thoroughgoing domestication of social life:

> The national popular culture . . . cannot be dissociated from the public consumption of red wine. Everywhere in France, throughout the nineteenth century, the people developed their very own 'Maisons de la Culture' which were the bars and dance halls . . . . Like the bistros and taverns elsewhere, in the Bigouden region it is the little 'buvette' which is the autonomous institution of popular culture, and which stands outside the bourgeois world and beyond the control of the Church. The 'buvette' is a completely secular institution, which in its total rejection of hierarchy is redolent of communitarian and anarchist notions of equality, although it is also permeated by secret and mystical rituals of communication. The 'buvette' is the oasis, the concrete utopia of plebeian life.[20]

By the early 1960s the 'traditional' forms of popular culture such as the 'buvette' were already being relegated to a less important role, as social life became ever more centred upon the home and television. People were increasingly aspiring to achieve what Morin characterised as 'the bourgeois life-style – the fully equipped, comfortable domestic interior'.[21] Plozevet could be seen to be being inexorably drawn into national life and to be becoming an integral part of modern consumer society.[22]

Against this general background of social change, Morin focused on the new teenage culture in the chapter 'The old and the young'. At this point in time (1965) the teenagers of Plozevet were unanimous in wanting their own youth club which they could run themselves and where they could dance and play records. Morin promised to help them, and saw himself as someone who was accepted by the teenagers because he was not stuffy and authoritarian. No doubt we have here once again a further example of an intellectual's 'populist gesture'. What is more, as has usually been the case, the intellectual concerned refused to see it as such:

> As for myself, I was neither a moralizer nor a pedagogue nor an organizer; I liked these young people and I had no wish to influence them to take any particular direction. I was accompanied by young research workers who were as close to them as they were to me, and I was sufficiently unlike their idea of an adult to win their confidence. I was at one and the same time Captain Haddock (so nicknamed for my sailor's hat and for the beard I had then) to these Tintins and Quetzalcoatl to these clean-shaven youngsters – the protector of the autonomy of their movement.[23]
>
> I personified the model of the 'acceptable' adult: one who does not criticise, does not judge, understands enjoyment, and knows how to enjoy himself.[24]

Morin highlighted the way in which the adolescents' own youth club was, however, soon taken over by local adults, and integrated into the association 'Youth and Leisure' ['Jeunesse et Loisirs'], whose aim was to organise a variety of activities ranging from physical education and sport to the more cultural spheres of theatre, cinema and music. According to Morin, the more educational objectives of the 'animateurs' were an imposition of adult values on the adolescents' own desire for pure entertainment. However, he was also obliged to accept that the young of Plozevet did not really have any rebellious, anti-social instincts. Poking fun at his own 'lust for permanent revolution', he acknowledged that these particular young people did not live up to the subversive stereotype that he was tempted to project onto them. For instance, Marlon Brando was playing in *The Wild One* at the local Plozevet cinema at the time of Morin's sociological investigations, and although the film clearly impressed him, he recorded how it left the Plozevet adolescents unmoved and uncomprehending.[25] None the less, in his study of Plozevet teenagers, despite this tendency to project his own romantic fantasies onto the young, Morin in fact demonstrated a definite capacity to give a sympathetic account of their life and culture, even though they hardly corresponded to his own libertarian ideas, and even though they were in reality fully integrated into the provincial society that he himself found stifling and limited. What he did respond to, however, was the way in which youth culture, even in its 'integrated' forms, represented a desire for pleasure and fun, and an openness to mobility and change. Morin obviously regarded it as a very positive feature of youth culture that it challenged the puritanism and earnestness of an older militant culture solely preoccupied with political and educational goals:

> Adolescent entertainment seems like debauchery in the puritanical eyes of those numerous militants and teachers who have devoted their lives to the public good. More than just an opposition between work and entertainment, it becomes for them rather a conflict between public-spiritedness and selfishness, reason and madness.[26]

There seems no doubt that Morin sympathised with the adolescent quest to escape from the constrictions of a pedagogical and militant culture because, a generation earlier, he himself had escaped from the prison of his own communist, even Stalinist, past. In his *Autocritique* ['Self-criticism'], first published in 1959, Morin recounted the miserable years of his own blinkered acceptance of communist doctrine and of his toeing of the Party line. Above all he stressed the suffocating feeling of being trapped within the narrow-minded and programmatic culture of socialist realism, and of being cut off from the vital and open culture that was to be found outside the Party. When he actually found himself excluded from the Party in the early 1950s (because of an article he had published in *L'Observateur*), he suddenly experienced an exhilarating sense of complete liberation. He now felt his destiny as an intellectual lay henceforward in pursuing his critical work in a totally open culture alongside 'the unfrocked, the homeless, the cosmopolitan, the excluded'.[27] Morin's sympathetic treatment of youth culture – in both its mass cultural and countercultural forms – must, therefore, be seen against the background of his own political experience. He himself saw youth culture and counterculture as refreshing antidotes to the closed, sclerotic, gerontocratic world that he associated with communist culture. In his shrewd contemporary analysis of the events of 1968 he picked out the key element in that 'cultural revolution' as being a generalised youth revolt against authority and father figures.[28] In fact, he suggested that the new revolutionary struggle was now to be understood not in terms of a conflict between capital and labour, but rather as a battle between youth (liberty) and old age (authority).[29] A crucial aspect of this new challenge to authority was the rejection of obsolete communism in its Stalinist, Marxist-Leninist and Bolshevik forms. However, Morin deeply disapproved of what happened in 1968 in so far as it had also encouraged a resurgence of the dogmatic spirit which had been only too painfully familiar to him in his former communist existence:

> Intellectual terrorism endeavours to establish itself wherever revolutionary inspiration begins to weaken. The strict Marxist-Leninists proclaim the law of Althusser; Marxism (which is supposed to free people) becomes arrogant and intimidating; the Poujades of the intellectual world begin to shout very loud; the words 'revolution' and 'working class' become once again imbued with magical power; the Situationists start physically assaulting people – which they deem to be a poetic act (especially when it is several against one); all those involved in the world of art and literature – painters, actors, directors, writers and students – replay (this time in even more caricatural a form) the old story of a search for proletarian art, which inevitably ends in a few intimidating dogmas about art in the service of the revolution, or revolution in the service of art.[30]

Morin was, therefore, dismayed when libertarianism turned into another manifestation of fanatical intolerance. He severely criticised the 1968 'enragés' for regarding liberalism as a corrupt and hypocritical bourgeois doctrine. However, although Morin was fully aware of the extent to which May 68 had encouraged such a return to old-style rigorism, he none the less responded enthusiastically to the way in which youth had come forward and called into question all aspects of authority. In this more optimistic vein, he saw the events of 1968 as the sign that the future cultural revolution would be brought about by an alliance of students and intellectuals (yet another populist gesture) working inside or from the base of universities.

Morin was to respond even more eagerly to what he took to be the new youth cultural revolution, when he went to California in late 1969 and caught the end of the flower-power era. Here he felt exhilarated by the way in which the old, rigid, oppressive framework of conventional life was being broken down.[31] In Morin's eyes, the Californians he met in 1969 allowed him to take a critical distance from the ethos of intellectual life in France:

> I felt more strongly than ever to what degree life was despised by intellectuals in France . . . . The gap between ideas and life was obviously the norm among our intellectuals. Ideas were revolutionary, socialist, proletarian. But life was petit-bourgeois, institutionalised, mean, repetitive and self-centred.[32]

The stiflingly cerebral nature of French culture was for Morin part and parcel of a French puritanism whose inhibitions and constrictions only became fully evident when set against a new counterculture which accorded a priority to 'dance, play, tenderness, laughter'.[33] The 'puritanism' of French intellectual culture was intimately bound up in Morin's mind with the repressive nature of French political life, and this also he set against the new youth culture that he encountered in America:

> I am one of those people who see the activism of the party militant as reactionary. What is revolutionary is being militant in life – it is the commune and the new network of human, social and, indeed, economic relationships; it is the rock festival and the love-in.[34]

America offered Morin at this time the opportunity to cast off his intellectual, political and cultural inhibitions and join 'la grande fête' – life as one long festival. What is more, it also allowed him to give himself up guiltlessly to American mass culture and discover in the process the life-enhancing performances of their show-business stars:

> Yesterday evening, five uninterrupted hours of television. 'The Tom Jones Show', 'The Dean Martin Show', and even one or two other shows. And the evening before I had already seen 'The Dionne Warwick Show'.
> In all these shows there is nothing that grates, nothing that

is heavy or boring . . . . On the contrary, what one finds in them is a combination of a good deal of talent and hard work (all those rehearsals) together with an inspired kind of spontaneity – nothing like the stilted versions one meets with in France. There is no hint of effort in the pure and full voices of Dionne Warwick and Eartha Kitt. What a wonderful moment when these two sublime black dolls [sic] appear on stage. And what a feeling of euphoria when it is all so happy, apparently unforced, and everything is carried along by such natural talent.[35]

Morin had, however, been far more guarded than this in his major work on mass culture published in 1962, *L'Esprit du temps* ['The spirit of the age'].[36] At first glance this work seems to have been written in order to counter the traditional, entrenched resistance to mass culture to be found across all sections of the French intelligentsia.[37] Indeed, Morin began the work by saying as much in a very direct way:

Intellectuals consign mass culture to a subcultural Hell. Those with a 'humanist' point of view deplore the invasion of inferior cultural products . . . . Those with a right-wing attitude tend to regard mass culture as entertainment for helots, a plebeian form of barbarism. Those who are on the Left, and who have derived their ideas from vulgar Marxism, look upon mass culture as a kind of barbiturate (the new opium of the people), or as a deliberate form of mystification (capitalism is diverting the masses away from their real problems). Those who have developed a more profound Marxist analysis criticise the new forms of alienation to be found in bourgeois society: the alienation of man in his work now extends to his alienation in his consumer habits and in his leisure time . . . . No matter how different the origins of humanist, left-wing or right-wing contempt for mass culture, all parties judge it to be cultural junk, trash, or, as they say in the United States, kitsch. Even if we put to one side the question of value judgements, one still has to register the global resistance of the 'intellectual class' or the 'cultural class' to mass culture.[38]

Within the overall context of French intellectual attitudes to mass culture in postwar France, Morin's own self-conscious and self-critical approach can be seen to have been most exceptional.

He realised how French intellectuals experienced a crisis of identity when faced with a culture that they had not created and did not control. No longer could they play the role of cultural policemen, since it had become impossible to draw hard and fast rules about culture in a society where an undifferentiated pluralism was rapidly becoming the order of the day.[39] Morin was, therefore, attempting to explode the intellectual's smug and outdated confidence that he was in possession of a self-contained and superior culture. Morin felt he was himself in a particularly good position to do this, in that, unlike most of his kind, he considered he had an intuitive sympathy for, and understanding of mass culture:

> It is important that the observer participates in what he is observing. In a certain sense he has to like going to the cinema, putting a coin in a juke-box, playing slot-machines, following sport on radio and television, humming the latest song. He himself must be to some degree one of the crowd, whether at a dance, strolling along the streets or joining in games. He has to know this world without feeling an outsider. He has to like wandering about on the grand boulevards of mass culture. Perhaps one of the tasks of the modern Narodnik, eager as ever to 'go and meet the people', is to 'go and meet Dalida'.[40]

This nice final touch of ironic self-awareness placed Morin's own concerns within the long historical tradition of naïve populist attempts to understand and join the people. However, this does not diminish the importance of Morin's claim that mass culture could only be understood by those who relished its pleasures. Morin's initial aim in *L'Esprit du temps* was, therefore, to offer a positive reevaluation of mass culture. In fact, the volume soon turned into a standard critique of it. Whatever fertility of mind and range of reference Morin brought to the study of mass culture in *L'Esprit du temps*, his analyses came down in the end to the usual view of it as a culture that homogenises, standardises, simplifies, sentimentalises and so forth. Ultimately he saw the whole of mass culture as an industry which, in its many forms, produced dreams and myths of comfort, leisure, success, happiness and love – all of which were designed to 'integrate' people into capitalist society. Thus, for instance, when Morin observed that mass culture, as in the case of cinema,[41] had the power to draw people deeply into its imaginary world of sex and violence through processes of projection and identification,[42] he did not point out that this was arguably also a feature of the aesthetic experience offered by much of high culture. Instead, he saw it rather as capitalism's way of draining off potentially subversive drives, and of conditioning people all the more effectively to live standardised, stereotyped existences.[43]

Morin's treatment of mass culture would seem to resemble in certain key ways that to be found in Roland Barthes' celebrated text *Mythologies* (1957), a collection of essays on mass culture written in the years 1954–56. As with Morin, one of Barthes' aims seems to have been to challenge the dogmatic and complacent views of the educated and cultured classes, and to destabilise their fixed notions of high culture and mass culture. In his witty, paradoxical and attentive analyses of mass culture, Barthes seems on one level to have been seeking to grant it a value and a complexity equal to high culture. This can be seen in his attempts to show that the consumers of mass culture were capable of aesthetic responses every bit as sophisticated and disinterested as those normally associated with the audience for high culture. The famous example of his treatment of wrestling is an obvious case in point. Since wrestling has commonly been thought to be one of the most vulgar forms of entertainment, it was of course a particularly provocative gesture of Barthes to take it as his first example of the complex aesthetic status of an activity commonly regarded as the essence of cultural inferiority and illegitimacy. However, instead of heaping contempt upon the spectators at wrestling matches, and seeing them as ignorant dupes of a contest that was so obviously fixed, Barthes proceeded to compare them with the cultured audience of the prestigious cultural form of high theatre. He presented them as equally able to differentiate between art and reality, and equally able to delight in art as formal spectacle:

> There are people who think that wrestling is an ignoble sport. Wrestling is not a sport, it is a spectacle, and it is no more ignoble to attend a wrestled performance of Suffering than a performance of the sorrows of Arnolphe or Andromaque.[44]

As well as to wrestling Barthes turned to the music hall, and claimed to find there also the purest features of high art:

> In its most essential form variety is not simply a technique of entertainment, it is a condition of artifice (in the Baudelairean

sense of the term). To extract gesture from the sickly sweet pulp of repeated time, and present it in its superlative, definitive form, giving it a purely visual character, disengaging it from all causation, exploiting all its potential as spectacle and not as signification – such is the original aesthetic of music hall. The props (of trapeze artists) and gestures (of acrobats), detached from the viscosity of time (that is to say, both from any emotional or rational meaning), shine out as examples of pure artifice, which to a certain degree are reminiscent of the cold precision of Baudelaire's hashish visions of a world which has been completely purified of all spirituality precisely because it has renounced time.[45]

At one level, therefore, Barthes obviously felt the inadequacies of the binary opposition between high and low culture. In a later text, in fact, he welcomed the prospect that by adopting the idea of culture as 'différentielle et collective' – that is to say, 'plural' – one could be freed from those rigid cultural categories which have led people to set high culture against low culture and mass culture.[46] In reality, however, it would be quite wrong to think of Barthes as someone who in any important sense wanted to accord positive value to mass culture, or who thought of mass culture as existing with equal validity alongside high culture in an undifferentiated aesthetic field. The two cases of wrestling and music hall were, in any case, hardly representative of Barthes' general attitude to mass culture in *Mythologies*. He clearly saw these as essentially popular or working-class spectacles and for this reason he seems to have felt happy, like so many other French intellectuals before him, to make a dramatic populist gesture in their direction. According to Barthes, when French intellectuals dreamed of abandoning their condition as intellectuals, they did so by conjuring up fantasies of becoming like working men. For instance, in the essay 'Wine and Milk' Barthes claimed that when the intellectual drank red wine he felt he was himself actually taking on a proletarian identity:

Wine will deliver him [the intellectual] from myths, will remove some of his intellectualism, will make him the equal of the proletarian; through wine the intellectual comes nearer to a natural virility, and believes he can thus escape the curse that a century and a half of romanticism still brings to bear on the purely cerebral.[47]

What, however, French intellectuals have never been willing to do is, of course, to make a sympathetic gesture towards anything relating to the bourgeoisie – the traditional 'bête noire' of the French artistic and intellectual classes. If Barthes was ready to claim that popular spectacles such as wrestling and music hall achieved the disinterested and formal qualities of true art, he was certainly not prepared to say the same for bourgeois, or rather petit-bourgeois 'art forms'. What is more, since he considered the whole of mass culture to be an orchestrated expression of the petit-bourgeois ethos, it becomes obvious that, far from wanting to grant any status or value to it, he sought on the contrary to demonstrate that it was precisely an inferior, degraded form of culture. Unlike Morin, Barthes in no sense called into question his own situation as an intellectual, nor did he seek to make a populist gesture towards mass culture of the kind that one saw in Morin. There was obviously no chance that Barthes might think the appropriate cultural role of the intellectual was now to 'go and meet Dalida'! Nor for one moment did Barthes see himself as the kind of intellectual who was in a position to understand mass culture because he was part of it, and because like any other consumer he enjoyed taking his pleasures there. Despite the fact that Barthes claimed he himself experienced 'the contradictions of modernity'[48] and that he was not analysing mass culture from an Olympian point of view, it is obvious that he did not pretend to experience mass culture in the same way that others did. For Barthes, the challenge of mass culture was not, as it was for Morin, that it called into question the intellectual and the artistic status that separated him from, and made him different from the masses. On the contrary, Barthes was provoked by what he saw as the conformist, consensualist nature of mass culture into fighting against it, in the name of his own separateness and difference from 'the bourgeois Norm'.[49]

There is a distinct Marxist strain in *Mythologies*, and the essays can be seen as an attempt to show how the whole of mass culture is a capitalist mystification of social and cultural reality. According to Barthes, the mass media encouraged people to accept as 'natural' what was, in fact, merely a mythological reality, constructed in order to mask injustice and inequality and condition people into following the norms of bourgeois, capitalist society. However, rather than concentrating on the workers as the classic victims of capitalist mystification, Barthes focused on intellectuals, writers and artists, that is to say, those whose difference and otherness were considered dangerous and unacceptable by bourgeois society. A major aim of *Mythologies* was, in fact, to counter the specific assault of Poujade on intellectuals.[50] In the face of Poujade's contemptuous characterisation of intellectuals as airy-fairy, idle, overly cerebral, sterile and weedy creatures, Barthes put up a determined defence not only of the right to difference and otherness,[51] but also of the intrinsic virtue of the intellectual's critical perspective and of the sceptical gaze that the intellectual directed upon society.[52] In Barthes' view, to desire to identify onself with the mass of other people ('to find salvation by joining with the majority of French people, the 'common herd' whose numerical superiority is set against the lassitude of 'distinguished' intellectuals'), would have been to want to abandon one's historic task as an intellectual – namely, that of 'decomposing bourgeois consciousness'.[53] Since mass culture constituted one enormous project to neutralise all potential sources of difference and disorder and to integrate these into the cosy world of petit-bourgeois stereotype and prejudice, it had to remain the duty and the desire of the intellectual to resist such pressures and remain a free, subversive agent.

One of the aspects of mass culture mythology that obviously filled Barthes with particular disgust was the way it promoted the life of the petit-bourgeois married couple as the ideal form of human relationship. His essay 'Conjugales', for instance, revealed his remorseless contempt for the domestic dreams of everyman and everywoman. Such dreams were clearly for Barthes a grotesque parody of human possibility:

The marriage of Sylviane Carpentier, Miss Europe 53, to her childhood friend, the electrician Michel Warembourg, is a pretext for the elaboration of the image of the happy little home. Thanks to her title, Sylviane could have had a brilliant career as a star. She could have travelled, made films and earned lots of money. Instead, being sensible and modest, she gave up 'temporary fame' and, staying true to her past, she married an electrician from Palaiseau. The young married pair are now presented to us after their wedding in the process of setting themselves up in their anonymous, comfortable little home and getting down to their happy routine: they are sorting out their two-room flat, taking breakfast, visiting the cinema, going off to market. Here one can see how the life of the couple is being presented as such a natural and wonderful thing, and is being used to promote the petit-bourgeois style of life. But it is the fact that this intrinsically paltry ideal of happiness could be consciously chosen which will make millions of French people who share the same condition feel happy and justified.[54]

This small example is enough to indicate that Barthes was obviously never going to sing the praises of everyday life, nor was he going to extend any profound sympathy for 'ordinary' people as they performed their customary rituals and routines. He was, of course, attacking here the way in which the media and the powers that be used people for their own political purposes, but Barthes' unashamed contempt for these 'ordinary' lives was in reality an essential element in his critique. It was not only in his capacity as demythologising intellectual or as refined aesthete, that Barthes felt such horror for ordinary lives. It seems that it was also in his capacity as a homosexual that he experienced a distaste for the cloying sentimentality and the meagre pleasures that he associated with the ordinary heterosexual couple. Being outside heterosexual society (or, as he would have it, consensualist, conformist, petit-bourgeois society) presumably allowed him, in his view, to carry out his critical, subversive tasks, as a writer and an intellectual. Being a homosexual, moreover, also offered him, in his opinion, a constantly changing, exciting and more intense range of pleasures than was open to heterosexual couples:

> The potential for enjoyment that follows from a perversion (in this instance, that of the two H's: homosexuality and hashish) is always underestimated. The Law, the Doxa, Science do not want to understand that perversion, quite simply, *makes you happy*; or to be more precise, it creates a plus: I am more sensitive, more perceptive, more loquacious, more capable of being entertained etc . . . – and in this *plus* there comes to reside difference.[55]

Heterosexuality was the condition of the mass of others and, like the Doxa, it limited human possibility by confining people within rigid, conformist structures. On the other hand, homosexuality was said to allow for an infinity of special, individual pleasures. The restrictiveness of heterosexual mass society was replaced by the freedom of a 'plural' society in which individual pleasure was not subject in any way to the pressures of the group.[56] For Barthes 'pluralism' was not therefore – as it came to be for many commentators – a democratic concept that acknowledged the otherness, and the right to existence, of different social, sexual and ethnic groups. It was, rather, a deeply individualistic notion that allowed for infinite possibilities of 'dispersion' and 'multiplication'.[57] In other words, pluralism in Barthes' sense was certainly not intended to lead to another humanism. Difference and otherness were not to be acknowledged, simply to be enclosed once again within the confines of a broader notion of human collectivity:

> A pluralist philosophy is emerging. It is hostile to the process of massification, and its tendency is towards difference. It is ultimately Fourierist in kind. Such a philosophy imagines a society which would be divided up into infinite individual elements, but these would not be social divisions, and therefore would not be in conflict with each other.[58]

Barthes' radically individualistic notions of plurality differ considerably from the broadly humanist concepts of pluralism that were to come to the fore in the writings of many French cultural commentators in subsequent years. For instance, Jean-Pierre Colin in *La Beauté du manchot: culture et différence* (1986) ['The beauty of the one-armed man: culture and difference'] has shown how the notion of difference was taken up by the State in the early 1980s as a major focus of socialist cultural policy.[59] Colin worked in Jack Lang's Ministry of Culture and had special responsibility for cultural development in such previously neglected areas as the army, hospitals and prisons, although he himself seems to have been principally involved with the disabled. In Colin's view, this concern for a whole range of newly identified marginal and repressed groups was evidence that socialist cultural policy was still pursuing its original aim of opening up cultural life to those individuals and groups that had formerly been excluded from it.[60] However, this new socialist interest in minority groups was also founded on a recognition that the old socialist cultural discourse had to abandon its exclusive concern with the working class. What is more, Colin acknowledged that modern socialism had to let go of its revolutionary Marxist pretensions and return to a more broadly-based humanist tradition which worked for the well-being of all categories of under-privileged people.[61]

Colin was fully aware that this return to humanism marked an explicit break with all those many anti-humanist tendencies which had come to dominate left-wing intellectual approaches to politics and culture and which had been particularly prominent in the late 1960s and early 1970s.[62] For Colin, 'the right to difference' was the basis of a new humanism, and he did not accept that to proclaim and support this right in any way threatened the solidarity and unity of the French nation. He did, however, recognise that there was no socialist unanimity on this matter, and pointed to those Socialists who resisted the development towards multiculturalism and who still insisted on the continuing importance of a national secular education system as the best means of creating a unified culture, and a unified people.[63] In Colin's view, the future of France lay not only in accepting, but also in actively embracing cultural diversity. Since France had so evidently become a multicultural nation, it was essential that French people transcended their fear of others and recognised their rights. What is more, it was vital that people should be willing to accept that the culture of France would inevitably be transformed under the influence of all the new cultural groups which were pressing for their own culture to be granted full status. According to Colin, only if the French State, and French people in general, showed themselves ready and able to welcome these changes, could France look forward to a secure and stable future:

> In the France of 1981 the groups of people who want to press their own individual case regarding the exercise of their rights, particularly in the cultural sphere, are legion. Simplifying somewhat, it seems to me that there are three basic demands here which are connected to each other, contradict each other and encroach upon each other, but which in the end come together in the central question which faces not so much the institution of State as society in general: *do you accept difference?* Do you admit that, at the moment of time in which we are now living, man can freely exercise his cultural rights in the most important sense of the term? Are you prepared to see everything change before your eyes, including the most sacred heritage – that of the Nation? But is not this the only way the Nation will once again find its dynamism, and perhaps will manage to survive in a world totally taken over by the process of standardisation?[64]

In this final characterisation of the modern world as one in which everything conspires to produce standardisation, one recognises the persistence of the 68 spirit within Langian cultural policy. Indeed, Colin explicitly acknowledged the crucial role played by the events of 1968 in promoting the desire for self-expression and the quest for cultural identity.[65] In his concern to press for the rights of underprivileged and repressed minority groups, Colin felt the need to attack the two chief targets of 1968 – the State and the media. These he still saw as guilty of imposing uniform cultural standards on people, and of not permitting the expression of a diversity of cultural views within their institutions. On the other hand, according to Colin, the living popular culture of today – that of young people – was one that had fully embraced ethnic differences. The key area of popular music demonstrated this beyond any doubt, and in Colin's eyes this was evidence of the emergence of a more democratic and humanist culture:

> From reggae to the music of the Far East, and not forgetting African and Arab music, the youth of many countries are today demanding the right to get to know other cultures intimately, and to share in them. In a world threatened by war and violence this offers great hope. In our opinion, minorities of all kinds have their own role to play within this movement towards a genuinely 'hybrid culture'.[66]

Although the notion of a 'hybrid culture', in Colin's sense, seems to give priority to the question of ethnic diversity, he was, in fact, trying to emphasise that all minority groups could enrich national culture by offering their own distinctive contribution. In Colin's judgement, it was Jack Lang who was truly 'the harbinger of different cultures'.[67] It was Lang who was willing to accept the validity of what every group had to offer, and who refused to use hierarchical, traditional, conformist norms of culture as a way of excluding what had previously been perceived as inferior, but which, it was now recognised, had been excluded simply because it was different. Lang was, therefore, always ready to give State support to cultural activities that had no traditional cultural legitimacy. Not least of these were such quintessential mass cultural forms as rock 'n' roll and strip cartoons.[68] In providing State funding for such popular cultural forms, however, Lang believed he was still working within the established tradition of socialist cultural objectives, even though it was now less a case of providing access to high culture than of supporting a whole diverse range of cultural practices:

> Jack Lang is the driving-force behind a cultural policy which operates on all fronts and in all directions. It covers all areas of

creativity (even including gastronomy, fashion and the furniture industry). It always attempts to reach as many types of people as possible, and gives those who want it the means to express themselves . . . . The governing idea is, indeed, that of a reduction of cultural inequality through the intervention of the public authorities . . . . What is original in the Minister's programme is that he is ready to take on board new forms of expression that are very popular with the young, and in so doing he is giving them a legitimacy in adult eyes that they did not have previously, and for the first time he is prepared to provide financial help.[69]

Colin rejected any suggestion that Lang's cultural policy led, as his many critics and political opponents have claimed, to a superficial and indiscriminate form of cultural pluralism, or to an acceptance of the show-business values of the media.[70] In fact, he emphasised that Lang's cultural policy was deeply humanist in its readiness to accord full dignity and validity to all marginal and repressed groups, and in its refusal to exclude these groups by applying to them the destructive norms of the dominant culture. To make this claim truly convincing, Colin did not choose to take the case of youth and mass culture, but focused instead upon the way society dealt with the disabled. In Colin's view, the disabled were a group who were still genuinely excluded from national culture, and who were still experiencing indifference, neglect and even cruelty at the hands of the dominant culture. In seeking to help the disabled, therefore, the Socialists could continue to present their cultural policy as a heroic moral mission whose purpose was to fight for justice and equality in the cultural sphere on behalf of those who were still suffering deprivation, exclusion and repression. Taking a longer historical view, Colin related the situation of the disabled in modern France to that of Breton children of an earlier period who, because of their different language, had from the time of the Third Republic been treated in a most brutal and insensitive fashion by the State education system. The particular contemporary example chosen by Colin was that of deaf people who for many years had not been allowed by the educational authorities to use sign language:

Sign language has been practically *forbidden* in the country which gave birth to it, and it remains today widely prohibited in numerous educational institutions. This astounding prohibition goes back to the establishment by the State of an obligatory school system at the beginning of the Third Republic. It was at this period that those in favour of oral communication (the oralists) were successful in imposing their pedagogical views. They only allowed the children to learn the spoken language. This, of course, never led to anyone speaking it properly, and in any case the language was never heard, but was only read on the lips of other people. Learning the spoken language was supposed to guarantee the integration of deaf children into the national community, whereas, because it was different, sign language was alleged to cut them off from it. This was the period when the Breton language was prohibited in schools. Indeed, until the Second World War the child who was caught speaking his mother tongue in the playground was subjected to official punishment. A clog would be tied to his arm until he denounced the friend he was talking to. The oralists behaved in much the same way. They tied together the hands of those children caught communicating with each other through sign language. This same refusal to accept difference is highly symbolic. There is no connection between the fact of hearing Breton in the mouth of one's parents and that of being born deaf, other than this determination of a centralised State to annihilate all differences – except, of course, differences in social situation – so as to ensure the perfect working of the republican system.[71]

By this example one can seen how the Socialists have come to look upon their cultural policies, with their new stress on 'difference', as playing an important part in a general 'humanist' project. In the view of contemporary Socialists, one is most definitely not forced to abandon humanist perspectives because one has challenged and extended traditional and conventional definitions of culture. Neither, for that matter, is one obliged to give up ideas of national community because one has rejected monolithic definitions of 'the Nation'. In fact, by insisting on the essentially 'humanistic' quality of their cultural policies, the Socialists try precisely to push back the boundaries of people's notions of culture and the Nation, while at the same time making sure that their discourse remains within the mainstream tradition of the rhetoric of cultural democratisation, which has itself always been characterised by its attachment to humanist values.[72] In recent years in France, however, there have also been some notable critics who have refused to share the optimistic faith of the Socialists, and who, indeed, have insisted that modern culture, even in its State-promoted forms, cannot be made to fit within a humanist frame of reference. The Georges Pompidou Centre, more commonly known as Beaubourg, has been cited by such critics as a crucial case in point. Beaubourg can, with some justice, be seen as the quintessential modern State cultural institution in France. It was intended to embody the new, open, pluralist cultural policies of the French State, which in this instance happened to be in the hands of the Gaullists and not the Socialists. In his study of Beaubourg, *L'Enjeu du Centre Georges Pompidou* (1976), ['The challenge of the Georges Pompidou Centre'], Claude Mollard emphasised the extent to which the Centre, although it might have appeared to mark a dramatic shift in policy, was, in fact, thought of by the State as simply a logical continuation of the project of cultural democratisation.[73] According to Mollard, the State accepted that much had changed in the cultural sphere since 1968, and indeed conceded that the cultural revolution of 1968 had itself contributed in a positive sense to these changes. Consequently, Mollard refused to agree with those who simply saw Beaubourg as an institution that had been specifically designed to 'recuperate' the 68 style of cultural activity:[74]

Beaubourg was denounced as useless, as a State strategy to take over and defuse all the popular cultural activities that had grown up in the wake of 1968 – in brief, it was denounced as a prestigious and grandiose operation mounted by the Authorities, as a way of countering the spontaneous, joyful and popular cultural activity that had developed in the Baltard pavilions.[75]

For Mollard (who was Secretary General of the Centre), there was, however, nothing remotely sinister and repressive about Beaubourg. Far from killing off the true spirit of 1968, and using a watered-down, controllable version of it for State purposes, Beaubourg was a genuine response to the 1968 demand that culture should be a form of 'everyday practice' and involve new and more open forms of human interaction.[76] A major aim of Beaubourg, in fact, was to facilitate through its architectural design natural and easy modes of human communication. It attempted to bring into being a completely new idea of what a modern museum and cultural institution ought to be – namely a place where the public was accepted as 'king of the domain'.[77] No longer should such a place be closed, stuffy and elitist. It should on the contrary, be a truly democratic centre, available to everyone. A modern museum such as Beaubourg should rid itself of the sacred aura of a cultural temple, and try to be more like a department store in which everyone felt free to enter and move around.[78] There should be a total and unimpeded interaction between the building and the 'quartier', between the street, the piazza and the foyer.[79] Above all else, it ought to be fun and proclaim its belief that 'dreary culture is dead'.[80] For Mollard, therefore, Beaubourg was an imaginative way of carrying out a truly 'popular cultural policy',[81] that is to say, of furthering the ambition of facilitating access to culture for vast numbers of people, and not least for the working class, since, as Mollard stressed, a working-class district of Paris had been deliberately chosen as the site for the Centre.[82] Beaubourg was designed to be an institution which would not intimidate people, which they would happily come into, and which would give them the feeling that culture was a lively and amusing part of everyday life:

> There will be constant interchange between the Centre and the surrounding 'quartier', which will be partly converted into a pedestrian precinct, and which will be linked to the Centre by an embankment which must not be a dreary esplanade, but a place where people meet, gather together and enjoy themselves – a focus of constant movement and life. There will be a perpetual sense of being swept along by the circulation of the public, who will be visible through the glass walls as they are attracted inside from the square and carried up by the constantly ascending escalators in one rising column. The enormous façade will offer a picture of incessant life and gaiety, and it will also be able to serve as a screen reflecting day by day all the spectacles that are going on in the world.[83]

The most notorious critic of Beaubourg at the time of its opening was Jean Baudrillard, who has since been much vaunted as a postmodernist commentator on mass society and mass culture.[84] In *L'Effet Beaubourg: implosion et dissuasion*, published in 1977 soon after the opening of the Georges Pompidou Centre, Baudrillard countered the optimism of the rhetoric of cultural democratisation as it had been applied to Beaubourg, and offered instead a bleak and Satanic portrait of the institution as symbol of the death of culture. In the immediate aftermath of 1968, and within the context of his critique of mass consumer society, Baudrillard had, in fact, already pronounced the death of traditional high culture.[85] In his opinion, high culture had become just a part of consumer society and was indistinguishable from mass culture itself.[86] In a world of constant change and movement, where reality had been exchanged for its representation on the television screen, and where experience had simply become the vicarious consumption of images offered by the media, there was no longer any room for the old humanist culture which claimed to embody permanent and profound aesthetic and moral values. According to Baudrillard, anyone who still held on to ideas of humanist high culture was a dinosaur in the modern world. This was as true of the autodidact who had been the heroic outsider of the cultural world, bravely battling all his life to acquire the supreme prize, as it was of the genuinely cultured person who allegedly represented the humanist ideal which everyone aspired to imitate.[87] In his text on Beaubourg, Baudrillard continued his miserabilist portrait of a society taken over by mass culture, and he added an apocalyptic evocation of a world evacuated of all meaning, hurtling towards barbarism and destruction. According to Baudrillard, Beaubourg did not have the courage of its own lack of convictions. Its architecture was a spectacular acknowledgement that the modern world was all process and no product, endless movement to no purpose, gaudy show without inner substance. In Baudrillard's opinion, the logic of Beaubourg's architecture was that it should as a museum contain nothing.[88] Instead of which, the corpse of traditional high culture and, what is worse, the corpse of avant-garde culture (which had long lost its power to shock or transform) were to be endlessly laid out in this new museum space for the necrophiliac hordes to come and see. The deeply black joke for Baudrillard was that what was claimed by the State to be the democratic cultural institution par excellence, the main purpose of which was to satisfy the people's alleged need and desire for culture, was in reality a mausoleum to which the masses flocked in order to spit on the dead body of culture:

One has to begin by accepting the obvious truth: Beaubourg is a *monument of cultural dissuasion*. This new museum presents itself in such a way as to try and salvage the humanist myth of culture, but in truth what one is witnessing in Beaubourg is the death of culture, and in reality the masses are blithely being invited to come along and help mourn its passing. And they come in their hordes. That is the supreme irony of Beaubourg: the masses come thronging in, not because they are drooling over the idea of having access to culture – of which they have supposedly been deprived for centuries – but because, for the first time, they have in their thousands the opportunity to join in a massive act of mourning over a culture which they have basically always loathed.[89]

According to Baudrillard, therefore, Beaubourg was living proof of the folly and futility of the attempt to offer culture to the masses. All those multitudes of people who bore down upon Beaubourg did not, in any way, prove the success of a policy of cultural democratisation, since they did not come for the reasons that the policy-makers had hoped. Like all those people who rush to the scene of catastrophes, they were simply a prey to the herd instinct. They were, according to Baudrillard, a mindless mass of human matter being fed through a factory process. Warming to his subject, he gleefully evoked the prospect of the whole structure of Beaubourg buckling under the strain of the heaving crowds. Indeed, he pictured it being brutally vandalised by all those visitors who had no interest in 'looking, deciphering, learning', but who, like all masses, manhandled and destroyed whatever happened to be in their path. At Beaubourg the traditional, elitist sanctuary of art had truly been taken by storm and desecrated. In reality, however, this gives too purposive an idea of popular behaviour for Baudrillard. He did not think of the masses as made up of individual agents acting out of any deeply held views or beliefs. Rather, he saw them as primitive, mindless units moving around in a mechanical fashion. For this reason he preferred not to attribute to them even consciously aggressive intentions. He imagined Beaubourg not as being destroyed by anything that might resemble the mythical insurrectionary action of 'the people', but simply as 'imploding' under the pressure of its own overloaded circuits.

Jacques Rigaud has responded to Baudrillard's Satanic, apocalyptic portrayal of culture in mass society with sanguine good humour. Refusing to be deflected from his own continued faith in the worthwhileness of a policy of cultural democratisation, Rigaud has insisted on seeing Beaubourg as one of the undeniable successes of State cultural policy:

> It is true that the peasants from the Rouergue and the miners from Hénin-Liétard are not to be seen there every day. But, viewed overall, the Pompidou Centre cannot be regarded as one of those places of cultural intimidation which are reserved for the initiates of bourgeois culture . . . and it is clear that the Beaubourg public is truly the public, and a young one to boot.[90]

In Rigaud's judgement it was, therefore, impossible to deny that Beaubourg was quite simply 'popular'.[91] In being willing to assert this so confidently and so unapologetically, one can see how Rigaud was intent on showing that he was fully prepared to regard as 'popular' whatever was liked, chosen or practised by large numbers of people. Rigaud's short essay on Beaubourg is, in fact, only one small instance of a widespread determination in modern France to put forward a positive interpretation of mass society, and one which rejects the pessimistic analyses of postmodernist commentators, as well as the Marxist critiques of consumer society that had such currency in 1968 and afterwards. From Rigaud's perspective, Baudrillard was not only expressing extremely reactionary views when he attacked Beaubourg, he was also repeating the outdated ideas of 1968:

> The case against consumer society, as it was formulated around 1968 (and in which Baudrillard was one of the sincere if rather belated witnesses for the prosecution when he wrote his book in 1977) was quickly dropped, and now seems very out of date in relation to other dangers and other more important issues. It is not Beaubourg which has imploded, but the ideas of those who challenged Beaubourg in the name of some kind of spontaneist new culture.[92]

Rigaud was not, however, being quite honest in claiming that Baudrillard's analyses of mass culture had a very outmoded quality about them. He himself in fact conceded at one point that Baudrillard seemed to have hit on an essential truth when he detected a hollowness in the behaviour of those who tramped through Beaubourg. Other postmodernist cultural commentators, as well as Baudrillard, have also pointed to a void at the centre of modern mass society, but rather than following Baudrillard and seeing this as a cause for lamentations over the mindlessness and meaninglessness of mass culture, some of these commentators have come to interpret this 'void' in a far more optimistic and positive sense. One finds this, for example, in a very characteristic text such as Gilles Lipovetsky's *L'Ere du vide. Essais sur l'individualisme contemporain* (1983) ['The age of the void. Essays on contemporary individualism']. In *L'Effet Beaubourg*, Baudrillard presented the masses as having finally escaped the repressive control of dominant culture and as having surfaced in the form of a barbaric and destructive force. In *L'Ere du vide* Lipovetsky also saw dominant culture as having lost its ability to repress and discipline people, but, unlike Baudrillard, he considered this to be a major and positive development towards the achievement of greater individual freedom. One of the most striking and revealing features of Lipovetsky's text is that, given its exclusive stress on the individual nature of modern society and culture, he could obviously barely bring himself to use the adjective 'popular' at all, since this would have clearly risked giving the impression that individuals might have common tastes and common practices. Rather than 'mass culture' or 'popular culture', Lipovetsky now preferred, therefore, to talk of a 'personalised culture' ['culture personnalisée'].[93] People were not, for Lipovetsky, the frightening, mindless brutes that one encountered in the analyses of all those who articulated a pessimistic critique of mass society. Nor were they the homogeneous members of a collectivity called 'the People', beloved of patriots and the Socialists and Communists of old. People were now simply individuals, liberated at last from 'the disciplinary – revolutionary – conventional order' which had held total sway over them until recently. Modern individuals were now free to follow their own desires and make their own choices in a society where the whole social, political and institutional order was in the process of adjusting itself to these profound changes. According to Lipovetsky, the 'void' at the centre of this new utopia was to be explained by the fact that these modern individuals held no fixed beliefs, had no deep attachments and lived by no established codes. Humorous and flexible, they were perfectly adjusted to living their lives against the constantly changing backdrop of mass consumer society. They felt no anxiety that their lives were not guided or controlled by any overarching religious, philosophical, moral or political imperatives. Neither did they feel the need to have an ultimate goal towards which they were working. On the contrary, they were completely at ease in their unchecked hedonistic quest for immediate self-realisation. For Lipovetsky, postmodern society was a pluralist society in which each individual was free to create his own separate and different existence, and in which the quest for personal autonomy did not encroach upon the liberty of others. It hardly needs to be stressed that, according to Lipovetsky, modern society had lost all the 'antagonism' essential to Marxist ideas of social relations. If anything, people were now 'indifferent' to each other, as they pursued their own individual ends. At the centre of Lipovetsky's account was his conviction that the old political world of ideological commitment and sacrifice of the self to a grand cause had gone for ever. In political or civic terms, people were now only concerned when their own private individual sphere was affected.

In the specifically cultural sphere, Lipovetsky noted the coming of the age of self-service culture, in which individuals were free to make their own cultural choices from an infinitely various range of possibilities. No longer was one's own personal taste in culture, and one's own access to culture, guided or controlled by political or educational intermediaries. The modern individual did not need, nor would he take kindly to, any form of authoritarian intervention in his cultural tastes and choices, for he desired to become himself a fully-fledged cultural practitioner:

The modern age was obsessed with production and revolution. The postmodern age is obsessed with information and expression. Now people are said to be expressing themselves in their work, in social relations, in sport, in leisure – so much so that there soon will not be any activity that is not graced with the label of 'cultural'. Culture is no longer an ideological discourse, it is a mass aspiration, the latest manifestation of which is the extraordinary proliferation of free radio stations. Now we are all disc jockeys, presenters and 'animateurs': just switch on your FM radio, and you are seized by a flood of intimacies, of people finding a platform for their own cultural, regional, local, neighbourhood, school, minority group point of view. This represents an unprecedented democratisation of speech: everyone is encouraged to ring the switchboard; everyone wants to say something on the basis of his private experience, everyone can get on the airwaves and be listened to.[94]

The time when it was a question of enabling the masses

191

to gain access to the great cultural works is now in the past and has been superseded by a spontaneous and very real democratisation of artistic practices.[95]

Far from resisting the mass media, the modern individual enjoyed a guiltless and endless relationship with it. Moreover, Lipovetsky completely refuted the contemporary relevance of 1968 attacks on mass culture, since he did not consider that it was a system of indoctrination that produced passivity in its consumers. On the contrary, he saw mass culture as 'seducing' individuals, that is to say, as offering them something which they, as individuals, genuinely desired and which they judged would contribute to their 'well-being, freedom and self-interest'.[96] In fact, Lipovetsky stressed that contemporary French society was to be understood specifically in terms of the degree to which it had been fundamentally transformed since the political agitation of the late 1960s. In his view, class consciousness and political consciousness had completely given way to narcissism and hedonism. In this new situation, culture was no longer to be thought of as a moral, political or aesthetic imperative, for it had now become simply just another hedonistic possibility which individuals were free to take or leave. Least of all was culture what it had been for Bourdieu – a key factor in the struggle for symbolic dominance. According to Lipovetsky, modern individuals were not engaged in a competitive struggle against each other. Rather, they sought their own individual ends with a lack of concern for other people. In addition, the world of culture, aesthetics and style, like every other area of modern life, had become a plural, undifferentiated world characterised by peaceful coexistence.[97] There were no longer any ideal forms held up as supreme and universal models to imitate. Nor were there any strict criteria or conventions which one felt obliged to follow. In any case, styles and tastes changed so rapidly that no fixed system of distinction could possibly operate. What is more, the world of culture, fashion and style was based on humour, and individuals were more concerned to play with conventions and develop their own idiosyncratic 'look', rather than slavishly obey notions of good taste, or worry whether they had come up to some fixed standards of distinction:[98]

The humorous code has no affinity whatsoever with middle-class savoir-vivre and its preoccupation with tact and elegance. On the contrary, it is totally mixed up with the language of the street and constantly indulges in the familiar and the casual. The idea of a struggle between social classes for symbolic dominance is of very little help in explaining a phenomenon whose origin is to be found in the general revolution of life style, and not in the competition for distinction and prestige. Far from being a means of conferring cultural nobility, the humorous code evacuates all the meaning from those signs of distinction and respectability that belonged to a former age, and subverts all previous systems of hierarchy and precedence by bringing everything down to the same informal level of relaxed equality, which is henceforth set up as a cultural value . . . . In reality, the humorous code works towards a loosening-up of all signs, and removes from them all the weight of their seriousness. The humorous code is, therefore, truly a force which democratises discourse by relieving it of its substance and playfully neutralising it. But this process of democratisation owes less to egalitarian ideology than it does to the success of consumer society which extends individualist passions, induces a desire in the masses to live freely and in the here and now, and at the same time undermines all forms of strictness.[99]

In Lipovetsky's view, therefore, culture was not, as it had been for Bourdieu, something that people had diligently to study and understand in order to prove they were every bit as good as the next person. According to Lipovetsky, the world of culture had totally changed since the time of the 1950s and early 1960s when Bourdieu had developed his ideas. Lipovetsky did not even consider that there was now one privileged sphere of high culture in which people needed to be initiated. One can take Lipovetsky's attitude to Beaubourg as an example of his general ideas upon culture. Although Bourdieu had wanted to make museums less stuffy and more accessible to users, he had still considered that their central purpose was the educational one of teaching a body of knowledge relating to a circumscribed and prestigious area of art. For Lipovetsky, on the other hand, a museum's primary purpose was quite simply to provide fun, and not, as it had been for Bourdieu, to contribute to the education service's aim of creating fully cultured people. Lipovetsky judged Beaubourg to be a great success, because he saw it as the first important museum not only to have recognised that humour lay at the centre of modern culture, but also to have acknowledged that the museum itself should be a gadget with which people would want to play. In general, therefore, Lipovetsky insisted on drawing a thoroughly positive and optimistic portrait of modern mass culture, which he saw as offering freedom, choice and fun to individuals. As a writer for the influential journal *Le Débat* and for the Beaubourg house journal *Traverses* – most of *L'Ere du vide* appeared originally in these two periodicals – Lipovetsky was developing an analysis of contemporary society which was highly congenial to progressive liberals and social democrats in France who were keen to show that they were ready to take all aspects of modern culture on board, and thereby demonstrate that they were going to have no truck with stuffy, traditional, elitist values. Above all, such groups wanted to make it clear that they had rejected what they saw as the dogmatic, puritanical and repressive heritage of the Left which to them now seemed outdated and bankrupt. In fact, Lipovetsky's euphoric portrayal of the modern individual as some-one who availed himself freely of the multiple pleasures offered by mass culture, has to be understood in terms of his characterisation of French people as having previously been dominated by cultural and political authoritarianism and rigorism.

Another writer for *Le Débat* who has argued passionately against the oppressive weight of French cultural and political traditions is Paul Yonnet, whose study offers the most sustained and coherent account of mass culture and popular culture in modern France. In his *Jeux, modes et masses. La société française et le moderne 1945–1985* (1985) ['Games, fashions and the masses. French society and the modern 1945–1985'], Yonnet's overriding purpose is to give a positive interpretation of modern mass culture and to rescue it from the elitist and miserabilist treatment to which he believes it has been subjected by academics and intellectuals since 1945. He criticises the popular education and popular culture movement for insisting that leisure time had to be the occasion for moral and cultural self-improvement.[100] He also criticises Bourdieu for his obsessional stress on the class basis of culture.[101] But, above all, he charges the whole body of French intellectuals and academics with having shared contemptuous and repressive high cultural attitudes towards the leisure and cultural practices of the vast majority of other French people.[102] In Yonnet's view, French intellectuals, and French sociologists in particular, have manifested an extraordinary degree of ignorance and prejudice in their treatment of mass culture. They have refused to see themselves as 'men within the mass of other men',[103] and have constantly analysed mass cultural practices from the outside, without any empathy for the people they have studied and whom they have preferred to see as ignorant dupes, or passive victims, rather than as the conscious agents that Yonnet holds them to be.

According to Yonnet, modern leisure needs to be seen as a genuinely 'empty' sphere within which individuals freely choose to act according to their desires. One of Yonnet's principal examples of free leisure activity is that of betting on the horses ['le tiercé'] which he regards as offering a crucial example of the way in which the dominant culture ['la Grande Culture'] has consistently presented a miserabilist critique of practices which in reality are not only perfectly valid in themselves, but which could also be said to constitute a desirable model of leisure and cultural behaviour in a mass society. To begin with, Yonnet is perfectly convinced that the dominant culture has always despised the practice of betting on the horses. To prove his point, he cites the persistent attitude of contempt shown by the prestigious newspaper *Le Monde*. Yonnet is, however, far from impressed by this scorn, since he believes that the attitude of *Le Monde* simply reveals that its readers prefer to gamble on the Stock Exchange rather than back the horses:

> The fact that the readers of *Le Monde* prefer to play the Stock Exchange rather than bet on the horses allows one to understand the true significance of the miserabilist descriptions of 'the little punter', the vague lamentations based on what they have read in books, the inquisitorial humanism of those with the best educational qualifications who, having inherited the earth (and having deserved to do so!), prefer the prestigious calculations that are required for chess, the game of go and structural linguistics to the contemptible free act of placing a strategic bet on the chances of a horse winning a race.[104]

Far from deserving the contempt of dominant culture, betting on the horses, according to Yonnet, is a practice which shows how people in a modern mass society can participate in a leisure activity which allows them to be free and individual agents who do not encroach upon the liberties of others and who do not come together to form a brutal and threatening mass. Moreover, an essential element in this free activity is that the individual enters into the open space of leisure divested of social identity and political affiliation:

The ludic community of punters is like a society of anonymous people. In order to back the horses, the punter does not
need to have a history. He is the individual who, for the space
of a morning, relieves himself of all proofs of his identity, of
what marks him out socially. He leaves behind the stamp of
his daily self . . . he frees himself from all constraints, be they
professional, administrative, economic, political or domestic.
He floats in a strange, airy atmosphere of freedom. In so
doing, one could almost say that he neutralises himself as
a social agent. The only thing that counts for him is the
horse-race and the runners.[105]

Above and beyond the specific arguments he brings forward
in favour of betting on the horses, it is obvious that Yonnet is
attempting to build up a general case which will enable him to
'revalorise' mass culture and popular culture in the face of the
persistent contempt demonstrated by intellectuals and academics
in postwar France. However, although Yonnet is deeply conscious
of the continuing power of dominant culture to exercise its tyranny,
and although he feels very strongly that the traditional bastions of
high culture (the schools, the universities etc.) are still sticking to
their old criteria, he does, in fact, tend to adopt the triumphalist
position that popular culture has, in reality, finally won the day.
This can be seen most clearly in his ample treatment of rock and
pop music. Yonnet fully recognises that France was initially very
slow to respond to the new youth culture of rock and pop. On
the one hand, he explains this by stressing the extent to which
France in the 1950s was locked in its own self-contained world
of popular song and popular entertainment which drew on exclusively French cultural myths and stereotypes (Chevalier, Montand,
Piaf, and so forth).[106] It was, therefore, the very strength of the
tradition of French popular song which prevented rock and pop
music developing in France at the same rate and on the same scale
as had happened, for instance, in Anglo-Saxon countries. On the
other hand, Yonnet is also convinced that it was the enormous
importance of literary high culture in France that prevented the
early development of rock and pop music. He even goes so far as
to say that 'the French ideology of high culture' became even more
prevalent and tyrannical in French society after 1945, as a result of
the efforts of the popular culture, popular education and popular
theatre movements, which tried to foist literary high culture on

French people as a whole, whereas previously it had been restricted to relatively small circles:[107]

> This French ideology of high culture, as we have said, spread to large sections of the population, to the point at which it exerted an almost total dominance in the cultural sector. This ideology was taken up and propagated by teachers at all levels keen on democratising the educational system. It was also taken up by artistic, political and union institutions at the time of the TNP, Jean Vilar and Gérard Philipe (when the Avignon Festival was just beginning). It was passed on by the early sociologists of free time (Joffre Dumazedier, for example), and since then its influence can be seen in the very name given to one of the State radio channels: France-Culture. Its influence still carries on today, and it is not irrelevant to note that the French ideology of high culture is without doubt largely responsible for the impasse in which the whole area of French creativity has found itself, in literature as well as in social science . . . . The French ideology of high culture also explains the original rejection of American rock 'n' roll by our country.[108]

However, although Yonnet emphasises the enormous obstacles initially put in the way of pop culture in France by the deeply entrenched literary values of high culture, he claims that in the end rock and pop culture gained the upper hand and now has to be recognised as a key element in the true living culture of French people. It is this new *aural* culture which Yonnet describes as the ever-present, oceanic feature of modern French life, and this is not something to be feared or regretted.[109] More generally, Yonnet, like Lipovetsky, believes that high culture ['la Grande Culture'] has suffered 'its final defeat'.[110] It has lost its power to direct and regiment the leisure and cultural tastes and practices of the mass of French people. One may dispute the truth of this assertion of Yonnet's. One also may not share his view that the defeat of high culture marks a triumphant liberation from intimidation and a sense of guilt and inferiority. However, after having studied the discourse on culture in modern France, one is at least in a better position to understand Yonnet's assertion and to see it within the context of this cultural discourse which has been, and still remains, such a vital component of French intellectual life.

NOTES

1 FROM HIGH CULTURE
TO ORDINARY CULTURE

1 H. Cueco, quoted in C. Clément, *Rêver chacun pour l'autre*, Paris, Fayard, 1982, p. 55.
2 For a glossary of key terms in the institutional area of modern French culture, see R. Labourie, *Les Institutions socio-culturelles. Les mots-clés*, Paris, Presses Universitaires de France, 1978.
3 P. Bénéton, *Histoire de mots: culture et civilisation*, Paris, Presses de la Fondation Nationale des Sciences Politiques, 1975, p. 142. Unless otherwise indicated, all translations are by the author.
4 See G. Lipovetsky, *L'Ere du vide: essais sur l'individualisme contemporain*, Paris, Gallimard, 1983, p. 17; R. Debray, *Le Pouvoir intellectuel en France*, Paris, Folio, 1986, p.24 (1st edn 1979).
5 H. Lefebvre, *La Vie quotidienne dans le monde moderne*, Paris, Gallimard, 1968, p. 67.
6 An important example of a contemporary defence of a humanist notion of high culture is: P. Emmanuel, *Culture, noblesse du monde. Histoire d'une politique*, Paris, Stock, 1980.
7 P.-H. Simon, 'Contestation et culture', *Le Monde*, 24–5 July 1968.
8 See, for example, M. Druon, *L'Avenir en désarroi*, Paris, Plon, 1968; J. Dutourd, *L'Ecole des jocrisses*, Paris, Flammarion, 1970; J. Cau, *Discours de la décadence*, Paris, Copernic, 1978; P. Guth, *Lettre ouverte aux futurs illettrés*, Paris, Albin Michel, 1980.
9 See P. Gaudibert, *De l'Ordre moral*, Paris, Grasset, 1973.
10 P. Combes, *La Littérature et le mouvement de Mai 68: écriture, mythes, critique, écrivains 1968–1981*, Paris, Seghers, 1984, p. 284, n. 26.
11 C. Javeau, *Haro sur la culture*, Brussels, Editions de l'Université de Bruxelles, 1974, p. 49.
12 See P. Gaudibert, op. cit., pp. 9–10.
13 P. Bourdieu, *La Distinction, critique sociale du jugement*, Paris, Minuit, 1979 (Eng. tr.: *Distinction: a social critique of the judgement of taste*, London, Routledge and Kegan Paul, 1984, pp. 318ff).
14 ibid., p. 250.

15 ibid.
16 ibid., pp. 318ff.
17 ibid., p. 321.
18 ibid., p. 319.
19 These terms, and those that follow, have been taken particularly from texts written in the early 1960s.
20 P. Ory (ed.), *Mots de passe, 1945–1985: petit abécédaire des modes de vie*, Paris, Autrement, 1985.
21 Quoted in C. Javeau, op. cit., p. 42.
22 A. Kimmel and J. Poujol, *Certaines Idées de la France*, Sèvres, Centre international d'études pédagogiques, 1980.
23 See A. Salon, *L'Action culturelle de la France dans le monde*, Paris, Nathan, 1984; D. C. Gordon, *The French Language and National Identity 1930–1975*, The Hague, Mouton, 1978.
24 P. Gaudibert, op. cit., p. 10.
25 See C. Billard and P. Guibbert, *Histoire mythologique des Français*, Paris, Galilée, 1976.
26 E. Weber, *Peasants into Frenchmen: the modernization of rural France 1870–1914*, London, Chatto and Windus, 1979, p. 486.
27 R. Mandrou, 'Cultures populaire et savante', in J. Beauroy *et al.*, *The Wolf and the Lamb. Popular culture in France from the old regime to the twentieth century*, Saratoga, Anma Libri, 1976, p. 37.
28 M. Marrus, 'Folklore as an ethnographic source', in J. Beauroy, ibid., p. 113.
29 J. Cuisenier, *French Folk Art*, New York, Kodansha International, 1977 (Fr. edn: *L'Art populaire en France*, Freiburg, Office du Livre, 1976).
30 P. Bourdieu and L. Boltanski, 'La Production de l'idéologie dominante', *Actes de la recherche en sciences sociales*, 2–3, 1976.
31 J. Cuisenier and M. Segalen, *Ethnologie de la France*, Paris, Presses Universitaires de France, 1986, p. 38.
32 M. Guillaume, *La Politique du patrimoine*, Paris, Galilée, 1980.
33 P. Yonnet, *Jeux, modes et masses. La société française et le moderne 1945–1985*, Paris, Gallimard, 1985.
34 ibid., p. 73.
35 M. de Certeau, *La Culture au pluriel*, Paris, Christian Bourgeois, 1980 (1st edn 1974).
36 M. de Certeau, *La Prise de parole*, Paris, Desclée de Brouwer, 1968.
37 P. Bourdieu, 'Vous avez dit "populaire"', *Actes de la recherche en sciences sociales*, 46, 1984.
38 M. de Certeau, D. Julia and J. Revel, *Une Politique de la langue: la Révolution française et les patois*, Paris, Gallimard, 1975.
39 Quoted in M. de Certeau, *La Culture au pluriel*, op. cit. p. 56.
40 ibid., p. 57.
41 ibid.
42 ibid., p. 59.
43 ibid., p. 74.
44 ibid.
45 ibid., p. 136.
46 ibid., p. 118.

47 ibid., p. 248.

48 ibid., p. 239.

49 ibid., pp. 240–1.

50 ibid., pp. 241–2.

51 ibid., p. 245.

52 P. Gaudibert, *Action culturelle: intégration et/ou subversion*, Paris, Casterman, 1972.

53 ibid., 1977 edition, pp. 165–6.

54 One hardly needs to stress that interest in the 'everyday' and the 'fête' has also given rise in recent years to a considerable body of historical scholarship on these topics. See, for instance, G. Thuillier, *Pour une histoire du quotidien au XIXe siècle en Nivernais*, Paris/The Hague, Mouton, 1977; M. Ozouf, *La Fête révolutionnaire*, Paris, Gallimard, 1976.

55 See the review *Autrement*, 7 Nov. 1976, special number on 'La Fête cette hantise'; *Yale French Studies*, 73, 1987, special number on 'Everyday Life'.

56 L. Giard and P. Mayol, *L'Invention du quotidien*, vol. 2: *Habiter, cuisiner*, Paris, 10/18, 1980.

57 M. de Certeau, *L'Invention du quotidien*, vol. 1, Paris, 10/18, 1980.

58 L. Giard and P. Mayol, op. cit., p. 146.

59 ibid., pp. 64–5.

60 ibid., p. 64.

61 For examples of explicit attempts to do this, see M. Soriano, 'Popular Traditions and Consumer Society: the situation in France', *Cultures*, 1, 2, 1973, pp. 39–66 and 'Radio and Television "live" programming in the long term', *Cultures*, 8, 1, 1982, pp. 91–9; C. Lalive d'Epinay *et al.*, 'Persistance de la culture populaire dans les sociétés industrielles avancées', *Revue française de sociologie*, 23, 1, 1982, pp. 87–109.

62 L. Giard and P. Mayol, op. cit., pp. 18–19.

63 ibid., p. 22.

64 ibid., pp. 130–1.

65 ibid., p. 137.

66 The work of M. Bakhtin has had a great influence in France, as elsewhere. See, for instance, *L'Oeuvre de François Rabelais et la culture populaire au Moyen-Age et sous la Renaissance*, Paris, Gallimard, 1970.

67 L. Giard and P. Mayol, op. cit., p. 48.

68 ibid., pp. 132–3.

69 ibid., pp. 143–4.

70 For a British use of the term, see the essay 'Culture is Ordinary', in R. Williams, *Resources of Hope*, London, Verso, 1989.

71 M. de Certeau, 'Pratiques quotidiennes', in G. Poujol and R. Labourie (eds), *Les Cultures populaires*, Toulouse, Privat, 1979, p. 23.

72 L. Giard and P. Mayol, op. cit., p. 155.

73 ibid., pp. 155–6.

74 ibid., p. 153.

75 op.cit.

76 See, for instance, E. Morin, *Commune en France. La métamorphose de Plodémet*, Paris, Fayard, 1967. (Eng. tr.: *Plodémet. Report from a French Village*, London, Allen Lane, 1971).

77 op. cit. See also the review article of Guillaume's book by Y. de Kerorguen, 'L'Effet patrimoine', *Esprit*, 12, 1981, pp. 91–106.

78 M. Guillaume, op. cit., pp. 107–8.

79 ibid., p. 144.

80 ibid., pp. 187–8.

81 See, for instance, A. Duhamel, *Le Complexe d'Astérix: essai sur le
caractère politique des Français*, Paris, Gallimard, 1985.

82 H. Lefebvre, op. cit., pp. 73–4.

83 ibid., p. 74.

84 See G. Debord, *La Société du spectacle*, Paris, Edns Buchet-Chastel,
1967. (Eng. tr. *Society of the Spectacle*, Detroit, Black and Red, 1970.
See also, G. Debord, *Commentaires sur la société du spectacle*, Paris,
Lebovici, 1988.

85 H. Lefebvre, op. cit., p. 321.

86 ibid., pp. 339–40.

87 ibid., pp. 346–7.

88 ibid., pp. 105–6.

89 ibid., p. 205.

90 ibid., pp. 184–5.

2 POPULAR CULTURE AND POPULAR EDUCATION: LEISURE, WORK AND CULTURE

1 J. Charpentreau and R. Kaës, *La Culture populaire en France*, Paris, Editions ouvrières, 1962.

2 See B. Cacérès, *Histoire de l'éducation populaire*, Paris, Seuil, 1964.

3 On the role of 'associations' in French social and cultural life, see J.
Dumazedier and A. Ripert, *Société éducative et pouvoir culturel*, Paris,
Seuil, 1976.

4 See R. Mandrou, 'Cultures populaire et savante', in J. Beauroy *et al.*,
*The Wolf and the Lamb. Popular culture in France from the old regime to the
twentieth century*, Saratoga, Anma Libri, 1976, pp. 17–18.

5 J. Charpentreau and R. Kaës, op. cit., p. 7.

6 ibid., p. 59.

7 See B. Rigby, 'French Intellectuals and Leisure: the case of Emmanuel
Mounier', in T. Winnifrith and C. Barrett (eds), *The Philosophy of
Leisure*, London, Macmillan, 1989.

8 J. Boniface, *Arts de masse et grand public*, Paris, Editions ouvrières, 1962.
See also B. Rigby, 'The *Vivre son Temps* collection: intellectuals,
modernity and mass culture', in B. Rigby and N. Hewitt (eds), *France
and the Mass Media*, London, Macmillan, 1991.

9 J. Charpentreau and R. Kaës, op. cit., p. 74.

10 ibid., p. 158.

11 ibid., p. 58, emphasis added.

12 ibid., p. 159.

13 ibid., pp. 49–50.

14 ibid., p. 90.

15 ibid., p. 174.

16 J. Charpentreau, *Pour une politique culturelle*, Paris, Editions ouvrières, 1967.
17 ibid., p. 40.
18 See, for instance, J. Dumazedier, 'Culture de masse-Culture populaire', *Raison présente*, 64, 1982, pp. 81–95; *Révolution culturelle du temps libre 1968–1988*, Paris, Klincksieck, 1988.
19 On Dumazedier, see B. Cacérès, *Le Président*, Paris, Peuple et Culture, 1957; J.-P. Saez (ed.), *Peuple et Culture: histoire et mémoires*, Paris, Peuple et Culture, 1986; E. Ritaine, *Les Stratèges de la culture*, Paris, Presses de la Fondation Nationale des Sciences Politiques, 1983.
20 J. Dumazedier, *Vers une civilisation du loisir?* Paris, Seuil, 1962 (Eng. tr.: *Toward a Society of Leisure?*, New York, Free Press, 1967).
21 J. Dumazedier, ibid. p. 26.
22 ibid., p. 35.
23 ibid., p. 31.
24 ibid., p. 209.
25 ibid., p. 236.
26 ibid., pp. 230ff.
27 ibid., p. 40.
28 See C. Bouglé, *The French Conception of 'Culture Générale' and its Influence upon Instruction*, New York, Columbia University Press, 1938.
29 J. Dumazedier, op. cit., p. 36.
30 ibid., pp. 74–5.
31 E. Raude and G. Prouteau, *Le Message de Léo Lagrange*, Paris, La Compagnie du Livre, 1950, p. 117.
32 ibid., p. 129.
33 ibid., pp. 137–8.
34 See B. Rigby, 'The Reconstruction of Culture: Peuple et Culture and the Popular Education Movement', in N. Hewitt (ed.) *The Culture of Reconstruction*, London, Macmillan, 1989.
35 B. Cacérès, *Allons au-devant de la vie: la naissance du temps des loisirs en 1936*, Paris, La Découverte, 1981.
36 ibid., p. 28.
37 ibid., p. 29.
38 ibid., p. 68. See also R.-H. Guerrand, *La Conquête des vacances*, Paris, Editions ouvrières, 1963.
39 B. Cacérès, *Allons-au devant* op. cit., p. 67.
40 ibid., pp. 67–8.
41 B. Cacérès, *L'Espoir au coeur*, Paris, Seuil, 1967.
42 See M. Kelly, 'Humanism and National Unity: the Ideological Reconstruction of France', in N. Hewitt (ed.) *The Culture of Reconstruction*, op. cit.
43 B. Cacérès, *Histoire de l'éducation populaire*, op. cit., p. 164.
44 ibid., pp. 153–4.
45 ibid., p. 183.
46 ibid., pp. 149–50.
47 ibid., p. 177.
48 B. Cacérès, *La Rencontre des hommes*, Paris, Seuil, 1950.
49 ibid., p. 205.

50 J. Larrue, *Loisirs ouvriers chez les métallurgistes toulousains*, Paris, Mouton, 1965.
51 On Friedmann, see the chapter 'Humanism and the Labour process', in M. Rose, *Servants of Post-Industrial Power? 'Sociologie du Travail' in Modern France*, London, Macmillan, 1979. See also M. Rose (ed.), *Industrial Sociology: Work in the French Tradition*, London, Sage, 1987.
52 G. Friedmann, *Le Travail en miettes: spécialisation et loisirs*, Paris, Gallimard, 1956 (Eng. tr.: *The Anatomy of Work*, London, Heinemann, 1961).
53 ibid., p. 258.
54 J. Larrue, op. cit., p. 189.
55 J. Frisch-Gautier and P. Louchet, *La Colombophilie chez les mineurs du Nord*, Paris, Centre national de la recherche scientifique, 1960.
56 ibid., pp. 58–63.

3 CULTURE AND THE WORKING CLASS AND WORKING-CLASS CULTURE

1 J. Larrue, *Loisirs ouvriers chez les métallurgistes toulousains*, Paris, Mouton, 1965, pp. 107–8.
2 ibid., pp. 112–13.
3 ibid., p. 188.
4 J. Rigaud, *La Culture pour vivre*, Paris, Gallimard, 1975, pp. 49, 68.
5 J. Frémontier, *La Vie en bleu: voyage en culture ouvrière*, Paris, Fayard, 1980.
6 ibid., p. 220.
7 ibid., p. 120.
8 ibid., p. 202.
9 D. Mothé, 'Les ouvriers et la culture', *Socialisme ou barbarie*, 30, April–May 1960, pp. 1–44. See also D. Mothé, *Journal d'un ouvrier (1956–1958)*, Paris, Minuit, 1959.
10 For a similarly disabused account of the project to cultivate the workers, see F. George, 'Critique de la culture populaire', *Cahiers des saisons*, 36, 1964, pp. 6–16. George calls the State's attempt to cultivate the people through such institutions as the TNP 'national-populism'. He foreshadows the 1968 assault on culture when he writes: 'The TNP is "par excellence" the temple of recuperation through culture.'
11 D. Mothé, 'Les ouvriers et la culture', op. cit., p. 21.
12 ibid., p. 20.
13 ibid., p. 23.
14 ibid.
15 ibid., pp. 12–13.
16 ibid., p. 33.
17 ibid., pp. 32–3.
18 ibid., p. 16.
19 ibid., p. 32.
20 ibid., p. 15.
21 ibid., p. 28.

22 ibid., p. 30.
23 ibid., p. 42.
24 ibid., p. 39.
25 ibid., p. 46.
26 R. Kaës, *Images de la culture chez les ouvriers français*, Paris, Cujas, 1968.
27 ibid., p. 224.
28 ibid., p. 218.
29 See N. Racine, 'Marcel Martinet et la culture ouvrière', *Le Mouvement social*, 90, 1975, pp. 59–78.
30 R. Kaës, op. cit., p. 272.
31 See A. Touraine, *La Société post-industrielle*, Paris, Denoël, 1969.
32 A. Touraine, 'Travail, loisirs et sociéte', *Esprit*, special number on leisure, June 1959, p. 981.
33 ibid., p. 986.
34 ibid., p. 996.
35 J. Verdès-Leroux, *Au service du parti: le parti communiste, les intellectuels et la culture (1944–1956)*, Paris, Fayard, 1983. See also her second volume: *Le Réveil des somnambules: le parti communiste, les intellectuels et la culture* (1956–1985), Paris, Fayard/Minuit, 1987.
36 J. Verdès-Leroux, *Au service du parti*, op. cit., p. 9.
37 ibid., p. 297.
38 ibid., p. 325.
39 ibid., p. 424.
40 L. Aragon, 'La Culture des masses ou le titre refusé', in *La Culture et les hommes*, Paris, Editions sociales, 1947.
41 ibid., p. 7.
42 ibid., p. 9.
43 ibid., p. 13.
44 ibid., p. 27.
45 R. Leroy, *La Culture au présent*, Paris, Editions Sociales, 1972.
46 ibid., pp. 7–8.
47 ibid., p. 35.
48 ibid., pp. 27–8.
49 ibid., p. 49.
50 ibid., pp. 134–5.
51 G. Lavau, 'The PCF, the state and the revolution: an analysis of party policies, communication and popular culture', in D. Blackmer and S. Tarrou, *Communism in Italy and France*, Princeton, Princeton University Press, 1975.
52 ibid., pp. 130–1.
53 ibid., p. 132.
54 G. Lavau, *A Quoi sert le parti communiste français?* Paris, Fayard, 1981.
55 J. Verdès-Leroux, op. cit., p. 419.
56 For another account of communist culture, see *Autrement*, 78, March, 1986, 'La Culture des camarades'.

4 POPULAR CULTURE AS BARBARIC CULTURE: THE SOCIOLOGY OF PIERRE BOURDIEU

1 P. Bourdieu, *La Distinction: critique sociale du jugement*, Paris, Minuit, 1979 (Eng. tr.: *Distinction. A social critique of the judgement of taste*, London, Routledge and Kegan Paul, 1984).
2 P. Bourdieu and A. Darbel, *L'Amour de l'art: les musées d'art européens et leur public*, Paris, Minuit, 1966.
3 ibid., p. 151.
4 ibid., p. 65.
5 ibid., pp. 93–4.
6 ibid., p. 108.
7 ibid., p. 17.
8 ibid., p. 73.
9 ibid., p. 88.
10 ibid., p. 89.
11 ibid., pp. 13–15. Bourdieu ridicules the popular culture militants by dubbing them 'les populiculteurs' in *La Distinction*, op. cit., p. 366.
12 P. Bourdieu and A. Darbel, *L'Amour de l'art*, op. cit., p. 141.
13 ibid., p. 156.
14 ibid., p. 151.
15 P. Bourdieu *et al.*, *Un Art moyen: essai sur les usages sociaux de la photographie*, Paris, Minuit, 1965 (Eng. tr.: *Photography: The Social Uses of an Ordinary Art*, Oxford, Polity, 1989).
16 P. Bourdieu, *Un Art moyen*, op. cit., pp. 133–34.
17 ibid., p. 115.
18 P. Bourdieu, *Choses dites*, Paris, Minuit, 1987, pp. 159ff.
19 P. Bourdieu, *Un Art moyen*, op. cit., p. 122.
20 ibid., pp. 73–4.
21 ibid., p. 28.
22 ibid., p. 101.
23 P. Bourdieu, 'Différences et distinctions', in Darras, *Le Partage des bénéfices: expansion et inégalités en France*, Paris, Minuit, 1966.
24 ibid., p. 125.
25 ibid., p. 118.
26 ibid., pp. 126–7.
27 P. Bourdieu, *Distinction*, op. cit., pp. 54 and 251.
28 P. Bourdieu, *Choses dites*, op. cit., p. 30.
29 P. Bourdieu, *Distinction*, op. cit., p. 11.
30 ibid., p. 511.
31 See chapter 1 for the discussion of Luce Giard's reaction to Bourdieu.
32 P. Bourdieu, *Distinction*, op. cit., pp. 197–9.
33 ibid., p. 32.
34 ibid., pp. 394–5.
35 ibid., p. 43.
36 ibid., p. 372.
37 ibid., p. 376.
38 ibid., p. 386.

39 ibid., p. 381.
40 ibid.
41 P. Bourdieu, 'La transmission de l'héritage culturel', in Darras, *Le Partage des bénéfices*, op. cit., pp. 383–420.
42 ibid., p. 398.
43 ibid., p. 412.
44 P. Bourdieu, *Distinction*, op. cit., p. 251.
45 ibid., p. 283.
46 P. Bourdieu, 'La transmission de l'héritage culturel', op. cit., p. 409.
47 P. Bourdieu, *Distinction*, op. cit., p. 179.
48 P. Bourdieu, 'La sociologie de la culture populaire', in *Le Handicap socioculturel en question*, Paris, Editions ESF, 1978, p. 119.
49 ibid., p. 118.
50 P. Bourdieu, *Choses dites*, op. cit., p. 164.
51 P. Bourdieu, 'La sociologie de la culture populaire', op. cit., p. 118.
52 P. Bourdieu, *La Distinction*, op. cit., p. 459.
53 P. Bourdieu, *Choses dites*, op. cit., pp. 69–70.
54 P. Bourdieu, *Distinction*, op. cit., p. 395.
55 P. Bourdieu, *Choses dites*, op. cit., p. 178.
56 ibid., p. 70.
57 ibid., p. 182.
58 ibid., p. 184.
59 P. Bourdieu, *Ce que parler veut dire: l'économie des échanges linguistiques*, Paris, Fayard, 1982.
60 ibid., p. 42.
61 See, for instance, the chapter on Bourdieu in L. Ferry and A. Renaut, *La Pensée 68: essai sur l'anti-humanisme contemporain*, Paris, Gallimard, 1985.
62 P. Bourdieu and J.-C. Passeron, *Les Héritiers: les étudiants et la culture*, Paris, Minuit, 1964; *La Reproduction*, Paris, Minuit, 1970.
63 J.-C. Passeron, 'Introduction' to R. Hoggart, *La Culture du pauvre: étude sur le style de vie des classes populaires en Angleterre*, Paris, Minuit, 1970 (Eng. tr. of Passeron's introduction in *Working Papers in Cultural Studies*, Birmingham, Centre for Contemporary Cultural Studies, Spring, 1971. Slight alterations have been made to the translation here).
64 ibid., p. 121.
65 ibid., p. 126.
66 ibid., pp. 127–8.
67 R. Hoggart, *The Uses of Literacy: Aspects of working-class life with special reference to publications and entertainments*, Harmondsworth, Penguin, 1963, p. 177 (1st edn 1957).
68 ibid., p. 37.
69 C. Grignon and J.-C. Passeron, *A Propos des cultures populaires*, Cahiers du CERCOM, 1, Marseille, EHESS, April 1985. The text is in the form of a debate and Grignon and Passeron are not always unanimous in their views.
70 ibid., p. 65.
71 R. Hoggart, *The Uses of Literacy*, op. cit., p. 32.

72 See W. Labov, *Language in the Inner City: Studies in the black vernacular*, Oxford, Blackwell, 1977.
73 R. Hoggart, op. cit., p. 32.
74 C. Grignon and J.-C. Passeron, *A Propos des cultures populaires*, op. cit., p. 31.

5 CULTURE, THE STATE AND 1968

1 E. Ritaine, *Les Stratèges de la culture*, Paris, Presses de la Fondation Nationale des Sciences Politiques, Paris, 1983, p. 65.
2 See, for example, Peuple et Culture's role in the Colloque de Bourges, held in late 1964, on the theme of 'Scientific research and cultural development': 'The Bourges colloquium was organised as a result of a meeting between the leaders of Peuple et Culture and researchers from both the Ministry of Cultural Affairs and the Association d'étude pour l'expansion de la recherche scientifique'. (*Expansion de la recherche scientifique*, 22, April-May, 1965, p. 51.)
3 Ritaine calls this a shift 'from a revolutionary hope to a demand to the State to take culture on board', *Les Stratèges de la culture*, op. cit., p. 61.
4 The State's quantitative, statistical approach to culture is best demonstrated in the many texts issuing from the Ministry of Culture on the whole area of cultural practices and cultural development. See, for example, *Pratiques culturelles des Français. Description socio-démographique: évolution 1973–1981*, Paris, Dalloz, 1982.
5 For a violently critical account of Malraux's role in the Ministry of Cultural Affairs, see P. Cabanne, *Le Pouvoir culturel sous la Vème République*, Paris, Olivier Orban, 1981.
6 According to Emile Copfermann: 'The reappearance of the Popular Theatre movement in France in 1944 coincided with the expectation that there would soon be a "social democracy", which, it was hoped, would usher in a popular culture supported by an equally popular theatre – a popular culture whose guiding principle would be: "let us give the greatest works to the greatest number of people".' (*Le Théâtre populaire pourquoi?* Paris, Maspero, 1969, p. 11.)
7 See, J.-J. Queyranne, *Les Maisons de la Culture*, Lyon, Editions de l'AGEL, 1975, pp. 177–9. For my discussion of the Maisons de la Culture, I have relied particularly on Queyranne's thesis.
8 ibid., p. 53.
9 ibid., pp. 42–3.
10 ibid., p. 130.
11 ibid.
12 ibid., p. 417.
13 On the term, and the idea, of the 'non-public', see F. Jeanson, *L'Action culturelle dans la cité*, Paris, Seuil, 1973.
14 See the section 'Cathédrales ou "ligne Maginot" de la culture', in Queyranne, *Les Maisons de la Culture*, op. cit., pp. 464ff.
15 ibid., p. 704.

16 ibid., pp. 680–1; 718–24.
17 Quoted in F. Jeanson, *L'Action culturelle dans la cité*, op. cit., p. 119.
18 ibid.
19 For an example of greater resistance by the popular culture movement to the events of 1968, see J. Dumazedier, 'A un étudiant révolutionnaire', *Esprit*, 8–9, August–September 1968, pp. 61–80.
20 See E. Ritaine, *Les Stratèges de la culture*, op. cit., pp. 114ff.
21 ibid., pp. 126ff.
22 Part two of Ritaine's book is entitled: 'Populist gestures: taking militant action in the cause of culture'.
23 ibid., p. 139.
24 ibid., p. 146.
25 See M. Manceaux, *Les Maos en France* (Avant-propos de Jean-Paul Sartre), Paris, Gallimard, 1972.
26 J.-P. Sartre, *On a raison de se révolter*, Paris, Gallimard, 1974, pp. 73–4.
27 J.-P. Sartre, 'Avant-propos', in M. Manceaux, *Les Maos en France*, op. cit., p. 14.
28 See, for instance, the story of Georges, a 26-year-old engineer and maths graduate, ibid., pp. 51–69.
29 ibid., p. 241.
30 On the Situationists, see the key text by Guy Debord, *La Société du spectacle*, Paris, Edns Buchet-Chastel, 1967 (Eng. tr.: *Society of the Spectacle*, Detroit, Black and Red, 1970); also Debord's *Commentaires sur la Société du spectacle*, Paris, Lebovici, 1988. See also J.-F. Martos, *Histoire de l'Internationale situationniste*, Paris, Lebovici, 1989.
31 *De la misère en milieu étudiant considérée sous ses aspects économique, politique, psychologique, sexuel et notamment intellectuel, et de quelques moyens pour y remédier*, Strasbourg, AFGES, 1966. The text can most easily be consulted in R. Viénet, *Enragés et situationnistes dans le mouvement des occupations*, Paris, Gallimard, 1968, pp. 219–43.
32 ibid., pp. 224–5.
33 J.-J. Lebel, *Procès du festival d'Avignon, supermarché de la culture*, Paris, Pierre Belfond, 1968.
34 ibid., p. 74.
35 ibid., p. 170.
36 ibid., pp. 10ff and passim.
37 ibid., p. 24.
38 Lebel quoted a review by Edith Rappoport in *France nouvelle*, August 1968, in which she pinpointed the fact that the whole question of 'the popular' was what was at stake in the Avignon conflict, ibid., p. 171.
39 ibid., p. 14.
40 To realise the cruel irony of the attack on Vilar, one needs to recognise the extent to which the popular theatre movement, and Jean Vilar in particular, had been previously idealised. See, for example, B. Cacérès, *Allons au-devant de la vie: la naissance du temps des loisirs en 1936*, Paris, La Découverte, 1981, pp. 105ff.
41 J.-J. Lebel, *Procès du festival d'Avignon*, op. cit., p. 169.
42 ibid., p. 28.
43 ibid., p. 49.

44 ibid., p. 29.

45 ibid., pp. 29ff.

46 ibid., p. 36.

47 ibid., p. 59.

48 ibid., p. 21.

49 For a parallel, but more purely Marxist assault, see E. Copfermann, *Le Théâtre populaire pourquoi?* op. cit.

50 On the importance of Vaneigem's text, see P. Combes, *La Littérature et le mouvement de Mai 68: écriture, mythes, critique, écrivains 1968–1981*, Paris, Seghers, 1984, pp. 27, 124.

51 R. Vaneigem, *Traité de savoir-vivre l'usage des jeunes générations*, Paris, Gallimard, 1967, p. 35.

52 ibid., p. 51.

53 ibid., p. 17.

54 ibid., p. 8.

55 ibid., pp. 111–13.

56 ibid., p. 265.

57 ibid., p. 55.

58 ibid., p. 67.

59 ibid., p. 115.

60 ibid., p. 209.

61 ibid., p. 229.

62 ibid., pp. 206, 256.

63 See *L'Atelier populaire présenté par lui-même*, Paris, Usines, Universités, Union, 1968; J. Besançon (ed.), *Les Murs ont la parole: journal mural mai 1968*, Paris, Tchou, 1968.

64 M. de Certeau, *La Prise de parole*, Paris, Desclée de Brouwer, 1968, pp. 139–40.

65 J. Besançon (ed.), *Les Murs ont la parole*, op. cit., p. 83.

66 See L. Althusser, 'Idéologie et appareils idéologiques d'Etat', *La Pensée*, 151, June 1970.

67 B. Miège, J. Ion, A.-N. Roux, *L'Appareil d'action culturelle*, Paris, Editions universitaires, 1974, p. 13.

68 ibid., p. 44.

69 ibid., pp. 79, 179.

70 ibid., p. 62.

71 P. Gaudibert, *Action culturelle: intégration et/ou subversion*, Paris, Casterman, 1977, pp. 162–3.

72 M. de Certeau, *La Prise de parole*, op. cit., p. 66.

73 ibid., ch. IV.

74 ibid.

75 M. de Certeau, *La Culture au pluriel*, Paris, Christian Bourgeois, 1980 (1st edn 1974).

76 J. Dumazedier, 'Culture vivante et pouvoirs', in G. Poujol and R. Labourie, *Les Cultures populaires: Permanences et émergences des cultures minoritaires, locales, ethniques, sociales et religieuses*, Toulouse, Privat, 1979, pp. 65–77.

77 P. Besnard, 'La Culture populaire, discours et théories', ibid., pp. 53–63.

78 J.-C. Barthez, 'Culture populaire ou culture dominée?', ibid., pp. 41–52.
79 M. De Certeau, 'Pratiques quotidiennes', ibid., pp. 23–30.
80 *Autrement*, 16, Nov. 1978: 'Flagrants délits d'imaginaire'.
81 P. Besnard, in *Les Cultures populaires*, op. cit., p. 56.
82 G. Poujol, 'La Résistance à l'inculcation: résistants ou handicapés?', ibid., pp. 31–39.
83 Quoted in L.-J. Calvet, *La Production révolutionnaire: slogans, affiches, chansons*, Paris, Payot, 1976, p. 140.
84 ibid., p. 188.
85 M. de Certeau, 'Pratiques quotidiennes', in *Les Cultures populaires*, op. cit., p. 24.
86 ibid., pp. 28–9.
87 G. Poujol, in *Les Cultures populaires*, ibid., p. 36.
88 M. de Certeau, *La Prise de parole*, op. cit., ch. IV.
89 The volume *Les Cultures populaires* was the publication of the proceedings of a conference held in 1977.

6 MASS CULTURE, POP CULTURE AND PLURALISM

1 See for instance, P. Ory, *L'Entre-deux-mai: histoire culturelle de la France: mai 1968 – mai 1981*, Paris, Seuil, 1983.
2 Much of modern cultural commentary is, in fact, characterised by playfulness and jokiness. See, for instance, P. Ory (ed.), *Mots de passe 1945–1985: petit abécédaire des modes de vie*, Paris, Autrement, 1985.
3 For a socialist critique that does not share the euphoria over the mass media, see R. Debray, *Le Pouvoir intellectuel en France*, Paris, Ramsay, 1979 (Eng. tr.: *Teachers, Writers, Celebrities*, London, New Left Books, 1981).
4 D. Pinto, 'La Conversion de l'intelligentsia', in D. Lacorne *et al.* (eds), *L'Amérique dans les têtes. Un siècle de fascinations et d'aversions*, Paris, Hachette, 1986, pp. 124–36.
5 See, in particular, S. and J. Charpentreau, *Veillées en chansons: des disques et des thèmes*, Paris, Edns ouvrières, 1961 (2nd edn).
6 See, for instance, A. Willener, *The Action-Image of Society: On Cultural Politicization*, London, Tavistock, 1970.
7 P. Bourdieu and J.-C. Passeron, *Les Héritiers: les étudiants et la culture*, Paris, Minuit, 1964, p. 65 (Eng. tr.: *The Inheritors. French students and their culture*, Chicago, Chicago University Press, 1979).
8 R. Vaneigem, *Traité de savoir-vivre l'usage des jeunes générations*, Paris, Gallimard, 1967, p. 69.
9 A. Schnapp and P. Vidal-Naquet (eds), *Journal de la Commune étudiante (textes et documents nov. 1967 – juin 68)*, Paris, Seuil, 1969, p. 552.
10 ibid., p. 431.
11 E. Copfermann, *La Génération des blousons noirs: problèmes de la jeunesse française*, Paris, Maspero, 1962.
12 ibid., p. 96.
13 ibid., pp. 101–2. The Chaussettes noires were an early French rock

group (1961–64) whose lead singer was Eddie Mitchell. For a more sympathetic, retrospective assessment, see the entry for Eddie Mitchell in C. Brunschwig, L.-J. Calvet and J.-C Klein, *Cent ans de chanson française*, Paris, Seuil, 1981. This song dictionary in itself demonstrates how French academics and intellectuals have come to acknowledge the significance of the whole area of popular song, including pop music and rock 'n' roll. A writer such as L.-J.Calvet also demonstrates in his own works the shift from a political approach to popular song to a more accepting, pluralist position.

14 R. Vaneigem, op. cit., pp. 251–2. In fact, some contemporary commentators on 1968 pointed out that the 'blousons noirs' did, indeed, play a key role in the first outbreaks of spontaneous revolt. See, for instance, E. Morin *et al.*, *Mai 68: la brèche*, Paris, Fayard, 1968, p. 70.

15 Out of many impressive examples see, for instance, D. Hebdige, *Subculture. The Meaning of Style*, London, Methuen, 1979.

16 *Autrement*, 1, Spring 1975, special number on 'Jeunesses en rupture: dupes ou prophètes'.

17 See, for instance, Alice Hubel's piece on 'Le Golfe Drouot' in P. Ory (ed.), *Mots de passe*, op. cit., pp. 120–3.

18 See Edgar Morin's comment in his *Journal de Californie*, Paris, Seuil, 1970, p. 240, where he calls the hippy fashion 'the new populism': 'Because there is no longer such a thing as the people, they are trying to make themselves into the people: rustic, shabbily-dressed, grubby'.

19 E. Morin, *Commune en France. La Métamorphose de Plodémet*, Paris, Fayard, 1967 (Eng. tr.: *Plodémet. Report from a French Village*, London, Allen Lane, 1971). The reissued French version has now reinstated the real name of the village – Plozevet.

20 E. Morin, *Commune en France*, op. cit., p. 69.

21 ibid., pp. 91ff.

22 ibid., pp. 111ff.

23 E. Morin, *Plodémet. Report*, op. cit., p. 128. I have supplemented the English translation.

24 ibid., p. 141.

25 ibid., pp. 141–2.

26 E. Morin, *Commune en France*, op. cit., p. 218.

27 E. Morin, *Autocritique*, Paris, Seuil, 1975, p. 171.

28 E. Morin *et al.*, *Mai 1968: la brèche*, op. cit., pp. 77–78.

29 ibid., p. 83.

30 ibid., pp. 29–30.

31 E. Morin, *Journal de Californie*, op. cit., p. 5.

32 ibid., p. 7.

33 ibid., p. 122.

34 ibid., p. 143.

35 ibid., p. 60.

36 E. Morin, *L'Esprit du temps*, Paris, Grasset Fasquelle. 1962. This is now most easily available in the Livre de Poche biblio 'essais' series. Another fuller edition (containing several other essays on cultural matters) was published in 1983 in two volumes by Grasset: *L'Esprit du temps 1. Névrose*; *L'Esprit du temps 2.Nécrose*.

37 Much of what I go on to say about Morin in particular can be applied in general to the group of academics and intellectuals who wrote for the periodical *Communications* in the 1960s. See in particular number 5, 1965, 'Culture supérieure et culture de masse', where an interest in, and apparent openness to, mass culture is accompanied by a traditional high cultural resistance, fear, and even disdain.
38 E. Morin, *L'Esprit du temps 1. Névrose*, op. cit., pp. 18–19. On the intellectual resistance to mass culture, see also B. Rigby 'The *Vivre son Temps* collection: intellectuals. modernity and mass culture' in B. Rigby and N. Hewitt (eds), *France and the Mass Media*, London, Macmillan, 1991.
39 E. Morin, *L'Esprit du temps 1. Névrose*, op. cit., p. 20.
40 ibid., p. 24.
41 See also E. Morin, *Les Stars*, Paris, Seuil, 1962.
42 *L'Esprit du temps 1. Névrose*, op. cit., p. 157.
43 ibid., pp. 161, 190, 218–19.
44 R. Barthes, *Mythologies*, (selected and translated by A. Lavers), London, Jonathan Cape, 1972, p. 15.
45 R. Barthes, *Mythologies*, Paris, Seuil, 1970, p. 177 (1st edn 1957).
46 *Roland Barthes par Roland Barthes*, Paris, Seuil, 1975, p. 59.
47 R. Barthes, *Mythologies*, London, Jonathan Cape, op. cit., p. 75.
48 R. Barthes, *Mythologies*, Paris, Seuil, op. cit., p. 10.
49 ibid., p. 8.
50 See the essays in *Mythologies* on Poujade: 'Quelques paroles de M. Poujade' and 'Poujade et les intellectuels'.
51 ibid., p. 87: 'the whole of petit-bourgeois mythology implies the rejection of otherness, the negation of difference, the happiness of identity and the euphoria of sameness'.
52 ibid., pp. 182–90.
53 *Roland Barthes par Roland Barthes*, op. cit., p. 67.
54 R. Barthes, *Mythologies*, Paris, Seuil, op. cit., p. 48.
55 *Roland Barthes par Roland Barthes*, op. cit., p. 68.
56 ibid., pp. 69–70.
57 ibid., pp. 73–4.
58 ibid., p. 81.
59 See also H. Giordan, *Démocratie culturelle et droit à la différence*, Paris, La Documentation française, 1982.
60 J.-P. Colin, *La Beauté du manchot: culture et différence*, Paris, Publisud, 1986, p. 9.
61 ibid., p. 12.
62 See R. Geerlandt, *Garaudy et Althusser: le débat sur l'humanisme dans le parti communiste français et son enjeu*, Paris, Presses Universitaires de France, 1978; L. Ferry and A. Renaut, *La Pensée 68: essai sur l'anti-humanisme contemporain*, Paris, Gallimard, 1985.
63 J.-P. Colin, *La Beauté du manchot*, op. cit., p. 106.
64 ibid., pp. 55–6.
65 ibid., p. 26.
66 ibid., p. 124.
67 ibid., p. 112. On Lang's early cultural activities and ideas, see J.-D.

Bredin and J. Lang, Eclats, Paris, J.-C. Simoën, 1978; D. Looseley, 'Jack Lang and the Politics of Festival', *French Cultural Studies*, 1, February 1990. For a work written in enthusiastic support of socialist cultural policy, see C. Clément, *Rêver chacun pour l'autre*, Paris, Fayard, 1982. For a more balanced academic assessment, see D. Wachtel, *Cultural Policy and Socialist France*, New York, Greenwood Press, 1987. For a detailed survey of current State cultural policy, see R. Wangermée and B. Gournay, *La Politique culturelle de la France*, Paris, La Documentation française, 1988.

68 ibid., p. 90.
69 ibid. p. 88.
70 For highly critical assessments of Lang's cultural policies, see P. de Plunkett, *La Culture en veston rose*, Paris, La Table Ronde, 1982; J. Dutourd, *Le Spectre de la rose*, Paris, Flammarion, 1986. As well as these Right-wing attacks, see also the violent assault on Lang and modern trendy media culture by a figure who insisted on staying true to the spirit of 1968, and who saw Lang and his acolytes as traitors to the cause: G. Hocquenghem, *Lettre ouverte à ceux qui sont passés du col Mao au Rotary*, Paris, Albin Michel, 1986.
71 J.-P. Colin, *La Beauté du manchot*, op. cit.,p. 73.
72 See P. Emmanuel, *Culture, noblesse du monde. Histoire d'une politique*, Paris, Stock, 1980; J. Rigaud, *La Culture pour vivre*, Paris, Gallimard, 1975.
73 See also R. Bordaz, *Le Centre Pompidou: une nouvelle culture*, Paris, Ramsay, 1977; F. Ponge, *L'Ecrit Beaubourg*, Paris, Centre Georges Pompidou, 1977. For the cultural discourse which Beaubourg itself was to engender, see in particular the house journal *Traverses*.
74 For an account of Beaubourg both as recuperation of 1968 and as Althusserian Ideological Apparatus of State, see M. Baldwin's TV programme on Beaubourg in the Open University Course A315 'Modern Art and Modernism'.
75 C. Mollard, *L'Enjeu du Centre Georges Pompidou*, Paris, 10/18, 1976, p. 77.
76 ibid., p. 15.
77 ibid., p. 37.
78 ibid., p. 26.
79 ibid., p. 37.
80 ibid., p. 38.
81 ibid., p. 101.
82 ibid., p. 114.
83 ibid., p. 37.
84 See, for instance, J. Baudrillard, *In the Shadow of the Silent Majorities or the End of the Social and Other Essays*, New York, Semiotexte, 1983.
85 See J. Baudrillard, *La Société de consommation, ses mythes, ses structures*, Paris, Denoël, 1970.
86 ibid., pp. 149–53.
87 ibid., pp. 163–4.
88 J. Baudrillard, *L'Effet Beaubourg: implosion et dissuasion*, Paris, Galilée, 1977, pp. 14–15.

89 ibid., pp. 22–4.
90 J. Rigaud, 'L'Effet', in P. Ory (ed.), *Mots de passe*, op. cit., p. 41.
91 ibid.
92 ibid., pp. 43–4.
93 G. Lipovetsky, *L'Ere du vide. Essais sur l'individualisme contemporain*, Paris, Gallimard, 1983, p. 14.
94 ibid., p. 17.
95 ibid., p. 146.
96 ibid., p. 22.
97 ibid., p. 171.
98 On the whole question of 'le look' and 'le branché', see B. Couturier *Une Scène-jeunesse*, Paris, Autrement, 1983. In this text Couturier charts his own progress from 1968 Maoist to 1980s fashion journalist and media intellectual. He also explicitly states that the old Bourdieu-type class-based analysis of popular culture and high culture is now truly defunct, and was rendered so by people of his generation, that is those who belonged to the world of youth culture and pop music:

> The obsession with the divisions between social classes was a matter for the older generation, who were trying to hand down their class-based culture, which was altogether boring and archaic (accordion or Beethoven) and precisely what one wanted nothing to do with. But one also wanted nothing to do with national barriers and frontiers. Donovan was singing 'The Universal Soldier' . . . John Lennon, in proclaiming the obvious truth that the Beatles had become more popular than Jesus Christ, was simply registering the fact that Beatlemania was a world-wide phenomenon, as was the whole of youth culture and pop culture.
>
> (pp. 24–5)

99 G. Lipovetsky, *L'Ere du vide*, op. cit., p. 174.
100 P. Yonnet, *Jeux, modes et masses. La société française et le moderne 1945–1985*, Paris, Gallimard, 1985, pp. 63–4.
101 ibid., pp. 8, 10, 108–9.
102 ibid., pp. 8–11.
103 ibid., pp. 11–12.
104 ibid., p. 76.
105 ibid., p. 50.
106 ibid., pp. 192–3.
107 ibid., pp. 196–7.
108 ibid., pp. 197–8.
109 ibid., p. 188.
110 ibid., p. 198.

BIBLIOGRAPHY

Althusser, L., 'Idéologie et appareils idéologiques d'Etat', *La Pensée*, 151, June 1970; also in *Positions*, Paris, Editions sociales, 1976 (Eng. tr. in *Lenin and Philosophy*, London, New Left Books, 1971).

Aragon, L., *La Culture et les hommes*, Paris, Editions sociales, 1947.

L'Atelier populaire présenté par lui-même, Paris, Usines, Universités, Union, 1968.

Autrement, 1, Spring 1975, 'Jeunesses en rupture: dupes ou prophètes'.

    7, November 1976, 'La Fête cette hantise'.

    12, February 1978, '68/78. Dix Années sacrilèges'.

    16, November 1978, 'Flagrants délits d'imaginaire'.

    18, April 1979, 'La Culture et ses clients'.

    58, March 1984, 'Show-biz'.

    78, March 1986, 'La Culture des camarades'.

Bakhtin, M., *L'Oeuvre de François Rabelais et la culture populaire au Moyen-Age et sous la Renaissance*, Paris, Gallimard, 1970.

Barthes, R., *Mythologies*, Paris, Seuil, 1957 (Eng. tr: *Mythologies*, London, Jonathan Cape, 1972; *The Eiffel Tower and other Mythologies*, New York, Hill and Wang, 1979).

Barthes, R., *Roland Barthes par Roland Barthes*, Paris, Seuil, 1975.

Barthez, J.-C., 'Culture populaire ou culture dominée?', in G. Poujol and R. Labourie, *Les Cultures populaires: permanences et émergences des cultures minoritaires, locales, ethniques, sociales et religieuses*, Toulouse, Privat, 1979, pp. 41–52.

Baudrillard, J., *La Société de consommation, ses mythes, ses structures*, Paris, Denoël, 1970.

Baudrillard, J., *L'Effet Beaubourg: implosion et dissuasion*, Paris, Galilée, 1977.

Baudrillard, J., *In the Shadow of the Silent Majorities or the End of the Social and other Essays*, New York, Semiotexte, 1983.

Beauroy, J., M. Bertrand and E. T. Gargan (eds.), *The Wolf and the Lamb. Popular culture in France from the old regime to the twentieth century*, Saratoga, Anma Libri, 1976.

Bénéton, P., *Histoire de mots: culture et civilisation*, Paris, Presses de la Fondation Nationale des Sciences Politiques, 1975.

Bertrand, M. (ed.), *Popular Traditions and Learned Culture in France*, Saratoga, Anma Libri, 1985.

Besançon, J. (ed.), *Les Murs ont la parole: journal mural mai 1968*, Paris, Tchou, 1968.

Besnard, P., 'La Culture populaire, discours et théories', in G. Poujol and R. Labourie, *Les Cultures populaires: permanences et émergences des cultures minoritaires, locales, ethniques, sociales et religieuses*, Toulouse, Privat, 1979, pp. 53–63.

Billard, C. and P. Guibbert, *Histoire mythologique des Français*, Paris, Galilée, 1976.

Boniface, J., *Arts de masse et grand public*, Paris, Editions ouvrières, 1962.

Bordaz, R., *Le Centre Pompidou: une nouvelle culture*, Paris, Ramsay, 1977.

Bouglé, C., *The French Conception of 'Culture Générale' and its Influence upon Instruction*, New York, Columbia University Press, 1938.

Bourdieu, P., 'Différences et distinctions', in Darras, *Le Partage des bénéfices: expansion et inégalités en France*, Paris, Minuit, 1966, pp. 117–29.

Bourdieu, P., 'La transmission de l'héritage culturel', in Darras, *Le Partage des bénéfices: expansion et inégalités en France*, Paris, Minuit, 1966, pp. 383–420.

Bourdieu, P., 'La sociologie de la culture populaire', in *Le Handicap socioculturel en question*, Paris, Editions ESF, 1978.

Bourdieu, P., *La Distinction, critique sociale du jugement*, Paris, Minuit, 1979 (Eng. tr.: *Distinction. A social critique of the judgement of taste*, London, Routledge and Kegan Paul, 1984).

Bourdieu, P., *Ce que parler veut dire: l'économie des échanges linguistiques*, Paris, Fayard, 1982.

Bourdieu, P., 'Vous avez dit "populaire"', *Actes de la recherche en sciences sociales*, 46, 1984.

Bourdieu, P., *Choses dites*, Paris, Minuit, 1987.

Bourdieu, P., and L. Boltanski, 'La Production de l'idéologie dominante', *Actes de la recherche en sciences sociales*, 2–3, 1976.

Bourdieu, P., L. Boltanski, R. Castel and J. C. Chamboredon, *Un Art moyen: essai sur les usages sociaux de la photographie*, Paris, Minuit, 1965 (Eng. tr.: *Photography: the social uses of an ordinary art*, Oxford, Polity, 1989).

Bourdieu, P., and A. Darbel, *L'Amour de l'art: les musées d'art européens et leur public*, Paris, Minuit, 1966.

Bourdieu, P., and J.-C. Passeron, *Les Héritiers: les étudiants et la culture*, Paris, Minuit, 1964 (Eng. tr.: *The Inheritors. French students and their culture*, Chicago, Chicago University Press, 1979).

Bourdieu, P., and J.-C. Passeron, *La Reproduction*, Paris, Minuit, 1970 (Eng. tr.: *Reproduction in Education, Society and Culture*, London, Sage, 1977).

Bredin, J.-D., and J. Lang, *Eclats*, Paris, J.-C.Simoën, 1978.

Brunschwig, C., L.-J. Calvet and J.-C. Klein, *Cent ans de chanson française*, Paris, Seuil, 1981.

Cabanne, P., *Le Pouvoir culturel sous la Vème République*, Paris, Olivier Orban, 1981.

Cacérès, B., *La Rencontre des hommes*, Paris, Seuil, 1950.

Cacérès, B., *Le Président*, Paris, Peuple et Culture, 1957.

Cacérès, B., *Histoire de l'éducation populaire*, Paris, Seuil, 1964.

Cacérès, B., *L'Espoir au coeur*, Paris, Seuil, 1967.

Cacérès, B., *Allons au-devant de la vie: la naissance du temps des loisirs en 1936*, Paris, La Découverte, 1981.

Calvet, L.-J., *La Production révolutionnaire: slogans, affiches, chansons*, Paris, Payot, 1976.

Cau, J., *Discours de la décadence*, Paris, Copernic, 1978.

de Certeau, M., *La Prise de parole*, Paris, Desclée de Brouwer, 1968.

de Certeau, M., *La Culture au pluriel*, Paris, Christian Bourgeois, 1980 (1st edn 1974).

de Certeau, M., 'Pratiques quotidiennes', in G. Poujol and R. Labourie (eds), *Les Cultures populaires: permanences et émergences des cultures minoritaires, locales, ethniques, sociales et religieuses*, Toulouse, Privat, 1979, pp. 23–30.

de Certeau, M., *L'Invention du quotidien*, vol. 1, Paris, 10/18, 1980.

de Certeau, M., D. Julia and J. Revel, *Une Politique de la langue: la Révolution française et les patois*, Paris, Gallimard, 1975.

Charpentreau, J., *Pour une politique culturelle*, Paris, Editions ouvrières, 1967.

Charpentreau, J., and R. Kaës, *La Culture populaire en France*, Paris, Editions ouvrières, 1962.

Charpentreau, J., and L. Rocher, *L'Esthétique personnaliste d'Emmanuel Mounier*, Paris, Editions ouvrières, 1966.

Charpentreau, S. and J., *Veillées en chansons: des disques et des thèmes*, Paris, Editions ouvrières, 1961.

Chombart de Lauwe, P.-H., *Images de la culture*, Paris, Editions ouvrières, 1966.

Clément, C., *Rêver chacun pour l'autre*, Paris, Fayard, 1982.

Colin, J.-P., *La Beauté du manchot: culture et différence*, Paris, Publisud, 1986.

Combes, P., *La Littérature et le mouvement de Mai 68: écriture, mythes, critique, écrivains 1968–1981*, Paris, Seghers, 1984.

Communications, 5, 1965, 'Culture supérieure et culture de masse'.

Copfermann, E., *La Génération des blousons noirs: problèmes de la jeunesse française*, Paris, Maspero, 1962.

Copfermann, E., *Le Théâtre populaire pourquoi?* Paris, Maspero, 1969.

Couturier, B., *Une Scène-jeunesse*, Paris, Autrement, 1983.

Crubellier, M., *Histoire culturelle de la France XIX-XX siècles*, Paris, A. Colin, 1974.

Cuisenier, J., *French Folk Art*, New York, Kodansha International, 1977 (French edn: *L'Art populaire en France*, Freiburg, L'Office du Livre, 1976).

Cuisenier, J., and M. Segalen, *Ethnologie de la France*, Paris, Presses Universitaires de France, 1986.

Debord, G., *La Société du spectacle*, Paris, Editions Buchet-Chastel, 1967 (Eng. tr.: *Society of the Spectacle*, Detroit, Black and Red, 1970).

Debord, G., *Commentaires sur la société du spectacle*, Paris, Lebovici, 1988.

Debray, R., *Le Pouvoir intellectuel en France*, Paris, Ramsay, 1979 (Eng. tr.: *Teachers, Writers, Celebrities*, London, New Left Books, 1981).

De la misère en milieu étudiant, in R. Viénet, *Enragés et situationnistes dans le mouvement des occupations*, Paris, Gallimard, 1968 (1st edn, Strasbourg, AFGES, 1966).

Druon, M., *L'Avenir en désarroi*, Paris, Plon, 1968.

Duhamel, A., *Le Complexe d'Astérix: essai sur le caractère politique des Français*, Paris, Gallimard, 1985.

Dumazedier, J., *Vers une civilisation du loisir?* Paris, Seuil, 1962 (Eng. tr.: *Toward a Society of Leisure?*, New York, Free Press, 1967).

Dumazedier, J., 'A un étudiant révolutionnaire', *Esprit*, 8–9, Aug-Sept. 1968, pp. 61–80.

Dumazedier, J., 'Culture vivante et pouvoirs', in G. Poujol and R. Labourie, *Les Cultures populaires: permanences et émergences des cultures minoritaires, locales, ethniques, sociales et religieuses*, Toulouse, Privat, 1979, pp. 65–77.

Dumazedier, J., 'Culture de masse – Culture populaire', *Raison présente*, 64, 1982, pp. 81–95.

Dumazedier, J., *Révolution culturelle du temps libre 1968–1988*, Paris, Klincksieck, 1988.

Dumazedier, J. and A. Ripert, *Société éducative et pouvoir culturel*, Paris, Seuil, 1976.

Dutourd, J., *L'Ecole des jocrisses*, Paris, Flammarion, 1970.

Dutourd, J., *Le Spectre de la rose*, Paris, Flammarion, 1986.

Emmanuel, P., *Pour une politique de la culture*, Paris, Seuil, 1971.

Emmanuel, P., *Culture, noblesse du monde. Histoire d'une politique*, Paris, Stock, 1980.

Esprit, June 1959, special number on 'Le Loisir'.

Expansion de la recherche scientifique, 22, April–May 1965, 'Le Colloque de Bourges'.

Ferry, L. and A. Renaut, *La Pensée 68: essai sur l'anti-humanisme contemporain*, Paris, Gallimard, 1985.

Frémontier, J., *La Vie en bleu: voyage en culture ouvrière*, Paris, Fayard, 1980.

Friedmann, G., *Le Travail en miettes: spécialisation et loisirs*, Paris, Gallimard, 1956 (Eng. tr.: *The Anatomy of Work*, London, Heinemann, 1961).

Frisch-Gautier, J. and P. Louchet, *La Colombophilie chez les mineurs du Nord*, Paris, Centre national de la recherche scientifique, 1960.

Gaudibert, P., *Action culturelle: intégration et/ou subversion*, Paris, Casterman, 1977 (1st. ed. 1972).

Gaudibert, P., *De L'Ordre moral*, Paris, Grasset, 1973.

Geerlandt, R., *Garaudy et Althusser: le débat sur l'humanisme dans le parti communiste français et son enjeu*, Paris, Presses Universitaires de France, 1978.

George, F., 'Critique de la culture populaire', *Cahiers des saisons*, 36, 1964, pp. 6–16.

Giard, L. and P. Mayol, *L'Invention du quotidien*, vol. 2: Habiter, Cuisiner, Paris, 10/18, 1980.

Giordan, H., *Démocratie culturelle et droit à la différence*, Paris, La Documentation française, 1982.

Gordon, D. C., *The French Language and National Identity 1930–1975*, The Hague, Mouton, 1978.

Gorz, A., *Adieux au prolétariat. Au-delà du socialisme*, Paris, Galilée, 1980 (Eng. tr.: *Farewell to the Working Class*, London, Pluto, 1982).

Grignon, C. and J.-C. Passeron, *A Propos des cultures populaires*, Cahiers du Cercom, 1, Marseille, EHESS, April 1985.

Guerrand, R.-H., *La Conquête des vacances*, Paris, Editions ouvrières, 1963.

Guillaume, M., *La Politique du patrimoine*, Paris, Galilée, 1980.

Guth, P., *Lettre ouverte aux futurs illettrés*, Paris, Albin Michel, 1980.

Hebdige, D., *Subculture. The Meaning of Style*, London, Methuen, 1979.

Hocquenghem, G., *Lettre ouverte à ceux qui sont passés du col Mao au Rotary*, Paris, Albin Michel, 1986.

Hoggart, R., *La Culture du pauvre: étude sur le style de vie des classes populaires en Angleterre*, Paris, Minuit, 1970 (Fr. tr. of *Uses of Literacy: Aspects of working-class life with special reference to publications and entertainments*, Harmondsworth, Penguin, 1963, 1st edn 1957).

Javeau, C., *Haro sur la culture*, Brussels, Editions de l'Université de Bruxelles, 1974.

Jeanson, F., *L'Action culturelle dans la cité*, Paris, Seuil, 1973.

Kaës, R., *Images de la culture chez les ouvriers français*, Paris, Cujas, 1968.

Kelly, M., 'Humanism and National Unity: the Ideological Reconstruction of France' in N. Hewitt (ed.), *The Culture of Reconstruction. European literature, thought and film, 1945–50*, London, Macmillan, 1989.

de Kerorguen, Y., 'L'Effet patrimoine', *Esprit*, 12, 1981, pp. 99–106.

Kimmel, A. and J. Poujol, *Certaines idées de la France*, Sèvres, Centre international d'études pédagogiques, 1980.

Labourie, R., *Les Institutions socio-culturelles. Les mots-clés*, Paris, Presses Universitaires de France, 1978.

Labov, W., *Language in the Inner City: Studies in the black vernacular*, Oxford, Blackwell, 1977.

Lacorne D., J. Rupnik and M. F. Toinet (eds), *L'Amérique dans les têtes: un siècle de fascinations et d'aversions*, Paris, Hachette, 1986.

Lalive d'Epinay, C., M. Bassand, E. Christe and D. Gros, 'Persistance de la culture populaire dans les sociétés industrielles avancées', *Revue française de sociologie*, 23, 1982, pp. 87–109.

Lalive d'Epinay, C., M. Bassand, E. Christe and D. Gros, *Temps libre: culture de masse et cultures de classe aujourd'hui*, Lausanne, Editions P.-M. Favre, 1983.

Larrue, J., *Loisirs ouvriers chez les métallurgistes toulousains*, Paris, Mouton, 1965.

Lavau, G., 'The PCF, the state and the revolution: an analysis of party policies, communications and popular culture', in D. Blackmer and S. Tarrou, *Communism in Italy and France*, Princeton, Princeton University Press, 1975.

Lavau, G., *A Quoi sert le parti communiste français?* Paris, Fayard, 1981.

Lebel, J.-J., *Procès du Festival d'Avignon, supermarché de la culture*, Paris, Pierre Belfond, 1968.

Lefebvre, H., *La Vie quotidienne dans le monde moderne*, Paris, Gallimard, 1968 (Eng. tr.: *Everyday Life in the Modern World*, London, Allen Lane, 1971).

Leroy, R., *La Culture au présent*, Paris, Editions sociales, 1972.

Lipovetsky, G., *L'Ere du vide. Essais sur l'individualisme contemporain*, Paris, Gallimard, 1983.

Looseley, D., 'Jack Lang and the Politics of Festival', *French Cultural Studies*, 1, February 1990, pp.5–19.

Manceaux, M., *Les Maos en France* (Avant-propos de Jean-Paul Sartre), Paris, Gallimard, 1972.

Mandrou, R., 'Cultures populaire et savante' in J. Beauroy, M. Bertrand and E. T. Gargan, *The Wolf and the Lamb. Popular Culture in France from the Old Regime to the Twentieth Century*, Saratoga, Anma Libri, 1976.

Martos, J.-F., *Histoire de l'Internationale situationniste*, Paris, Lebovici, 1989.

Mass-Observation, *The Pub and the People. A worktown study*, Welwyn Garden City, Seven Dials Press, 1970 (1st edn 1943).

Miège, B., J. Ion and A.-N. Roux, *L'Appareil d'action culturelle*, Paris, Editions universitaires, 1974.

Ministère de la Culture, *Pratiques culturelles des Français. Description socio-démographique. Evolution 1973–1981*, Paris, Dalloz, 1982.

Mollard, C., *L'Enjeu du Centre Pompidou*, Paris, 10/18, 1976.

Morin, E., *Autocritique*, Paris, Seuil, 1975 (1st ed. 1959).

Morin, E., *Les Stars*, Paris, Seuil, 1962.

Morin, E., *L'Esprit du Temps*, Paris, Grasset Fasquelle, 1962. Reissued and enlarged as *L'Esprit du Temps l. Névrose; L'Esprit du Temps 2. Nécrose*, Paris, Grasset, 1983.

Morin, E., *Commune en France. La Métamorphose de Plodémet*, Paris, Fayard, 1967 (Eng. tr.: *Plodémet. Report from a French Village*, London, Allen Lane, 1971).

Morin E., C. Lefort and J.-M. Coudray, *Mai 68: la brèche*, Paris, Fayard, 1968.

Morin, E., *Journal de Californie*, Paris, Seuil, 1970.

Mothé, D., *Journal d'un ouvrier (1956–1958)*, Paris, Minuit, 1959.

Mothé, D., 'Les Ouvriers et la culture', *Socialisme ou barbarie*, 30, April–May 1960, pp. 1–44.

Mouralis, B., 'Discours du peuple et discours sur le peuple', in B. Mouralis, *Les Contre-littératures*, Paris, Presses Universitaires de France, 1975.

Nizan, P., *Les Chiens de garde*, Paris, Rieder, 1932.

Ory, P., *L'Entre-deux-mai: histoire culturelle de la France, mai 1968 – mai 1981*, Paris, Seuil, 1983.

Ory, P. (ed.), *Mots de passe 1945–1985: petit abécédaire des modes de vie*, Paris, Autrement, 1985.

Ozouf, M., *La Fête révolutionnaire*, Paris, Gallimard, 1976.

Passeron, J.-C., 'Introduction' to R. Hoggart, *La Culture du pauvre: etude sur le style de vie des classes populaires en Angleterre*, Paris, Minuit, 1970.

Pinto, D., 'La Conversion de l'intelligentsia', D. Lacorne, J. Rupnik and M. F. Toinet (eds), *L'Amérique dans les têtes. Un siècle de fascinations et d'aversions*, Paris, Hachette, 1986, pp. 124–36.

de Plunkett, P., *La Culture en veston rose*, Paris, La Table Ronde, 1982.

Ponge, F., *L'Ecrit Beaubourg*, Paris, Centre Georges Pompidou, 1977.

Poujol, G. and R. Labourie (eds), *Les Cultures populaires: permanences et émergences des cultures minoritaires, locales, ethniques, sociales et religieuses*, Toulouse, Privat, 1979.

Queyranne, J.-J., *Les Maisons de la Culture*, Lyon, Editions de l'AGEL, 1975, 2 vols.

Racine, N., 'Marcel Martinet et la culture ouvrière', *Le Mouvement social*, 90, 1975, pp. 59–78.

Raude, E. and G. Prouteau, *Le Message de Léo Lagrange*, Paris, La Compagnie du Livre, 1950.

Rigaud, J., *La Culture pour vivre*, Paris, Gallimard, 1975.

Rigby, B., 'French Intellectuals and Leisure: the case of Emmanuel Mounier', in T. Winnifrith and C. Barrett (eds), *The Philosophy of Leisure*, London, Macmillan, 1989.

Rigby, B., 'The Reconstruction of Culture: Peuple et Culture and the Popular Education Movement', in N. Hewitt (ed.), *The Culture of Reconstruction. European literature, thought and film, 1945–50*, London, Macmillan, 1989.

Rigby, B., 'The *Vivre son Temps* collection: intellectuals, modernity and mass culture', in B. Rigby and N. Hewitt (eds), *France and the Mass Media*, London, Macmillan, 1991.

Ritaine, E., *Les Stratèges de la culture*, Paris, Presses de la Fondation Nationale des Sciences Politiques, 1983.

Rose, M., *Servants of Post-Industrial Power? 'Sociologie du Travail' in modern France*, London, Macmillan, 1979.

Rose, M. (ed.), *Industrial Sociology: Work in the French tradition*, London, Sage, 1987.

Saez, J.-P. (ed.), *Peuple et Culture: histoire et mémoires*, Paris, Peuple et Culture, 1986.

Salon, A., *L'Action culturelle de la France dans le monde*, Paris, Nathan, 1984.

Sartre, J.-P., *Qu'est-ce-que la littérature?* Paris, Gallimard, 1948 (Eng. tr.: *What is Literature?* London, Methuen, 1950).

Sartre, J.-P., *On a raison de se révolter*, Paris, Gallimard, 1974.

Schnapp, A. and P. Vidal-Naquet (eds), *Journal de la Commune étudiante, (textes et documents nov. 67 – juin 68)*, Paris, Seuil, 1969.

Simon, P.-H., 'Contestation et culture', *Le Monde*, 24–5 July, 1968.

Soriano, M., 'Popular Traditions and Consumer Society: the situation in France', *Cultures*, 1(2), 1973, pp. 39–66.

Soriano, M., 'Radio and Television "Live" programming in the long term', *Cultures*, 8(1), 1982, pp. 91–9.

Touraine, A., 'Travail, loisirs et société', *Esprit*, June 1959.

Touraine, A., *La Société post-industrielle*, Paris, Denoël, 1969.

Thuillier, G., *Pour une histoire du quotidien au XIXe siècle en Nivernais*, Paris/The Hague, Mouton, 1977.

Vaneigem, R., *Traité de savoir-vivre à l'usage des jeunes générations*, Paris, Gallimard, 1967.

Verdès-Leroux, J., *Au Service du parti: le parti communiste, les intellectuels et la culture (1944–1956)*, Paris, Fayard, 1983.

Verdès-Leroux, J., *Le Réveil des somnambules: le parti communiste, les intellectuels et la culture (1956–1985)*, Paris, Fayard/Minuit, 1987.

Viénet, R., *Enragés et situationnistes dans le mouvement des occupations*, Paris, Gallimard, 1968.

Villadary, A., *Fête et vie quotidienne*, Paris, Editions ouvrières, 1968.

Wachtel, D., *Cultural Policy and Socialist France*, New York, Greenwood Press, 1987.

Wangermée, R. and B. Gournay, *La Politique culturelle de la France*, Paris, La Documentation française, 1988.

Weber, E., *Peasants into Frenchmen: the modernization of rural France 1870–1914*, London, Chatto and Windus, 1977.

Williams, R., 'Culture is Ordinary' in R. Williams, *Resources of Hope*, London, Verso, 1989.

Willener, A., *The Action-Image of Society: On cultural politicization*, London, Tavistock, 1970.

Yale French Studies, 73, 1987, 'Everyday Life'.

Yonnet, P., *Jeux, modes et masses. La société française et le moderne 1945–1985*, Paris, Gallimard, 1985.

INDEX